A Constructivist Approach to Block Play in Early Childhood

A Constructivist Approach to Block Play in Early Childhood

Karyn Wellhousen, Ph.D.
Associate Professor
University of New Orleans

Judith Kieff, Ed.D.
Associate Professor
University of New Orleans

DELMAR

™

THOMSON LEARNING

Australia Canada Mexico Singapore Spain United Kingdom United States

DELMAR
THOMSON LEARNING

A Constructivist Approach to Block Play in Early Childhood
by Karyn Wellhousen & Judith Kieff

Business Unit Director:
Susan L. Simpfenderfer

Executive Marketing Manager:
Donna J. Lewis

Production Editor:
J.P. Henkel

Acquisitions Editor:
Erin O'Connor Traylor

Channel Manager:
Nigar Hale

Cover Design:
Judi Orozco

Editorial Assistant:
Alexis Ferraro

Executive Production Manager:
Wendy A. Troeger

For permission to use material from this text or product,
contact us by
Tel   (800) 730-2214
Fax   (800) 730-2215
www.thomsonrights.com

Library of Congress Cataloging-in-Publication Data
Wellhousen, Karyn.
   A constructivist approach to block play in early childhood /
Karyn Wellhousen, Judith Kieff. — 1st ed.
      p. cm.
   Includes bibliographical references and index.
   ISBN 0-7668-1537-4
   1. Block building (Children's activity) 2. Early childhood
education. I. Kieff, Judith E. II. Title.

LB1139.C7 W45 2000
372.13--dc21   00-059044

NOTICE TO THE READER

Publisher does not warrant or guarantee any of the products described herein or perform any independent analysis in connection with any of the product information contained herein. Publisher does not assume, and expressly disclaims, any obligation to obtain and include information other than that provided to it by the manufacturer.

The reader is expressly warned to consider and adopt all safety precautions that might be indicated by the activities herein and to avoid all potential hazards. By following the instructions contained herein, the reader willingly assumes all risks in connection with such instructions.

The Publisher makes no representation or warranties of any kind, including but not limited to, the warranties of fitness for particular purpose or merchantability, nor are any such representations implied with respect to the material set forth herein, and the publisher takes no responsibility with respect to such material. The publisher shall not be liable for any special, consequential, or exemplary damages resulting, in whole or part, from the readers' use of, or reliance upon, this material.

To my grandparents, Millard "Sonny Boy" and Natalie Wakeford, for my earliest memories of the joy of blocks

—Karyn Wellhousen

To teachers everywhere who strive each day to provide all children authentic opportunities for optimal development

—Judith Kieff

Contents

Preface

Block play has been a part of early childhood education since the first kindergarten was created by Friedrich Froebel in Germany in 1837. The types of blocks and the ways they are used to enrich the lives of young children have evolved due to changes in society's attitudes toward children, scientific study, and political and social transformations. Today, the daily use of blocks and other play materials in early childhood programs are being threatened due to an emphasis on testing, accountability, and documenting narrow outcome-based goals. *A Constructivist Approach to Block Play in Early Childhood* provides readers with a fresh look at the continued relevance of block play in the lives of children today.

Section I, Chapter 1 reminds teachers, students of education, parents, and policymakers of the rich heritage of block play and its important role throughout the history of the early childhood profession. Chapter 2 alerts readers to the latest research on the development of the human brain and the subsequent need for children to be actively involved in their own learning with the support of appropriate play materials, such as blocks. Teachers and parents who care for and educate young children on a daily basis will learn how to recognize the stages of children's block building in Chapter 3.

In Section II, the needs of children in regard to block play are divided by age and ability. The developmental needs of children are reviewed and suggestions are provided for creating appropriate indoor and outdoor environments for block play, along with appropriate materials and accessories. The ages are divided as follows: infants and toddlers (Chapter 4), preschoolers and kindergartners (Chapter 5), and primary-grade students (Chapter 6).

Section III fully explores the role of the teacher in fostering block play. Chapter 7 provides concrete suggestions for creating an environment conducive to block play, including classroom arrangement and specific teacher intervention strategies. Guidelines and recommendations for including all children in block play, regardless of their abilities, are provided in Chapter 8. Strategies for observing and documenting learning are reviewed in Chapter 9.

A Constructivist Approach to Block Play in Early Childhood takes a comprehensive, wholistic look at block play consistent with a constructivist view of learning. This view provides learners with

> *"the opportunity for concrete, contextually meaningful experience through which they can search for patterns, raise their own questions, and construct their own models, concepts, and strategies"* (Fosnot, 1996, p. ix)

Current issues of interest receive special attention such as how gender influences block play, establishing home–school connections, choosing and implementing relevant assessments, strategies for incorporating IEP/IFSP goals for children with special needs and abilities, the role of parents, and findings regarding brain development and play.

Each chapter begins with Guiding Questions, which focus the reader on the main topics to be addressed, and concludes with Websites and Related Readings, which further the reader's understanding. Theory into Practice activities are suggested to help the reader take those important first steps into implementing the strategies discussed. Photographs and figures are provided to illustrate significant aspects of the text. An Instructor's Guide is available to provide additional suggestions for presenting materials from *A Constructivist Approach to Block Play in Early Childhood* for teacher education, early childhood training, or in-service activities.

Acknowledgments

The authors want to acknowledge the people whose time, talent, services, and encouragement made this book a reality. We deeply appreciate members of the Delmar Publishing Team: Erin O'Connor Traylor, who believed in our idea from the start; Alexis Ferraro, for patiently answering many questions; and J. P. Henkel and the other talented individuals who directed the art for this text.

The following reviewers played an invaluable role in critiquing and providing insightful feedback:

Jody Martin
Curriculum Specialist
Children's World Learning Centers
Aurora, CO

Sherry Nicholson
Saddlebrook College
Mission Viejo, CA

Betty Pearsall
Director, Child Development Center
Queens College
Flushing, NY

Linda Ruhmann
San Antonio College
San Antonio, TX

Christina Dias Ward
Trevecca Nazarene University
Nashville, TN

We want to thank the directors and parents who gave permission to photograph children from the following early childhood programs: Ecole Classique Learning Center in Metairie, Louisiana; Ellisville Head Start in Loxley, Alabama; Jubilee Child Development Center in Spanish Fort, Alabama; Mandeville Elementary School, Mandeville, Louisiana; Pine Grove Elementary School, Bay Minette, Alabama; Spanish Fort Presbyterian Church Preschool, Alabama; University of New Orleans Children's Center, New Orleans,

Louisiana; Granny's Child Care Center, New Orleans, Louisiana; and Jean Jones and Cathy Heath.

We gratefully acknowledge Shauntel Cenance, Bridget Smolcich, and Lisa Stewart, dedicated teachers who contributed photographs of their students and classrooms; Donna Everson, Patty Glaser, Becky Schmerbaugh, Angela Williams, and Linda Pruitt, for assuming the responsibility of obtaining permissions to photograph; Dr. Linda Flynn, for her expertise in the area of inclusion; and Adam Hill and Charles Harden, for providing technical assistance.

Karyn wants to personally acknowledge her husband, Jeff Tunks, and children, Katy Jo and Jackson, for their patience and commitment to this endeavor.

About the Authors

Karyn Wellhousen has more than 20 years of experience working with children and adult learners. After teaching preschool, kindergarten, and first grade, she obtained her Ph.D. from Florida State University. She has taught undergraduate and graduate students in The University of Texas System and at The University of New Orleans. Currently, she is a teacher/parent educator and freelance writer. She resides in Spanish Fort, Alabama, with her husband and two children.

Judith Kieff is Associate Professor in the Department of Curriculum and Instruction at the University of New Orleans. Dr. Kieff's career in early childhood education has included teaching children with special needs and children who are developing typically in kindergarten, primary grades, Head Start, and early intervention programs. Her research, publication, and in-service activities focus on integrating play into inclusive early childhood settings.

A Primer for Parents

Parents have long been recognized as their child's first teacher. Through modeling, demonstrating, talking, and listening, parents provide children with their first learning experiences. Many parents are choosing to spend time at home with their young children as opposed to returning to work within a few weeks after their birth. Parents who can make this choice recognize they have something unique to offer their children. Home schooling for children ages 6 to 18 is becoming a popular choice for many families. These parents believe they are the best teacher for imparting knowledge and instilling values. Even when there is not a full-time parent at home, mothers and fathers are interested in providing their children with valuable and fun learning experiences when they are together. Therefore, this primer has been written to summarize some of the information presented in the book and to direct parents to sections that will be of particular interest to them.

Selecting and Caring for Blocks

A primary role of parents in facilitating their children's learning through block play is the selection and purchase of materials. Approach this task by selecting basic block sets for infants and toddlers, and add to these as your child's interest and ability grows. Make available two to three different commercial block sets for infants and toddlers. (See Chapter 4 for useful descriptions of blocks for children this age.) Keep in mind that infants and toddlers are learning through their senses, so choose sets that offer variety in color, shape, and texture. Infants and toddlers also enjoy "homemade" blocks. Any items that are lightweight for safety reasons but sturdy enough to stack are suitable. An excellent homemade block set can be made from diaper wipe boxes, which are usually in great supply.

Add two to three additional block sets for preschoolers and kindergartners. Select at least one that is based on equal proportions, such as the table blocks or Kinder Blocks® described in Chapter 5. A child's progression through the stages of block play can be observed with these or other proportion-based block sets, such as the more expensive unit blocks (see Chapter 3). A snap-together block system such as Duplos®, which offer a different type of building experience, can also be added. As children enter first grade, they will be ready for more experimentation with their building. Legos®, Tree Blocks®, Marble Run®, and other sets suggested in Chapter 6 will provide new challenges.

Blocks have a long, rich history that is reviewed in Chapter 1. Friedrich Froebel, the creator of the kindergarten and the first set of blocks used in a classroom setting, emphasized the importance of demonstrating respect for blocks. This is an equally important lesson for children today. Parents can promote this by assisting children in putting blocks away after play. Rather than dumping blocks into a toy chest, they should be returned to a sturdy container and placed on a shelf. Storing blocks in clear plastic containers rather than their original packaging may reduce gender stereotyping associated with block play (see Chapter 7 for other suggestions). Sorting different block sets into their own separate container teaches classification skills, a basic mathematical process.

Parents' Role in Guiding Infants and Toddlers

Infants and toddlers experience rapid changes in growth and development. Many of the changes are obvious, such as physical growth, motor skills, and language learning. However, there are other significant changes occurring that are not as obvious, namely, the neural network within babies' brains. (See Chapter 2 for an overview of brain development research.) The primary vehicle for learning in the infant and toddler years is exploring using the senses. This is referred to as the sensory-motor stage. The rapid changes experienced during the first three years of life are discussed in Chapter 4.

Parents can stimulate learning during the infant and toddler years by following the child's lead in playing with blocks. Specific suggestions for effective ways to interact with infants and toddlers at play are provided in Chapter 4, along with safety features to keep in mind when choosing toys and preparing an environment for play. Periodical cleaning and disinfection methods are also described.

Parents' Role in Guiding Preschool and Kindergarten Children

Preschoolers and kindergartners who have had regular opportunities for block play move steadily through the seven stages of block building (see Chapter 3). They will have practiced stacking and bridging as a toddler, and will experiment with enclosures, patterns and symmetry, and early representational building by around age 5. Preschoolers and kindergartners begin learning important social skills during stage 7 of block building. At this stage, children build structures that they use for role play, such as a house, school, store, or fire station. They then incorporate people or animal figures into their play.

When children role play using figures, they are experimenting with how two or more people interact when they are together. They can often be heard resolving differences as they speak aloud for the figures: "You don't want to go to the store right now? Okay. What do you want to do?" This tells us that initial experiences with learning how to function as part of a group do not necessarily begin with their peers. Beatty (1990) referred to this behavior as solitary dramatic play and encourages adults to think of this behavior as "a step on the ladder of socialization." (See Chapter 5 for an in-depth discussion on how blocks enhance learning at this age.)

Preschool and kindergarten parents can observe children and the dialog used in their dramatic play. It will provide insight on how they are choosing to work out differences. They may use a broad range of strategies, including negotiation, persuasion, and even physical actions. (See Chapter 9 for a discussion on observing and documenting children's learning.)

By age 5, children may ask to keep their block structure in place over several days so they can continue their play scenario without having to rebuild the structure and start over each time. This is important because, when they can return to an ongoing play scenario, the play and dialog become more complex.

Parents' Role in Guiding Primary-Grade Children

Blocks offer many opportunities for learning, especially for children in the primary grades. Blocks promote learning in math and science, and allow children to begin exploring the world of architecture, engineering, and city planning. Primary-grade children are capable of solving problems that occur in block building using scientific and mathematical principles. They use logicomathematical knowledge learned from prior experiences with block building and other experiences to solve new, more difficult problems. According to Dreier (1996),

> *"Their discoveries are more sophisticated and involve the elaboration of concepts that build a solid foundation for classification, prediction, and hypothesis testing, which are essential to later work in science and to all clear thinking." (pp. 111)*

The parental role changes as children enter formal schooling. They must either step back and simply observe as their child's constructions become more sophisticated, or step-in and assist when new, challenging building sets have been introduced. Providing assistance when needed and then gradually allowing the child to take over is called "scaffolding" and is a crucial teaching technique.

Parents' Role in Guiding Children with Special Needs

Parents of children with special needs will find many ideas for adapting materials and the environment in Chapter 8. All children can and should be included in the fun and learning that blocks have to offer. Parents can share adaptations with teachers to ensure that block play is accessible in the classroom with peers as well as at home.

Conclusion

Parents are essential to their children's learning and development. Blocks offer a variety of learning opportunities for all children, regardless of gender, ability, ethnicity, or income. By providing children with appropriate materials and support, parents can instill in children a lifelong love for exploration and learning.

References

Beatty, J. (1990). *Observing the development of the young child.* Columbus, OH: Merrill.

Dreier, E. (1996). Blocks in the elementary school. In E. Hirsch (Ed.), *The block book* (3rd ed., pp. 103–116). Washington, DC: National Association for the Education of Young Children.

Fosnote, C. T. (Ed.). (1996). *Constructivism: Theory, perspective, and practice.* New York: Teachers College Press.

Overview of Blocks and Learning

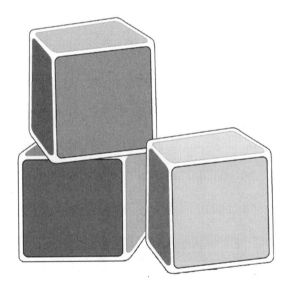

CHAPTER 1

Revisiting Tradition: History and Evolution of Blocks

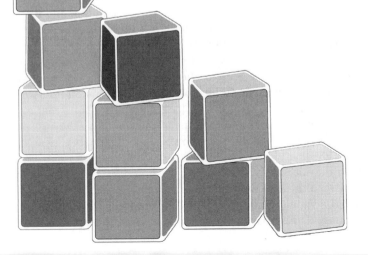

Guiding Questions

- *How have society's attitudes toward play evolved since the 1500s?*

- *What are the major contributions of people who shaped the early childhood profession—Friedrich Froebel, Patty Smith Hill, Caroline Pratt, Harriet Johnson, and Maria Montessori?*

- *How have political influences from the 1950s to the present affected early childhood programs today?*

History of Toys in Childhood

Prior to the eighteenth century, "toys" by today's definition did not exist. Instead of materials made specifically for children's play and learning, objects from the adult environment were transformed by children through their imagination. The absence of toys was the result of parental and society's attitudes toward children, childhood, and play in the sixteenth and seventeenth centuries (Brewer, 1979). Lack of regard for children's need for specific playthings during this period of history is explained in two ways. First, the high infant and child mortality rate prevented close parent–child attachments as adults tried to deal psychologically with the inevitable death of one or more children. Second, the idea that all humans are born into the world with original sin that must be eliminated required parents to be vigilant in their duty to control children, usually through frequent beatings (Schorsch, 1979). In addition, prior to the eighteenth century, society viewed play as not having a useful purpose or educational value. Instead, play was considered frivolous or even sinful. These prevailing views of childhood prevented parents from indulging their offspring with materials designed specifically for the child's enjoyment (Brewer, 1979).

A slow, gradual shift in attitudes toward children's play became evident during the early nineteenth century. People began to believe humans were not born in sin but as blank slates or *tabula rasa,* an idea popularized by educational philosopher, John Locke. He proposed that children were more likely to learn through play because it was pleasurable than as a result of physical punishment, which discouraged children's interest in learning. These ideas were most widely accepted by middle-class parents eager to improve their children's chances for success in the higher classes (Brewer, 1979) and became increasingly popular throughout the nineteenth century as toys were more widely available due to mass production (Schorsch, 1979). The idea of play in the nineteenth century, however, was narrow in comparison to today's definition. Toys were seen as didactic tools for rigidly educating children and were believed to have no other value. This attitude toward toys was evident in the cards, games, and puzzles that were sold with the intent of teaching morals and concepts such as geography, history, and spelling. Among the toys produced in the nineteenth century were the earliest known blocks. These were designed after a set first described by John Locke (1693) in his essay, *Some Thoughts Concerning Education,* as dice with letters on all six sides that are thrown to see how many words can be formed (Locke, 1693/1964). The "Locke blocks" as they were known are now called "Alphabet blocks" (Provenzo & Brett, 1983).

An exception to the idea that household toys should be rigidly used to educate children emerged through the work of Friedrich Froebel (1782–1852), who believed materials should be designed for children to explore and enjoy as well as for learning. This departure in attitude toward the value of toys and play was the impetus for the first kindergarten established by Froebel in Germany in 1837.

Froebel's Influence on Blocks for Early Childhood Education

The initial use of blocks as a vehicle for teaching young children in an educational setting is attributed to Froebel, German educator and "father of the kindergarten." Significant events in Froebel's childhood contributed to his unique ideas for educating young children. Froebel's mother died before he reached his first birthday and a neglectful stepmother left a sad and indelible impression that caring, nurturing, maternal figures are crucial in successfully rearing and educating healthy, happy children (Corbett, 1988). As he grew, he spent hours in solitude, exploring the forests surrounding his home, thus instilling in Froebel a deep appreciation for nature and science. His father's work as a Lutheran minister influenced Froebel's ideas on spirituality and the universal purpose of individuals. The correlation between these powerful childhood experiences and Froebel's work as an educator become evident when his life's work, the creation of the first kindergarten and its curriculum, is examined (Brosterman, 1997).

Froebel (1885) compiled a set of songs accompanied by a musical score, related illustrations, and instructions for mothers on how to best incorporate songs into purposeful play with their children. He emphasized the need for mothers to provide their children with these experiences beginning at the age of 4 months, as well as provided enough instruction to ensure the reader would spend substantial time interacting with their young offspring. These songs and movement games also became a part of the activities included in Froebel's kindergarten. His reverence for women and their maternal role was also made obvious by the important role they were given in the early kindergartens.

Before Froebel's involvement in education, women were generally not accepted into the teaching profession, but he saw the many contributions women could make in the kindergarten and trained them through an apprenticeship program. Froebel's love of nature was evident through the activities in the kindergarten that emphasized the study of plants and organic matter. Children routinely planted seeds in their individual garden plots and were responsible for caring for them until the seedlings reached maturity. Froebel believed these experiences would instill in children the inherent responsibility people have to one another in society (Brosterman, 1997). These educational principles were based on his theory of **unity** and **inner connection**. Through his teachings, Froebel emphasized the unity or wholeness of each child's cognitive, physical, and spiritual domains and the inner connection between individual children, the spiritual world, nature, and the human race as a whole (Corbett, 1988). To illustrate this concept in a concrete way, Froebel had the group of children sit in a circle for song and game activities. The circle, according to Froebel, represented the inner

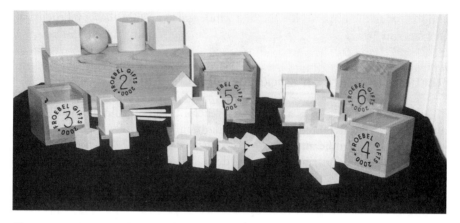

Figure 1–1   *Reproduction of Froebel's blocks, gifts 2–6.*

connection between children, whereas the unity of each individual was preserved by the space they filled in the circle.

These principles resulted in a curriculum based on a set of toylike materials Froebel called a "system of gifts and occupations." The 10 gifts included objects such as colored, woolen balls; divided wooden cubes or blocks; sticks; parquetry; rings; and jointed slats. Each gift was carefully kept in its own container to teach children respect for materials and a sense of order (Corbett, 1988). Of the 10 different gifts in Froebel's system, six were wooden block shapes. Gifts 2–6 are pictured in Figure 1–1. Froebel's blocks were undecorated to encourage discovery and creativity and were based on a modular system. Occupations consisted of art activities or handwork, including paper perforating, cutting, weaving, folding paper, sewing, modeling clay, and a unique set of materials called "peas work." Peas were soaked overnight and then dried, giving them the consistency of dough so they could be pierced with toothpick-like sticks to form three-dimensional figures. (It is believed that "peas work" was the predecessor of Tinkertoys.®) A distinction can be made between gifts and occupations by the fact that gifts can be restored to their original shape, whereas occupations cannot (B. Corbett, personal communication, April 1998).

Froebel's gifts and occupations were used to teach his beliefs of unity and inner connection through a prescribed regimen of exercises. The materials were not used for free play in the sense of the term today, but children were given more freedom to explore materials than was typical of this time. For example, the first task upon the introduction of each unique set of blocks (gifts 2–6) was to design *Forms of Life* or represent their physical world by manipulating the materials to mimic familiar objects from the child's environment. At this stage, children freely manipulate the blocks to create the object of their choosing, such as a house, chair, train, or tower. The creation of simplified, symbolic versions of objects familiar to the children in their daily life was to help them become more aware of their world and encourage children's thoughtful play.

The system also included a formal presentation and activities involving *Forms of Knowledge* (using objects to present specific concepts) and *Forms of Beauty* (maneuvering blocks to create symmetrical designs). When children are involved with creating *Forms of Knowledge,* they see how the blocks are used to teach specific mathematical and scientific concepts, such as the number of sides on a block, the movement of a cylinder-shaped block as it is rolled, or addition and subtraction theorems. *Forms of Beauty* correspond with elements of art such as design and pattern. Froebel's system required that *Forms of Beauty* using blocks be created on a gridded board. Children were encouraged to create and then modify their artistic constructions. Creating designs in this way introduced principles of symmetry, proportion, balance, rhythm, and simplicity (Bultman, 1997). A description of Froebel's gifts 2–6 and activities for teaching Forms of Life, Knowledge, and Beauty can be found in Figure 1–2.

Froebelian Kindergartens in America   The concept of kindergarten, with its curriculum designed specifically for children under the age of 7, spread to America via women who studied as apprentices in Froebel's German kindergarten (see Figure 1–3). In 1876, a model kindergarten was on display at the Centennial Exposition, the first World's Fair in the United States, held in Fairmount Park, Philadelphia. Ruth Burritt was appointed by the Froebel Society of Boston to serve as the teacher and demonstrator at the Kindergarten Cottage, a live exhibit at the exposition. She demonstrated Froebel's principles with a group of orphans who were transported to the Kindergarten Cottage 3 days per week. Burritt presented and explained the system to visitors as children followed a typical kindergarten routine of playing, singing, and movement games, and manipulating Froebel's gifts (Wortham, 1992).

Anna Wright, the mother of young Frank Lloyd Wright, attended the Centennial Exposition and was intrigued with the concept of the kindergarten and the materials used by the young children in the demonstration at the Kindergarten Cottage. She believed the blocks and teaching strategies on display would provide her son with the foundation needed to become a great architect, which was her vision for him. When she returned to Boston, she purchased a set of Froebel's gifts for her 9-year-old son, Frank (Wright, 1977). It is unknown whether Mrs. Wright purchased authentic Froebel's gifts or a variation which was rapidly being produced and marketed by toy manufacturers such as Milton Bradley. Regardless, Frank Lloyd Wright, a highly successful architect who has made enormous cultural contributions to design, often credited his experiences with the kindergarten materials for his success. Wright (1957) stated in his autobiography,

> *"Mother found the 'Gifts.' And gifts they were. Along with the gifts was the system . . . I sat at the little Kindergarten tabletop . . . and played . . . with the*

Gift	Contents	Life	Knowledge	Beauty
2	Two 2" cubes, one 2" cylinder, one 2" sphere, (each with holes drilled except for one cube), three sticks for spinning blocks	Build freely with blocks and container describe forms built	Name shapes, sort, count, concepts: up/down, front/back, on/under	Create patterns and designs by spinning blocks on sticks
3	2" cube divided into eight 1" cubes	Use blocks to represent familiar objects, create stories about objects built	Sorting, counting, arithmetic, fractions, vocabulary	Use symmetry, balance, and proportion to create designs on grid using all cubes
4	2" cube divided into eight 2" × 1" × ½" rectangular blocks	Use blocks as walls, fences, table, chairs when material is introduced with words such as brick, tile, steps	Fractions, proportion, concept of *vertical, horizontal, width, length, height*	Create symmetrical and asymmetrical designs
5	3" cube divided into 21 1" cubes, six half-cubes, and 12 quarter-cubes	Build representations with related stories, buildings, and familiar structures	Terms such as *angle, triangle, diagonal, rectangular prism,* size/shape differences, three cubed, Pythagorean Theorem $(A^2 + B^2 = C^2)$	Form complex patterns and symmetry by modifying constructions rather than destroying and rebuilding
6	3" cube divided into 18 rectangular blocks, 12 flat square blocks, and six narrow columns	Use new sizes and shapes for building forms	Fractions, area and volume, scale, proportion modularity	Form symmetrical designs using balance, simplicity, strength of center

Figure 1-2 *Froebel's gifts 2–6.*

From Bultman, S. (1997). *The Froebel Gifts 2000: The building gifts 2–6.* Grand Rapids: Uncle Goose Toys, Inc.

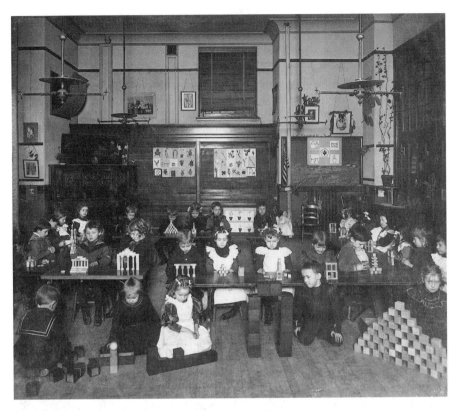

Figure 1–3 *Early 20th-century New York kindergarten using Froebel blocks.*

Courtesy of Photography Collection, Miriam & Ira D. Wallach, Division of Art, Prints & Photographs, The New York Public Library, Astor, Lenox & Tilden Foundations.

cube, the sphere, and the triangle—these were smooth maple wood blocks. . . . All are in my fingers to this day. . . . I soon became susceptible to constructive pattern evolving in everything I saw. I learned to 'see' this way and when I did, I did not care to draw casual incidentals of nature. I wanted to design." (pp. 19–20)

In *Inventing Kindergarten*, Brosterman (1997) supported Wright's claim that experiences with blocks and other kindergarten materials directly influenced his architectural designs and provided comparisons of forms typical of Froebel's gifts with Wright's architectural sketches. When the two are compared, the argument is quite convincing.

As the concept of kindergartens spread through Germany to America and beyond, kindergartens flourished. However, several factors led to changes in and finally abandonment of Froebel's original principles and curriculum. After Froebel's death in 1832, several books were written to describe the system of gifts and occupations. The authors presented different perspectives on the system, which led readers to believe there were a finite number of outcomes when using the materials. In fact, Froebel had designed the system to be open ended with infinite possibilities. A partial selection of sketched forms used by Froebel and his followers as examples came to be viewed as a standard for all to follow. A second factor resulting in the demise of the Froebel system was the mass production and redesign of Froebel's blocks. Several toy manufacturers, particularly Milton Bradley, altered the original designs, making what they believed to be improvements that changed educators' and the public's understanding of the original system. The most extreme deviation made by toy manufacturers was the inclusion of Alphabet blocks with Froebel's gifts, even though Froebel strongly criticized their use (Brosterman, 1997). Finally, the beginnings of the Child Study Movement caused psychologists and educators to question Froebel's teachings due to the lack of scientific proof of its effectiveness (Weber, 1969; Wortham, 1992).

Influence of Child Study Movement

It was Froebel's forward thinking concerning the need for educating children under the age of 7 that paved the way for the Child Study Movement. Before Froebel, young children were considered almost uneducable due to their active and spontaneous nature. The Child Study Movement, which began in the 1930s and continued through the 1950s, took a scientific approach to studying children's development and recommending appropriate methods for teaching. The research of G. Stanley Hall, John Dewey, and Edward Thorndike caused educators to question established Froebelian practices and incited great debate. Followers of Froebel's ideas and system found themselves struggling to defend the curriculum they believed in so fervently, while kindergarten reformers were making radical changes (Wortham, 1992).

One of the staunchest and most widely recognized kindergarten reformers was Patty Smith Hill (1868–1946) who was inspired by G. Stanley Hall, a founder of the Child Study Movement. It was Hill's goal to eliminate the prescribed methods associated with Froebel's system and replace them by giving children freedom to play. Similar to Froebel, her inspiration for ideas for a new kindergarten curriculum directly related to her early childhood experiences. Unlike Froebel, Hill enjoyed a happy childhood in which she and her siblings freely played and built with bricks, barrels, boards, and homemade constructions built in the carpenter shop at the female seminary established by her father (Fowlkes, 1984). One significant change Hill made to the Froebelian system was the design and introduction of new sets of blocks. The first set of blocks designed by Hill was roughly 16 times larger than those used by Froebel, and the table grid was omitted, thereby giving children permission to play with the blocks freely on the floor (Brosterman, 1997). In a

1941 description of changes to the kindergarten since Froebel's day, Hill (1999) stated,

> *"The tiny cubes, circles, squares, and triangles inherited from Froebel's day are poor materials for construction at this stage of child life, as one slip of immature fingers, or even a deep breath, may annihilate the child's production in the twinkling of an eye. (pp. 85–86)*

Later, she developed a set of floor blocks that were larger than the first set and adaptable for use in many ways, including building structures large enough for children to enter and dramatize familiar domestic scenes (Snyder, 1972). The set consisted of large, maple pillars; blocks; wheels; and rods, and ranged in size from $3' \times 3'' \times 1\frac{1}{4}''$ to $3'' \times 3'' \times 1''$. Two sizes of grooved pillars, 27″ and 15″ high, completed the set. According to Hill, the advantages of the larger blocks, and other homemade equipment typical to the kindergarten of her day (such as wooden kegs loaded with explosive powder) were that they required children to use large muscles and physical strength. Another advantage of the blocks was that, to build with the cumbersome materials, they typically required cooperation between two or more children (Fowlkes, 1984). The Patty Smith Hill blocks, as they were known, used a peg, hole, and groove system, which kept the blocks in place but eliminated the need for children to experiment with balance and stability (see Figure 1–4). Even though Hill's block systems are no longer manufactured or used, her legacy in the evolution of blocks still exists because her pioneering spirit inspired educators that followed.

Caroline Pratt (1867–1954) studied with and was inspired by Patty Smith Hill following a formal education in manual training, an innovation in education in the late nineteenth century. Similar to Hill, Pratt believed in the scientific study of children's learning as opposed to traditional Froebelian approaches to teaching kindergarten. Although she was intrigued by the methods and blocks designed by Patty Smith Hill, Pratt saw a need for a block system with a more organized approach to learning than the free play advocated by Hill. This desire led to the creation of the Unit Block System. The wooden blocks in this system are smaller than those designed by Hill and, therefore, easier for children to handle. In addition, the block system provides a standard proportion to promote children's understanding of mathematical relationships. Pratt first tried out her system in 1914 during a 2-month experiment in a barren settlement house in New York City. Later, she was able to fully implement her theory and practice at the City and Country School, a school she founded and that is still in existence (Driscoll, 1995; Winsor, 1996).

Harriet Johnson (1867–1934) was greatly interested in children's building with Unit Blocks and began to systematically observe and record children's structures. As she observed, she recognized a pattern in children's building that related to their prior experiences with blocks. In 1933, Johnson published a description of the seven stages of block play. This description is still considered valid and useful for understanding how children's block building changes with experience (see Chapter 2). Johnson's pioneering work was reprinted in

Figure 1–4 *Patty Smith Hill Blocks used at the Lincoln School, Teachers College, Columbia University, in the 1930s.*
Courtesy of Special Collections, Milbank Memorial Library, Teachers College, Columbia University.

1996, and Pratt's unit blocks are still widely used in early childhood classrooms today.

Montessori's Method

While Pratt was developing her system of Unit Blocks, across the Atlantic Ocean in Italy, Maria Montessori was developing a dramatically different learning system that partially relied on blocks as a basic learning tool. Montessori (1870–1952) was the first woman physician in Italy but was prevented from practicing medicine due to her gender. Because she could not care for others through the field of medicine, her interest turned to educating children who were poor and children who were considered disabled. Her method is considered scientific because it evolved from observing and studying children from

Figure 1–5 Montessori School student building the pink tower.

impoverished homes to children from middle- to high-income families. Montessori believed children need orderly, carefully prepared environments to encourage independence in thinking and actions. She developed a set of didactic (teacher-directed) materials that children were to use in the prescribed manner presented to them by a trained teacher. Montessori's method and materials were the basis of the curriculum used at the "Children's House," which opened in 1907 to provide social and education services to poor families and their children ages 3 to 6. The structured and self-correcting block activities are a crucial part of her method (Epstein, Schweinhart, & McAdoo, 1996; Montessori, 1964). One example of Montessori's materials is the pink tower (Figure 1–5). The initial block building begins with a series of 10 pink wooden cubes ranging in size from 1 to 10 centimeters. The task is successfully completed if the child, after observing the teacher perform it, stacks the blocks on top of one another in ascending order, thereby forming a tower. The children are expected to use Montessori materials as prescribed and demonstrated by the teacher, rather than playing with them as they freely choose. It is Montessori's *method* in conjunction with the materials that makes this educational philosophy unique.

Montessori received accolades for the cognitive advances made by what were to be considered "deficient" children and her ideas were disseminated through training and eventually introduced in the United States. Although the initial reception was positive, Montessori's methods were met with opposition as the Child Study Movement was strongly advocating the need for children to have open-ended experiences with blocks and other play materials. In fact, William Heard Kilpatrick, who advocated John Dewey's efforts in educational reform, stated both philosophies could not coexist in the United States. Time has of course proved Kilpatrick wrong because today there are many philosophies and related practices regarding the use of free play and exploration versus didactic teaching methods.

Influence of Social and Political Changes

The progressive philosophy of the early twentieth century lent strong support to the use of blocks and similar materials as important elements of early childhood education. Due to the beliefs of educational reformers, blocks were viewed as necessary for children's understanding of mathematical and spatial concepts, as well as for creativity and personal satisfaction (Franklin, 1950; Rudolph & Cohen, 1964). A shift in thinking toward educational goals emerged in the mid-20th century. In the 1950s and 1960s, funding for education increased as Americans sought ways to solve social and political problems. During this time, politicians and other facets of society looked toward education to resolve long-standing problems, such as poverty, and new concerns, such as advances in the Russian space program.

As a result, additional funding became available for innovative educational programs. Ironically, this occurred at a time when new theories on how children learn were emerging. These theories stimulated much interest in the educational arena, especially in early childhood education. However, the profound differences between behaviorist and constructivist theories that emerged during this period are still cause for controversy today.

B. F. Skinner's (1953) theory of behaviorism contends that human behavior is controlled by the environment and can be shaped through reinforcement and punishment. Behaviorist theory resulted in curriculum models dependent on direct instruction, detailed objectives, and a system of rewards and punishment. In extreme opposition was Piaget's constructivist theory of cognitive development. Piaget's tenet that a child's cognitive development could be influenced through meaningful experiences inspired child-centered curricula that encourage children to learn new concepts through active involvement with objects and resourceful people (DeVries & Kohlberg, 1987). Due to the teacher-directed nature of the behaviorist model, children in programs based on this philosophy had little opportunity to play with blocks; therefore, construction materials, along with other toys, began to vanish from preschool and kindergarten programs.

Children in classrooms with a constructivist philosophy, however, had multiple opportunities to freely interact with a variety of blocks, construction materials, and other toys. Blocks were viewed as valuable for creativity, oral language development, spatial orientation, and learning mathematical concepts (Gelfer & Perkins, 1988). Although there was no one clear victor in the debate over how children learn, variations on the theory of behaviorism became widespread and took a toll on the availability of blocks in early childhood classrooms. Constructivists held firm to their belief that children need ample opportunities for play as they continued to refine this philosophy.

The back-to-basics movement of the 1970s and 1980s rejected the constructivist theory that play is crucial to young children's learning (Gelfer & Perkins, 1988). Time spent playing with blocks and other materials was replaced with readiness workbooks and other paper-and-pencil tasks. Teaching basic skills was emphasized and teachers felt pressured to have students perform well on standardized tests which are believed by some to measure student learning. This trend affected early childhood education as curriculum requirements were continually pushed down to earlier grades. Golant and Golant (1997) illustrated this trickle-down phenomenon.

> *"Walk into a kindergarten classroom today and you'll see more than a pile of wooden blocks or a dress-up corner, a play kitchen, or an easel beckoning with blank paper and bright paints. You may be more likely to observe a sea of five-year-old heads bent over paper-and-pencil work-ditto sheets, workbooks, and the like." (p. 4)*

Even though these practices are challenged by professional education organizations, such as the National Association for the Education of Young Children (NAEYC) and the Association of Childhood Education International (ACEI), and renowned child-advocates, such as David Elkind (1987, 1988), the battle in favor of child-centered, play-oriented curriculum continues.

Conclusion

The presence and use of blocks in early childhood settings today varies dramatically according to the philosophy of the school or setting and the individual teacher. Emphasis on block play ranges in early childhood settings from a complete absence of blocks to the use of blocks as a mainstay in the curriculum. When blocks and other manipulative materials are replaced by workbook-driven teaching, children are missing out on great pleasure and crucial learning experiences. In addition, the early childhood profession is losing a significant piece of its long and rich history.

Theory into Practice

1. Read a complete original work by Froebel, Hill, Pratt, Johnson, or Montessori. Reflect on how their historical perspective affected your belief system.

2. Review how Froebel's and Hill's childhood influenced their philosophy and teaching. Reflect on your own childhood and how it may have affected your decision to work with children and your personal philosophy toward teaching.
3. Visit three different early childhood programs to determine if blocks are present and regularly available to children. Interview the director or teacher to determine their views on the importance of blocks.

Websites

www.froebelgifts.com

Website for Uncle Goose Toys, Inc., manufacturer of Froebel Gifts 2–9. A bibliography is provided on books related to Froebel's work.

www.geocities.com/froebel/web/forum/replies.html

Information is provided on Froebel's philosophy and life with a variety of links, including several on Frank Lloyd Wright.

www.amshq.org

Website for the American Montessori Society.

Related Readings

Brosterman, N. (1997). *Inventing kindergarten.* New York: Abrams.
Golant, S., & Golant, M. (1990). *Kindergarten—It isn't what it used to be.* Los Angeles: Lowell House.
Shapiro, M. S. (1983). *Child's garden: The kindergarten movement from Froebel to Dewey.* State College: Pennsylvania State University.

References

Brewer, J. (1979). *Childhood revisited: The genesis of the modern toy.* In Hewitt, K., & Roomet, L. (Eds.), *Educational toys in America: 1800 to the present* (pp. 3–10). Burlington: University of Vermont, The Robert Hull Fleming Museum.
Brosterman, N. (1997). *Inventing kindergarten.* New York: Abrams.
Bultman, S. (1997). *The Froebel Gifts 2000: The building gifts 2–6.* Grand Rapids: Uncle Goose Toys, Inc.
Corbett, B. (1988). *A garden of children.* Mississauga, Ontario, Canada: The Froebel Foundation.

DeVries, R., & Kohlberg, L. (1987). *Programs of early education: The constructivist view.* New York: Longman.

Driscoll, A. (1995). *Cases in early childhood education: Stories of programs and practices.* Boston, MA: Allyn & Bacon.

Elkind, D. (1987). *Miseducation: Preschoolers at risk.* New York: Alfred A. Knopf.

Elkind, D. (1988). *The hurried child: Growing up too fast too soon.* Reading, MA: Adisson-Wesley.

Epstein, A., Schweinhart, L., & McAdoo, L. (1996). *Models of early childhood education.* Ypsilanti, MI: High/Scope Press.

Fowlkes, M. A. (1984). Gifts from childhood's godmother: Patty Smith Hill. *Childhood Education, 61*(1), 44–49.

Franklin, A. (1950). Block—A tool of learning. *Childhood Education, 26,* 209–213.

Froebel, F. (1885). *Mother's songs, games and stories* (F. Lord & E. Lord, Trans.). London: William Rice. (Original work published 1844.)

Gelfer, J., & Perkins, P. (1988). Using blocks to build art concepts: A new look at an old friend. *Early Child Development and Care, 30,* 59–69.

Golant, S., & Golant, M. (1997). *Kindergarten—It isn't what it used to be: Getting your child ready for the positive experience of education.* Los Angeles: Lowell House.

Hill, P. (1999). Kindergarten. In K. Paciorek & J. Munro (Eds.), *Sources: Notable selections in early childhood education* (2nd edition) pp. 81–90. Guilford, CT: Brown & Benchmark.

Johnson, H. (1996). The art of blockbuilding. In E. Hirsch (Ed.), *The block book* (pp. 9–25). Washington, DC: National Association for the Education of Young Children.

Korver, J. (1985). *The Froebel gifts: A guide to gifts 2–6.* Boulder, CO: Korver/Thorpe, Ltd.

Locke, J. (1693/1964). *Some thoughts concerning education.* Woodbury, NY: Barron's.

Montessori, M. (1964). *The Montessori method.* New York: Schocken.

Provenzo, E., & Brett, A. (1983). *The complete block book.* Syracuse, NY: Syracuse University Press.

Rudolph, M., & Cohen, D. H. (1964). The many purposes of block building and woodwork. *Young Children, 20,* 40–44.

Schorsch, A. (1979). *Images of childhood: An illustrated social history.* New York: Mayflower Books.

Skinner, B. F. (1953). *Science and human behavior.* New York: Macmillan.

Snyder, A. (1972). *Dauntless women in childhood education: 1856–1931.* Washington, DC: Association for Childhood Education International.

Weber, E. (1969). *The kindergarten: Its encounter with educational thought in America.* New York: Teachers College Press.

Winsor, C. (1996). Blocks as a material for learning through play. In E. Hirsch (Ed.), *The block book* (pp. 1–8). Washington, DC: National Association for the Education of Young Children.

Wortham, S. (1992). *Childhood 1892–1992.* Wheaton, MD: Association for Childhood Education International.

Wright, F. L. (1977). *An autobiography.* New York: Duell, Sloan, and Pearce.

Wright, F. L. (1957). *A testament.* New York: Horizon Press.

CHAPTER 2

Brain Development and Learning

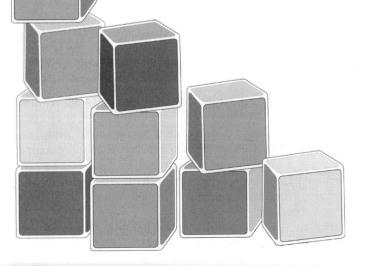

Guiding Questions

- *What effect does emotion, repetition, challenge, and rest have on the brain development of young children?*

- *What environmental conditions foster optimal brain development?*

- *How can play, specifically block play, enrich environments serving young children and thereby foster optimal brain development?*

Since the eighteenth century, adults have intuitively used toys, including blocks, to further learning and development as well as to entertain infants and young children. This practice has been consistently supported by psychological theories that point out the importance of play to learning and development (Erikson, 1963; Piaget, 1962; Vygotsky, 1978). Whereas psychology has focused attention on human learning and development, a second branch of science, **neuroscience,** has focused attention on how the brain develops and functions. These two branches of science developed independently for almost 100 years, and it was not until the late 1980s that a dialogue began between neuroscientists and psychologists (Bruer, 1999).

Subsequent communication between these two branches of science, plus new ways of studying the brain, have increased information regarding brain development and functioning and have changed how we view the human capacity for learning (Newberger, 1997; Schiller, 1997). In the early 1980s, many psychologists believed intelligence was determined mainly by our genetic makeup, but information gained through neuroscientific research has shed new light on the significance of environments to human learning. Figure 2–1 provides profiles of leading neuroscientists, psychologists, and educators as well as descriptions of technology involved in fostering collaboration leading to new understandings about brain development and educational practices.

It is important to understand that findings from brain research, as intriguing as they are, may not yet translate directly into classroom practice. Ideas proposed in the brain-based education literature are interpretations and suppositions based on the findings of neuroscience (Bruer, 1998, 1999; Wolfe & Brandt, 1998). Cognitive psychologists, neuroscientists, educational researchers, and practitioners continue to synthesize information to determine educational practice that will facilitate brain development and affect learning in the classroom (Lindsey, 1998/1999; Schiller, 1997; Wolfe & Brandt, 1998). This chapter summarizes existing knowledge related to brain development and, therefore, presents a rationale for the use of block and constructive play in early childhood programs.

Brain Development

The human brain consists of a complex multilevel system of synapses in the brain that develops in an integrated fashion over time (Diamond & Hopson, 1998; Wolfe & Brandt, 1998). This system is often referred to as **neural circuitry,** the **architecture of the brain,** or the **wiring of the brain.** Development of this system begins at conception with a single **neuron,** or brain cell. The main job of neurons is to receive information about the external environment (e.g., heat, cold) and internal environment (e.g., pain, hunger), interpret this information, and orchestrate appropriate responses.

Each neuron consists of a cell body with **axons** growing from one end and **dendrites** from the other. **Neurotransmitters** are chemical substances produced

The science of the mind (psychology) and the science of the brain (neuroscience) have been studied independently for almost a century. In the 1980s, new brain imaging technology was designed and psychologists, educators, and neuroscientists began a dialogue that lead to collaboration and formed a new field of study called cognitive psychology. This field has been responsible for interpreting neuroscientific findings and developing suggestions that may facilitate learning in homes, child care centers, and classrooms.

Following are profiles of leaders in cognitive psychology:

- *Marion Diamond* is a neuroscientist and professor of neuroanatomy at the University of California, Berkeley. Her research on rats documents the influence of the environment on the growth of brain cells.
- *Harry Chugani* and *Michael Phelps* of the University of California at Los Angeles invented positron emission tomography (PET), which measures energy used by the brain.
- *Pat Wolfe,* an education consultant, has studied brain research since the 1990s, drawing implications for classroom practice.
- *Robert Sylvester,* Professor Emeritus of Education, University of Oregon, has authored numerous articles and books about the brain and learning.
- *Geoffrey Caine* and *Renate Nummela Caine* are both educators who have authored several books interpreting brain research and describing implications for educational reform.
- *Eric Jensen's* work with underachieving students led to his interest in brain research. His 11 books and professional development programs offer suggestions for classroom practice.

Studying the Brain

Information about the brain was once only obtained through animal studies or human autopsies. However, in the 1990s, new technology in medical research affected our understanding of brain development and changed how we view the human capacity for learning. Technological advances have allowed scientists to study the brains of living people and determine the function, structure, and energy use of active human brains. Examples of this emerging technology include the following:

EEG   An electroencephalogram (EEG) is used to detect and record brain waves. It is often used to study the effects of certain environments on the brain. EEG readings are correlated with videotapes of children engaged in various activities, including play, and scientists draw conclusions about the effects of the event.

MRI   Magnetic resonance imaging (MRI) can produce images of internal body parts by exposing the body to a magnetic field and then measuring the energy that bounces off atoms within the body. Data are then translated, by computer, into detailed images that offer information about how the particular body part is (or is not) working.

PET   Positron emission tomography (PET) was developed by Harry Chugani and Michael Phelps of the University of California at Los Angeles. This technology not only shows the brain's structure and function, but also visually depicts how the brain uses energy.

Ultrasound   Ultrasound technology makes it possible to produce computerized images of internal body parts based on the echoes produced by sound waves.

Figure 2–1   *Bridging the gap between neuroscience and education.*

From Bruer, 1999; D'Arcongelo, 1998; Schiller, 1997; Shore, 1997.

in the brain that transfer information from one neuron to another across a minute gap, known as a **synapse,** which exists between one cell's axons and another cell's dendrites. This electrochemical process is the basis of all human behaviors. "Every thought we think, every move we make, and every word we say is based in the electrical and chemical communication between neurons" (Wolfe in D'Arcongelo, 1998, p. 22).

Synapses occur at thornlike protrusions called *spines.* These dendrite spines grow, change shape, or shrink as the individual experiences the world (Diamond & Hopson, 1998). The wiring of the brain, which is never truly complete, results from a series of complex interactions that occur between the brain's genetic composition and the stimuli produced by the environment in which the brain resides. Therefore, each human brain is wired in a truly unique way. Heredity determines the base number of neurons and their initial arrangement at birth, but the environment in which an infant lives has an enormous effect on dendrite growth as well as the actual strength and number of synaptic connections created in the brain (Schiller, 1997). These connections form **neural pathways** for the transmission of messages and, therefore, strongly influence an individual's learning potential.

The first stage of brain development occurs during the prenatal period. Neurons begin to develop as early as one week after conception and continue through the twenty-eighth week of gestation. At birth, the brain has approximately 100 billion neurons and 50 trillion synapses (Begley, 1996). Most humans have about the same number of brain cells at 28 weeks' gestation as they will have if they live to be 70 or 80 years old.

The second stage of brain development begins at birth. The size of a child's brain will continue to grow only until he or she reaches six or seven years of age, but the architecture of the brain will continue to change throughout the child's life. It is during this second stage of brain development that human experiences, to a great extent, begin to determine the actual level and quality of functioning of the brain's neural circuitry system (Simmons & Sheehan, 1997).

Synapse Development   During the first three years of life, synapses develop quickly in response to environmental stimulation. When stimuli are repeated, existing synapse connections are reinforced, growing stronger and more efficient. For example, when an infant has multiple opportunities to feel the surfaces of wooden blocks, synaptic connections that feed the brain information about texture are strengthened; therefore, subsequent information received by the brain concerning texture will be interpreted more efficiently. This facilitates the child's potential to identify concepts such as hard, soft, smooth, or rough, thus strengthening the child's general learning potential.

Synaptic density refers to the number of synapses per unit volume of brain tissue. Density changes over a person's life span and is generally much higher in infants and young children than in adolescents and adults (Bruer, 1998; Diamond & Hopson, 1998). Increased synaptic density is associated with initial emergence of skills and capacities, but the exact correlation between synaptic density and learning is yet to be discovered. There is no simple or direct relationship between synaptic density and intellectual functioning, and much learning occurs after the high synaptic density of childhood decreases to levels characteristic of adolescents or adults (Bruer, 1998, 1999).

Pruning   Another important aspect of brain development is **pruning.** During this process, dendrites that receive little stimulation do not sprout or develop and may even be eliminated or pruned away. However, dendrites that are used regularly strengthen, grow larger, and become permanent neural pathways in the brain (Newberger, 1997). Therefore, pruning directly affects synaptic density and the architecture of the brain. Pruning begins in the prenatal period and continues throughout a person's life. However, by puberty, pruning has reduced the high synaptic density characteristic of early childhood to lower levels generally associated with adulthood. The pruning process is not predetermined by genetic codes but is directly affected by the child's early experiences. Dendrites either grow or wither based on the stimulation or lack of stimulation present in the environment (Diamond & Hopson, 1998; Simmons & Sheehan, 1997; Wolfe & Brandt, 1998). Therefore, a child's early experiences strongly influence how the brain chooses to wire itself, affecting the child's ability to learn.

Neural Plasticity and Windows of Opportunity   Neural plasticity refers to the brain's amazing ability to reorganize its neural circuitry and rewire itself in response to experience, deprivation, or injury. Because dendrites retain the ability to grow and branch throughout a person's life, it is possible for them to regenerate after injury, or even to reorganize or adapt and take over functions meant for other areas of the brain (Diamond & Hopson, 1998; Wolfe & Brandt, 1998). However, even though the brain has the ability to develop new neural pathways and reshape existing pathways, infancy and early childhood are critical periods for the formation of the overall neurological network that foreshadows future learning and development. Diamond and Hopson (1998) stated that "many of our abilities, tendencies, talents, and reactions, those that get 'hardwired' in childhood become the collective mental platform upon which we stand and grow for the rest of our lives" (p. 57).

   Windows of opportunity are critical periods or special time slots for the development of synapse connections and neural pathways that lead to specific types of learning. During a window of opportunity, the presence of certain environmental stimuli serves to fine-tune the neural circuitry and strengthen neural pathways (Begley, 1996; Chugani, 1996; Diamond & Hopson, 1998). Examples of such types of learning include domains with a long course of development such as vision and hearing (Neville, 1995). In the visual domain, neurons begin transmitting messages related to visual perception when an infant is between 2 and 4 months old. Therefore, the first year of life represents a window of opportunity for optimal development of the brain's visual area.

Visual stimuli the child receives at this time will help develop neurological pathways, and repeated experience with stimuli will strengthen synaptic connections and facilitate the child's ability to process visual input. Likewise, lack of visual stimulation in infancy, or a low incidence of repetition of stimuli, may result in lower synapse density in the visual area. Synapse connections that exist but are not used consistently will not strengthen and are at risk of being pruned from the neural network. This would negatively affect the child's ability to learn through the visual domain.

Neuroscientists have yet to find evidence of windows of opportunity for the acquisition of many skills transmitted through culture and societal means, such as reading or math (Greenenough, 1997). However, language is transmitted through culture and societal means and neuroscientists believe there is a window of opportunity for language learning (Diamond & Hopson, 1998). Because there is a direct relationship between visual, auditory, and language development and learning to read or successfully solve math problems, the complex neural circuitry system developed in early childhood is a vital link to the development of literacy, numeric understanding, and problem-solving skills.

At first, the concepts of neural plasticity and windows of opportunity may seem contradictory in function. However, even though the brain retains the ability to change the shape of its neurological network throughout a person's life, these changes become more difficult to attain after certain windows of opportunity have passed. Diamond and Hopson (1998) stated:

> *Childhood, from conception to adolescence, just happens to be the optimum time for neural development because of the "exuberant connectivity" and neural pruning that takes place in these years. Scientists are still trying to understand the fine details of how synapses are strengthened, weakened, out-competed, and pruned back. If they understood this force of nature well enough, they could harness it and restore plasticity—and with it, perhaps seeing, hearing, speaking, walking—even after a critical period has passed. But that is the province of future research. (p. 63)*

It is, therefore, always important for individuals to seek out new opportunities to broaden their own capacities because the brain is always capable of changing its neural circuitry. However, it is vitally important for both parents and educators to take advantage of the windows of opportunity that exist in the early childhood years by providing young children with appropriate stimulation through enriched environments.

Emotion and Brain Development

One of the most outstanding findings of neuroscientific research is the direct relationship between emotions and brain development, and consequently, emotions and learning (Diamond & Hopson, 1998; Schiller, 1997; Wolfe & Brandt, 1998). Learning, thinking, and feelings are all connected because emotions trigger the brain's chemical system causing the brain to release neurotransmitters that affect the development of the brain's neurological pathways. When strong emotions are associated with a particular experience, the brain releases **adrenaline** (a neurotransmitter), which acts as a memory fixative and creates a memory trace within the neural pathways of the brain. The idea that memories may exist physically in the brain leads educators to consider pairing positive emotions such as joy, curiosity, pride, or delight with learning activities (Newberger, 1997; Schiller, 1997; Wolfe & Brandt, 1998).

Not all emotions will have a positive effect on the development of neural pathways or learning. When emotions are threatening or stressful, the neurotransmitter **cortisol** may be released (LeDoux, 1996). This hormone can cause death of brain cells and a reduction in synapses in certain areas of the brain, thereby reshaping a child's developing neural pathways and affecting learning potential (Gunnar, Broderson, Krueger, & Rigatuso, 1996). Excess cortisol in the brain is linked to impaired cognitive ability and to difficulty responding appropriately or productively in stressful situations. Neglected or abandoned children often have difficulty learning, experiencing empathy, developing attachments, and expressing emotion. This could be due, in part, to high levels of cortisol in the brain created by stress in their young lives (Newberger, 1997).

One way to prevent the negative effects of stress on the development of neural pathways is to foster strong attachments between children and their parents, family members, caregivers, and teachers. Positive interactions with caring adults have been shown to stimulate a child's brain, causing synapses to grow into neural pathways that strengthen and facilitate the child's learning potential (Newberger, 1997; Schiller, 1997; Shore, 1997). Studies measuring the level of cortisol in children's saliva showed those who received warm, responsive care were able to turn off this stress-sensitive response more quickly and efficiently than those who did not receive such care (Gunnar, 1996). Touch, interactive play, holding and rocking infants, and reading stories have been shown to foster positive attachments, counteract stress, and stimulate brain growth and development in infants and young children (Schiller, 1997) (see Figure 2–2).

Another way to prevent the negative effects of stress in classroom situations is to monitor the level of challenge each child faces as he or she participates in classroom activities. "Complex learning is enhanced by challenge and inhibited by threat" (Caine in D'Arcongelo, 1998, p. 24). To engage emotions in a classroom setting, a teacher or caregiver might use strategies such as play, humor, role modeling, competitions, journal writing, celebrations, drama, creative writing, or student presentations (Jensen, 1998). It is important for teachers to monitor each child's reactions carefully because different activities will evoke different emotions among children due to the amount of challenge the child perceives within the activity.

Figure 2–2   *Warm, nurturing, interactive block play fosters positive attachments and stimulates brain growth and development.*

Effect of Repetition on Brain Development   Neural pathways are strengthened each time they are used. Therefore, the repetition of any stimulus or experience may foster the development of more efficient neural pathways in the brain, thereby strengthening learning potential (Diamond & Hopson, 1998). **Automaticity** is the ability to produce a behavior pattern or thought sequence without focused concentration. For example, through the repeated experience of driving a car, a driver learns to automatically turn on the ignition, fasten the seat belt, and check the gas gauge before she begins to back out of the driveway. Because these actions are automatic, the driver's brain is freed to pay attention to other aspects of driving, such as the presence of other cars or the direction to her destination.

Automaticity is developed through the repetition of an action pattern or thought sequence and is key to fostering learning among young children (Schiller, 1997). If there is a behavior or thought pattern young children need to develop to the level of automaticity, the child should be encouraged to engage in consistent repetitions of this pattern. However, the use of repetition to strengthen neural pathways and foster learning is not a simple matter, because there are a variety of strategies and conditions in which repetition occurs. Some conditions may evoke strong positive emotions, strengthening neural connections, whereas others may evoke strong negative emotions that may create stress, thereby potentially weakening connections.

There are three broad categories of **repetition strategies** commonly used in classrooms: practice, drill, and rehearsal. There are subtle differences between these strategies. **Practice** is performing the same task repeatedly to improve performance. Practice is task specific and performed within a limited context; therefore, there is little transferability from one context to another (Lowery, 1998). For example, if you were to practice the skill of computer keyboarding on a regular basis, you would soon become more efficient, accurate, and speedy. You would be able to transfer this skill and maintain your efficiency as long as you were using similarly configured keyboards. Your efficiency would not necessarily be transferable to another type of keyboard such as a piano keyboard.

When a child is personally motivated to improve skills through practice, this motivation adds a positive emotional element to the learning context and increases the probability that what is practiced will become automatic. However, when a child has no personal stake in practice—that is, if she does not care about the intended learning or the motivation comes from fear or threat—practice becomes **drill** and may result in stress. Drill can sometimes cause a type of stress that is counterproductive to the learning process. As noted earlier, high levels of stress are actually detrimental to brain development and, therefore, to the learning process.

Rehearsal is activity in which previously learned behavior is repeated in a similar but not identical way. Young children often enjoy the repetitive activity of stacking blocks and knocking them down. These activities provide children with opportunities to develop concepts related to cause and effect, size, weight, balance, and gravity. If a child chooses to play in the block center everyday and constructs towers with the same type of blocks, she is practicing. If her teacher introduces a new type of block with a different feel or stacking quality, then the child's activity changes from practice to rehearsal. She is using the same actions and experiencing the same concepts but not in an identical way; therefore, the context of her learning has been extended. Rehearsal activities draw on and extend children's prior knowledge and experience, strengthening neural pathways that support learning and retention. Rehearsal strategies also strengthen the connections that exist among the visual, auditory, and language systems within the brain. As noted earlier, if these connections are not consistently used, they become vulnerable to pruning and may fade away (Diamond & Hopson, 1998).

Effect of Neural Rest on Brain Development   Evidence from neuroscience suggests the brain is unable to stay attentive for long periods of time; therefore, the brain needs **neural rest,** or downtime, to process information and strengthen neural circuitry (Jensen, 1998). Newly formed synapses can grow stronger only when no other neural stimuli compete for attention. "Downtime has to be nonchallenging time. As soon as you create challenge, interaction, and feedback, it is not downtime" (Jensen in D'Arcongelo, 1998, p. 25).

The normal human brain works most efficiently when periods of high levels of attention are followed by periods of lower levels of attention. Jensen (1998) suggested teachers directly engage student's attention only 20% to 40% of the teaching time and then provide a choice of interesting activities designed to help the student process the information. Jensen stated:

> *Teachers need to keep attentional demands to short bursts no longer than the age of their learners in minutes. For a 1st grader, that's about 6 consecutive minutes; for a high schooler, that's up to 15 minutes. Julie's teacher will want to use Julie's attention sparingly for introductions, key ideas, directions, lecturettes, reviews, stories, and closings. The rest of the overall learning time (processing, encoding, and "neural rest") ought to be student time, used for processing, projects, discussions, group work, partner work, self-assessment, journal writing, feedback, design, research, mapping, interviews, review, or memorization. (p. 43)*

Enriched Environments

Neuroscientists have studied the effects of environments on animal behavior since the 1950s (Bruer, 1998). Although a direct correlation between animal research and human research cannot be made, some general conclusions can be drawn. Diamond and Hopson (1998) studied the effect of enriched and impoverished environments on the brains of rats, concluding that enriched environments influence human brain growth and, therefore, learning potential.

Enriched home and school environments give children opportunities to make sense out of what they are learning, facilitating optimal development of mental capacities (Diamond & Hopson, 1998; Jensen, 1998; Lindsey, 1998/1999; Newberger, 1997; Schiller, 1997; Shore, 1997; Simmons & Sheehan, 1997; Wolfe & Brandt, 1998). Furthermore, a child's brain development suffers if the child is denied opportunities to live in a stimulating environment, has few opportunities to play, or is rarely touched by peers or adults (Nash, 1997). Wolfe and Brandt (1998) stated that environments, including classroom environments, are not neutral places but consistently influence brain growth and development and, subsequently, learning. "We educators are either growing dendrites or letting them wither and die. The trick is to determine what constitutes an enriched environment" (p. 11).

Elements of an enriched environment for young children include nurturing, interactive relationships between adults and children, sensory stimulation, consistent emotional support, challenging tasks that capitalize on children's prior knowledge and experience, opportunities to choose from a variety of activities that allow children to process information, and a nutritious diet (Diamond & Hopson, 1998). An impoverished environment would contain many opposing elements, including the following:

- *A diet low in protein, vitamins, and minerals, and too high or too low in calories*
- *A vacillating or negative emotional climate*
- *Sensory deprivation*
- *High levels of stress and pressure*
- *Unchanging conditions lacking novelty*
- *Long periods of isolation from caregivers and/or peers*
- *A heavy, dull atmosphere lacking in fun or in a sense of exploration and joy of learning*
- *A passive rather than active involvement in some or all activities*
- *Little personal choice of activities*
- *Little chance to evaluate the results or effects and change to different activities*
- *Development in a narrow, not broad range of interests (Diamond & Hopson, 1998, pp. 107–108)*

At first, it may appear that elements of enriched environments simply represent what is common-sense parenting and teaching, and that impoverished environments represent extreme conditions in our homes and schools. However, Diamond and Hopson (1998) painted a realistic picture of the day-to-day conditions of many children living in contemporary society:

> *It doesn't take an orphanage scene from David Copperfield to qualify as an impoverished environment. All it takes is a toddler sitting alone and passive for hours in front of a television set, dreaming eyes of wonder glazed over, imagination shelved, exploratory energy on hold. Then throw in a bowl of potato chips and a soda. (p. 109)*

Unfortunately, this scene repeats itself too often. Therefore, to promote brain development and facilitate learning, it is important for early childhood educators to understand how to enrich the environments of the children whose lives they influence. Figure 2–3 summarizes major findings from neuroscience that are important for educators to consider when developing environments for young children.

A synthesis of the literature related to brain development points to several major constructs or "big ideas" that are useful to educators and families of young children. These big ideas include the following:

1. Brain development is nonlinear and continues throughout a person's lifetime. However, during early childhood, the brain has the greatest capacity for change. Brain development results from a complex interplay between a person's heredity and environment, and the influence of the early environment on brain development is long lasting.
2. Warm, loving relationships enhance brain growth and development.
3. Learning is strongly influenced by emotion—the stronger the emotion connected with an experience, the stronger the memory of that experience will be.
4. There are critical periods—windows of opportunity—when the development of specific types of neural circuitry occurs most easily.
5. The brain needs downtime or neural rest to work efficiently.
6. The brain needs stimulation and enriched environments for optimal development and functioning.

Figure 2–3 *The "big ideas" from neuroscience.*
From Bruer, 1998; Chugani, 1996; D'Arcongelo, 1998; Diamond & Hopson, 1998; Jensen, 1998; Lindsey, 1998/1999; Newberger, 1997; Wolfe & Brandt, 1998.

Play and Brain Development

Psychologists, researchers, educators, and parents have long recognized the value of play in children's learning and development. Play is an absorbing activity and a fundamental means for gathering and processing information, learning new skills, and practicing old ones. It is the ultimate realization of learning by doing (Feeney, Christensen, & Moravcik, 1996; Scales, Almy, Nicolopoulou, & Ervin-Tripp, 1991; Spodek, 1986). Freud (1958) viewed play as an emotional release for children, whereas Erikson (1963) believed that play helped children develop self-esteem and gain mastery of their thoughts. Piaget (1952) discussed two important by-products of play, one being joy and the other learning. Vygotsky (1978) believed that through play children stretch beyond their own understanding and develop new skills and abilities that support further learning and development.

Play can be defined as "open-ended, self-chosen, enjoyable actions and activities that unite and integrate cognitive, language, social, emotional, and motor aspects of learning within rich, culturally sensitive, child-centered, and supportive contexts" (Kieff & Casbergue, 2000, p. xiii). Therefore, when children play, many elements of an enriched environment are present. They have opportunities to both experience and express many emotions such as joy, pleasure, surprise, curiosity, anticipation, and wonder. During interactive play, children have opportunities to build strong attachments to warm, responsive family members, peers, and caregivers. Because play is self-chosen, children bring their prior knowledge and experience into the play episode, are able to monitor the amount of challenge present in an environment, and thus extend their learning. At times, children spend much of their play time exploring new materials, phenomena, or relationships, trying to figure out and make sense of the people and objects in their world. At other times, children's play is restful and repetitive as they practice and rehearse new skills and develop automaticity or previously formed skills or concepts (see Figure 2–4). Therefore, through play, children have many opportunities to develop neural pathways that govern cognitive, motor, social, and emotional learning and development (Shore, 1997).

A person only has to observe children at play for a short period of time to realize there are many forms of play. Some forms are quite simple, whereas others are quite complex. Piaget (1954, 1962, 1965, 1969) described two stages of play: **functional play** and **symbolic play.** Functional play is also known as exploratory, sensorimotor, or practice play. During functional play, children repeat a particular action, for example, building and knocking down a stack of blocks. Because their actions are motivated by pleasure, children are mentally engrossed and the action sustains their interest and attention. Practice or functional play remains a major source of pleasure, development, and learning throughout a person's life (Van Hoorn, Nourot, Scales, & Alward, 1993).

Figure 2–4 *When children play, many elements of an enriched environment are present.*

Piaget's second stage of play is known as symbolic play. When children engage in symbolic play they use mental representations, thereby allowing one object to stand for another. A young child might use a block to represent a telephone and pretend to talk. Three major forms of symbolic play are **constructive play, dramatic play,** and **games with rules.** Constructive play provides a natural link between practice play and dramatic play. During constructive play, the child uses concrete materials to build or form a representation of objects in her environment or even objects that she imagines. For example, a child may use blocks to build a structure that represents a house. She may even extend her construction to represent a neighborhood. A child's ability to represent what she is thinking through constructions increases with age and experience.

Dramatic play involves the creation of imaginary roles and situations, and often accompanies constructive play (Van Hoorn et al., 1993). A child may use a block to represent a telephone and then pretend to be a doctor calling an ambulance. As with constructive play, dramatic play becomes more sophisticated and more abstract with age, opportunity, and experience. **Sociodramatic play** occurs when children interact with peers, siblings, parents, or caregivers during dramatic or constructive play. In preschools and kindergartens, it is common to see children and teachers working together to build structures and play out scenes as they create them in their imaginations. For example, four-year-old children, collaborating with their teachers, may use a combination of blocks and chairs to create a *school bus* and go on an imaginary trip to the *beach*. During this *trip,* the children are negotiating with each other and making up the rules for their play as they go along.

When children begin to create rules for their games or use rules created by others, they are engaging in the type of symbolic play described by Piaget (1954, 1965, 1969) as games with rules. Constructive play provides children with multiple opportunities to create their own rules or negotiate with others to change existing rules as they build and carry out dramatic play scenarios with blocks and other construction materials.

Conclusion

As a result of ongoing dialogue between educational psychologists and neuroscientists regarding brain development, parents and educators can now rely on more than theories, intuition, and anecdotal evidence to explain the significant changes in the brain during the early years. As we have seen, constructive play, is a fundamental activity of childhood that leads not only to cognitive, social, emotional, and physical growth; development; and learning, but also provides an enriched environment conducive to the growth and development of the brain's complex multilevel neural circuitry system. This system is the foundation for optimal learning throughout a person's life. In the following chapters, we explore, in depth, many aspects of block play and describe ways to facilitate functional and symbolic play in early childhood classrooms.

Theory into Practice

1. Take a casual walk through a mall or grocery store, observing interactions between young children and the adults who accompany them. Take note of actions or activities you see as enriching to the child's overall development. What differences do you see among the children you observe? What conclusions can you draw from these observations?
2. Observe young children at play with blocks. Write a running record of the children's actions and conversations during the play episode. Review your record and find events within the episode that could be described as repetition strategies or neural rest. Describe events that challenged the children. What conclusions can you draw from these observations?
3. Review the daily schedule of a program for young children. With a red pen, highlight times when children are indirectly challenged. With a green pen, highlight times when children are directly challenged. Evaluate the schedule based on information you have read about challenge and neural rest. What revisions would be necessary to bring about an optimal balance for the age group you are observing?

Websites

www.cainelearning.com

Caine Learning LLC: Renata and Geoffrey Caine offer information related to brain development and education. Site offers resources, articles, and links in its attempt to answer the basic question, "Why are we struggling in our ability to educate?"

www.brains.org

Brains.org with Kathie Nunley and Gene Van Tassell offers practical classroom applications for current research through articles and links.

Related Readings

Diamond, M., & Hopson, J. (1998). *Magic trees of the mind: How to nurture your child's intelligence, creativity, and healthy emotions from birth through adolescence.* New York: Plume.

Healy, J. (1994). *Your child's growing mind: A guide to learning and brain development from birth to adolescence.* New York: Main Street Books.

Shore, R. (1997). *Rethinking the brain: New insights into early development.* New York: Families and Work Institute.

References

Begley, S. (1996, February 19). Your child's brain. *Newsweek, 55–61.*

Bruer, J. T. (1998). Brain science: Brain fiction. *Educational Leadership, 56*(3), 14–18.

Bruer, J. T. (1999). In search of brain-based education. *Phi Delta Kappan, 80*(9), 648–657.

Chugani, H. T. (1996). *Functional maturation of the brain.* Paper presented at the Third Annual Brain Symposium, Berkeley, CA.

D'Arcongelo, M. (1998). The brains behind the brain. *Educational Leadership, 56*(3), 20–25.

Diamond, M., & Hopson, J. (1998). *Magic trees of the mind: How to nurture your child's intelligence, creativity, and healthy emotions from birth through adolescence.* New York: Plume.

Erikson, E. (1963). *Childhood and society* (2nd ed.). New York: Norton.

Feeney, S., Christensen, D., & Moravcik, E. (1996). *Who am I in the lives of children?* Englewood Cliffs NJ: Merrill.

Freud, S. (1958). *On creativity and the unconscious.* (I. F. Grant Doff, Trans.) New York: Harper & Row. (Original work published in 1928).

Greenenough, W. T. (1997). We can't focus just on ages zero to three. *APA Monitor, 28,* 19–20.

Gunnar, M. R. (1996). *Quality of care and buffering of stress physiology: Its potential in protecting the developing human brain.* Minneapolis: University of Minnesota Institute of Child Development.

Gunnar, M. R., Broderson, L., Krueger, K., & Rigatuso, R. (1996). Dampening of behavioral and adrenocortical reactivity during early infancy: Normal changes and individual differences. *Child Development, 67*(3), 877–889.

Jensen, E. (1998). How Julie's brain learns. *Educational Leadership, 56*(3), 41–45.

Kieff, J., & Casbergue, R. (2000). *Playful learning and teaching: Integrating play into preschool and primary programs.* Boston: Allyn & Bacon.

LeDoux, J. (1996). *The emotional brain: The mysterious underpinnings of emotional life.* New York: Simon & Shuster.

Lindsey, G. (1998/1999). Brain research and implications for early childhood education. *Childhood Education, 75*(2), 97–100.

Lowery, L. (1998). How new science curriculum reflects brain research. *Educational Leadership, 56*(3), 26–30.

Nash, M. (1997). Fertile minds. *Time, 149*(5), 48–56.

Neville, H. J. (1995). Developmental specificity in neurocognitive development in humans. In M. S. Gazzaniga (Ed.), *The cognitive neuroscience* (pp. 327–384.). Cambridge, MA: MIT Press.

Newberger, J. J. (1997). New brain development research—A wonderful window of opportunity to build public support for early childhood education! *Young Children, 52*(4), 4–9.

Piaget, J. (1952). *The origins of intelligence in children.* New York: International University Press.

Piaget, J. (1954). *The construction of reality in the child.* New York: Ballantine Books.

Piaget, J. (1962). *Play, dreams, and imitation in childhood.* New York: Norton.

Piaget, J. (1965). *The moral judgement of the child.* New York: Free Press.

Piaget, J. (1969). *The language and thought of the child.* New York: World.

Scales, B., Almy, M., Nicolopoulou, A., & Ervin-Tripp, S. (1991). *Play and the social context of development in early care and education.* New York: Teachers College Press.

Schiller, P. (1997). Brain development research: Support and challenges. *Child Care Information Exchange, 11*(7), 6–10.

Shore, R. (1997). *Rethinking the brain: New insights into early development.* New York: Families and Work Institute.

Simmons, T., & Sheehan, R. (1997, February 16). Brain research manifests importance of first years. *The News & Observer,* 42–57.

Spodek, B. (1986). *Today's kindergarten: Exploring the knowledge base, expanding the curriculum.* New York: Teachers College Press.

Van Hoorn, J., Nourot, P., Scales, B., & Alward, K. (1993). *Play at the center of the curriculum.* New York: Merrill.

Vygotsky, L. S. (1978). *Mind and society: The development of higher psychological processes.* Cambridge, MA: Harvard University Press.

Wolfe, P., & Brandt, R. (1998). What do we know from brain research. *Educational Leadership, 56*(3), 8–13.

Stages of Block Building

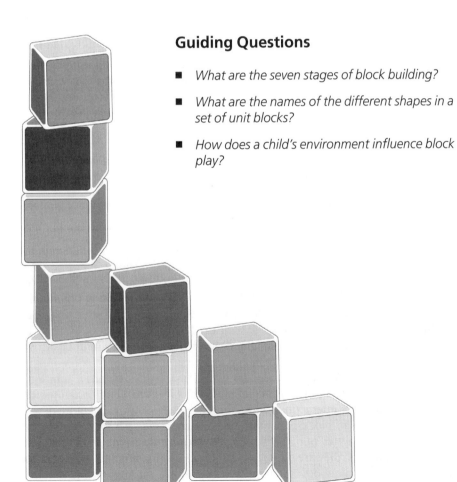

Guiding Questions

- *What are the seven stages of block building?*

- *What are the names of the different shapes in a set of unit blocks?*

- *How does a child's environment influence block play?*

As Ms. Hall passes by the block center, she watches how intently the children build and play with blocks. Upon closer observation, she notices Martin repeatedly stacking square unit blocks to form a tower that always tumbles after the sixth block is placed on top. Next to Martin, with their backs to his tower building, Sheri and Allison are engaged in dramatic play with a farm scene they built from a variety of unit blocks and small plastic animal figures. In another corner of the block center, Jackson has built two bridges side by side; each is identically decorated with triangles and pillars. As she observes these three different scenes, Ms. Hall reflects on her knowledge of children and the stages of block building.

It is important for teachers to be thoroughly familiar with the stages through which children pass as they explore block building. By recognizing the different stages of block building, teachers can note children's development and learning and can facilitate their play in ways that foster further learning. Identifying and understanding the stages of block building is similar to understanding children's sequential growth and milestones of motor development. In the first 18 months of life, infants experience an observable sequence of motor development—sitting with support, rocking on all fours, crawling, pulling to a standing position, holding on and walking around furniture, standing alone, and walking independently. The teacher who is familiar with stages of block building is able to observe and document learning just as new parents proudly note changes in their child's physical abilities. (The Block Play Rating Scale/Checklist for Preschoolers ages 3–5 is provided in Chapter 9 to assist teachers in documenting children's block building.)

Introduction to Unit Blocks and Building

Unit blocks, designed by Caroline Pratt, are made of hardwood, carefully cut to specification, sanded, and left natural with no embellishments to interfere with children's imaginative play. The dimensions of the basic unit are $5^1/_2''$ long $\times$ $3^3/_4''$ wide $\times$ $1^3/_8''$ thick. A half unit is exactly half the length of the unit block, a double unit is twice the length of the unit block, and a quadruple unit is four times the length of the basic unit. Other block shapes are designed to stack evenly, such as the pillar, half pillar, and large and small cylinders. There are more than 20 different block shapes, some of which are pictured in Figure 3–1.

The stages of block play are based on the seminal work of Harriet Johnson, teacher and author of *The Art of Blockbuilding* (1933/1996). Johnson observed and studied children's interactions with unit blocks for many years before devising the seven stages of block play that are still considered relevant to children's block building today (Hirsch, 1996). (*Note:* Because Johnson's work focused solely on unit blocks, they are the only type of building material described in this chapter. There are many other types of blocks suitable for young children, and these are discussed in subsequent chapters.)

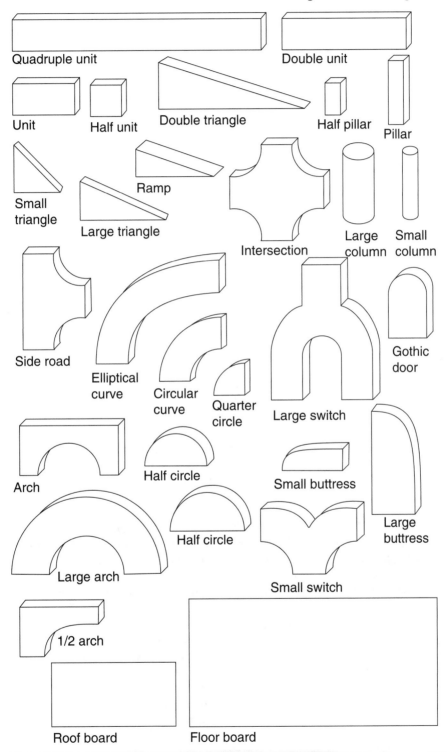

Figure 3–1 *Unit block shapes and names.*

Children move through the stages of block play in a sequential fashion, gradually adapting their block building as they move through the seven stages. As they reach new stages of building, strategies used in previous stages may still be apparent. They are in a sense building on what they already know and, therefore, maintain the elements of design from the previous stages. This is similar to stages of children's drawing development. Young children gradually refine rudimentary scribbles into geometric shapes. As their drawings become more representational, they still use the basic shapes, only now with a purpose—to resemble objects they want to depict.

Progression through the stages of block building represents changes in children's cognitive understanding of balance, spatial relationships, symmetry, and imaginative play. A child's current stage of block building is determined by the most sophisticated element of his block structure. For example, a child may build a farmyard with blocks for dramatic play by making an enclosure for a horse corral. Building enclosures is characteristic of stage 3, which occurs prior to using a block structure for dramatic play purposes, which is stage 7. Even though the child in this example adopted a building technique from stage 3, the current stage in which this child is building is best described as stage 7 because the structure was built and used for dramatic play.

The distinct characteristics of building at each stage make it possible to document and assess children's learning and development as they engage in block play over time. When discussing children's learning in stages, it is always important to point out that the learning is derived from the experimentation and repetition that occurs within each important stage. Adults should be familiar with the stages of block building so they understand children's repetitious play with blocks and support them as they try new methods of building. Adults should not attempt to move children through the stages of block building more quickly because this holds no value to the child. Coaxing children to create more sophisticated structures than they are naturally capable of robs them of time needed to do necessary experimenting and investigating to construct their own knowledge.

A preschool-age child who has not had prior experiences with blocks will move through the stages in the same sequence as a child who began experimenting with blocks in infancy, with the exception of the first stage (carrying). He will, however, pass through the early stages more quickly, due to his relevant experiences with other objects and materials. Variations in the stage of block building among children of the same age will occur in terms of "the rate at which children pass through these stages, the emphasis they place on each, and the lines of development that they subsequently follow" (Johnson, 1933/1996, p. 18). For example, after mastering a building technique at a particular stage, a child may spend time repeatedly performing the newly learned technique before moving on to learning new building strategies. Another child may engage in what Johnson refers to as "stunt building." This risk-taking behavior involves the child using what he knows about a particular building technique and pushing it to the limit, such as creating a tower so high a chair is needed to add blocks to the top and several assistants are required for safety purposes and to keep blocks balanced as the child continues to build upward. Through stunt building, children discover the limits of the material and their ability to manipulate it. The result of both of these experimental styles is a greater understanding, which may later be applied to solving problems with building.

Johnson's research is based on observing children from 2 to 6 years of age, but she refrains from associating specific ages with each stage. Gura (1992), however, identifies characteristics of block builders by age. She found children at 3 to 4 years of age spend more time exploring the physical properties of blocks, combining blocks at increasing levels of difficulty, and more time paying attention to space concerns than creating representations with blocks. Children 4 and 5 years of age spend about equal time exploring blocks and building and creating figurative representations. At age 6 and older, creating figurative representations of actual structures dominate block play.

Seven Stages of Block Building

Johnson (1933/1996) identified seven stages of block building:

- Stage 1: Carrying
- Stage 2: Stacking
- Stage 3: Bridging
- Stage 4: Enclosures
- Stage 5: Patterns and symmetry
- Stage 6: Early representational
- Stage 7: Later representational

Each stage is described in detail, and building scenarios are provided to describe a classroom scene related to block building at each stage, along with observer comments. A summary chart (see Figure 3–2) provides an overview of characteristics of each stage and sketches of examples. Johnson's research on block building focused solely on materials from Pratt's unit block system. Therefore, all descriptions, examples, scenes, and sketches portray the unit block system.

Stage 1: Carrying   The response of very young children to blocks is similar to their reactions to other unfamiliar objects. Their first inclination is to explore them using their senses; therefore, they visually examine, touch, and taste them (see Figure 3–3). They may also grasp one block in each hand and strike the two together to explore the new sound. This stage is further characterized by young children simply carrying the blocks from place to place, dumping blocks from their container, and knocking down structures built by others. No actual building takes place in the carrying stage. This stage of block play is analogous to the early scribbling stage in children's drawing development. Scribbling is a physical, sensory experience in which children enjoy the feel of the materials and the physical motion that accompanies scribbling. Early scribblers are not

Stage	Characteristics	Examples of Structures
1—Carrying	Carry blocks, explore with senses, hit blocks together or against other objects	No building takes place
2—Stacking	Stack the blocks either vertically (towers) or horizontally (rows)	
3—Bridging	Bridge the space between two upright blocks with a third block	
4—Enclosures	Purposefully place blocks to enclose a space	

Figure 3–2   *Stages of block building summary chart.*

Stage	Characteristics	Examples of Structures
5—Patterns and symmetry	Build structure with balance, symmetry, and decorative elements	
6—Early representational	Incorporate building techniques from stages 1–5, begin naming structure during or after construction	
7—Later representational	Announce name of structure before building begins, build familiar settings, use structure and related accessories for dramatic play	

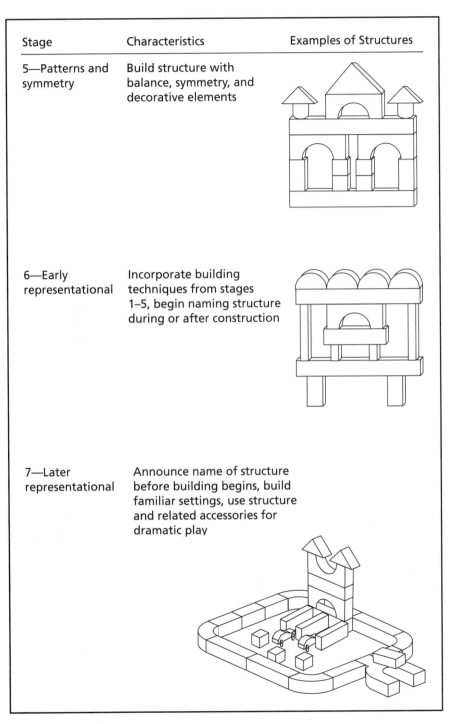

Figure 3–2 *Continued*

cognizant of making marks because creating a product is not the purpose of their actions (Kellogg, 1970; Lowenfeld & Brittain, 1982). Similarly, children in the carrying stage of block play are not concerned with building but with fully experiencing the materials. Young children's experiences in this first stage demonstrate growing physical knowledge (that is, an understanding of physical attributes of objects in the child's immediate environment).

Figure 3–3 *Jackson's block play consists of carrying blocks.*

Block Scenario 1

Robbie (male, 16 months) walks over to a small bucket containing unit blocks. He sits down and carefully takes out a square block, placing it purposefully on the floor next to him. He removes a unit block and places it on the floor also. He reaches into the bucket a third time, pulls out a small pillar, puts it in his mouth briefly, and drops the block on the floor. He picks up two blocks from the floor (square and pillar) and bangs them together as he winces at the sound. Robbie stands up, still holding onto the two blocks, and carries them to his caregiver who is seated on the floor. He drops them in her lap and joins two other children at the snack table.

Comments

Robbie is in the carrying stage (stage 1) of block play. He exhibits characteristics such as exploring the physical properties of blocks by tasting and banging. He carries them from one place to another—in this case to the caregiver. Robbie made no attempt to build.

Figure 3–4 *Blocks are balanced as they are stacked vertically.*

Stage 2: Stacking The second stage of block building is characterized by repeatedly stacking blocks, either vertically to create towers (see Figure 3–4) or horizontally to create rows (see Figure 3–5). Children's need for **functional play** (repetitive behavior for mental mastery and coordination of skills) is evident during this stage. They repeatedly experiment with stacking blocks

Figure 3–5 *This preschoolers places blocks in horizontal rows before stacking them vertically.*

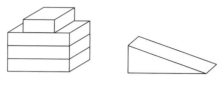

Figure 3–6 *Stage 2: Stacking.*

either vertically or horizontally. This repetition in block building is similar to other activities that intrigue young children, such as requesting that the same book be read over and over or repeatedly demanding one more turn on the slide at the playground. As emphasized in Chapter 2, repetition is important to children's brain growth and development. Furthermore, when they are choosing the activities they repeat, the sheer joy of the activity further promotes brain growth.

Individual children approach building towers and rows in different ways. Some will haphazardly stack blocks until they fall, whereas others carefully line up the blocks and push them into an even line. Regardless of how individual children build, they all possess a need to build rows and towers repeatedly before moving on to other types of structures. Once children have mastered building rows and towers, they begin to build them in multiples that, to the adult, resemble floors and walls. Soon after this is accomplished, they move to the next stage of building. Harriet Johnson did not determine whether the tower or row preceded the other or if one appeared easier to children. Instead, the significance of this stage is characterized by the action of placing first one block, then another, in a serial order (see Figure 3–6).

Block Scenario 2

Samantha (female, 4 years, 4 months) is encouraged by her teacher, Mr. James, to join him in the block corner. She takes her teacher's outstretched hand and walks slowly with no expression on her face. Mr. James takes several blocks from the shelf (five unit blocks, four squares, and one ramp) and lays them on the carpet. He places them on the floor and sits down opposite Samantha. Shyly, she takes a unit block and sets it flat in front of her. She then takes another unit and stacks it on top. Then a third unit block is stacked. She carefully straightens the blocks. Samantha concentrates on building, and her motions are slow and deliberate. Mr. James talks informally with Samantha as she builds, providing encouragement without overt enthusiasm.

Mr. James: *"You have stacked three blocks so far."*
Samantha: *"I'm going to make it taller."*

Samantha places the ramp on the stack next and then a square block, which slides off. Her teacher engages her in a conversation about why the square slid off, and she removes the ramp and replaces the square, which sits firmly on top of the three stacked unit blocks (see Figure 3–6). She smiles broadly at her accomplishment. Mr. James leaves the block area to assist arriving children. Samantha takes down each block one by one, and rebuilds and disassembles the tower again. The third time she builds the tower, she uses all five units and two squares. After replacing all the blocks on the shelf, she joins another child building with Legos®.

Comments

Four-year-old Samantha is in the stacking stage (stage 2). Samantha is highly verbal but has shown little interest or aptitude in the block corner. According to the Toy Preference Inventory, which her mother completed during registration, she had no experiences with blocks prior to entering prekindergarten. Although her mother has since purchased a set of blocks, Samantha does not freely choose block play at school. Her teacher, Mr. James, has devised a plan for slowly introducing her to block building and shows support by being physically available and providing encouraging remarks.

Stage 3: Bridging   Stage 3 of block play is made evident by children "bridging" or roofing the space between two upright blocks. The upright blocks must be placed the appropriate distance apart to support the bridging block, or a bridging block that is long enough to lie on both supporting blocks must be selected (see Figure 3–7). A typical point of confusion for children who are making their first attempts at bridging occurs when the upright, support blocks are placed on the floor at either end of a base block. When a bridging block of the same size as the base block is logically selected, children are confused by the fact that it is not long enough to bridge the upright blocks. Children who persistently experiment with different bridging attempts will find success earlier than those who are easily defeated and revert back to building towers and rows. Once a child learns how to bridge between blocks, he repeatedly practices his newfound skill in structure after structure. Uses of bridges also become more elaborate with practice as children build bridges on top of other bridges (see Figure 3–8).

Figure 3–7   *A preschooler carefully bridges three unit blocks.*

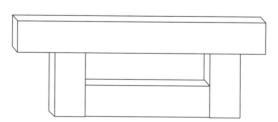

Figure 3–8   *Stage 3: Bridging.*

Block Scenario 3

After waking from a nap and enlisting the help of a teacher with putting on her new shoes, Rachel (female, 3 years, 4 months) runs to the block shelf and quickly selects two double units and four unit blocks. She builds one on top of the other—double unit lying flat, unit blocks on top standing vertically, and finally the double unit placed horizontally on top. The top block (double unit) is precariously balanced. She quickly pulls away the bottom unit block and squeals as the blocks tumble.

Next, she places the double unit on the floor, with the unit blocks standing on end on the floor at both ends of the double unit. She attempts to rest the second double unit on the tops of the two standing unit blocks. The unit blocks do not support the double unit because they are too far apart. Rachel returns to the block shelf and selects a quadruple unit, which she carefully rests across the top of the two unit blocks (See Figure 3–8). She seems satisfied as she beckons her teacher to come and see what she has done.

Comments

Rachel first demonstrates her skill at building towers (stage 2) with "stunt building" by attempting a difficult structure. She is in the beginning bridging stage (stage 3). The two unit blocks could not support the bridging block because they were held too far apart by the base double unit. Rather than moving the two units on top of the base so they could support the double unit, she selected a longer block to create the bridge.

Stage 4: Enclosures   In stage 4, children successfully use blocks to enclose space (see Figure 3–9). Children may initially intend to create block enclosures, but if they do not possess the cognitive understanding of spatial orientation (knowing which direction to turn the blocks), they will continue to place blocks end to end creating a roadlike effect. It often takes a great deal of practice and many attempts before children are successful at arranging even four blocks to create an enclosure in the shape of a square. Once the act of building an enclosure is accomplished, repetition takes over, and children will create a series of enclosures. Block enclosures also become more elaborate as children experiment by making new enclosed shapes, such as circles or ovals, varying the size of the enclosed space, or creating a series of joined enclosures. According to Johnson, children at this stage begin wrestling with the material in their desire to make it less rigid and more flexible (see Figure 3–10).

Figure 3–9   *Katie uses trial and error to find the blocks needed to form an enclosure.*

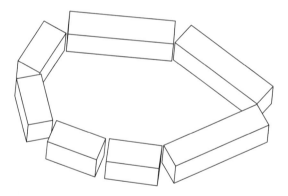

Figure 3–10   *Stage 4: Enclosures.*

Block Scenario 4

Michael (male, 4 years, 10 months) takes three double unit blocks from the shelf and places the long, narrow side of each on the floor. The ends are almost touching at the edges as he turns each block at an angle. He returns to the shelf, carries two unit blocks to his building place, and continues turning each at an angle. He stands to look at this structure with the open gap. He takes two more units from the shelf and places them carefully so they fill in the gap and form an enclosed space (see Figure 3–10). He stands back and smiles at the block enclosure he created. Michael calls to the teacher to show her his latest accomplishment.

Comments

Michael demonstrates his ability to enclose a space (stage 4). He understands the basic principle of turning blocks at an angle to create a rounded shape. He solved a problem by selecting smaller blocks (units) to fill in the open area. He is proud of the control he had over the inflexible blocks and wants to share his success with his teacher.

Stage 5: Patterns and Symmetry   Children at this stage build balanced structures with decorative or symmetrical patterns. The principles of design learned previously (towers, rows, bridging, and enclosures) are evident with the addition of attention to pattern (see Figures 3–11 and 3–12). It is not certain whether this attention to design is visual or kinesthetic, that is, if children are building so there is visual symmetry or if the physical act of building is the predominant force. As children build, they appear rhythmic and intentional in the physical act of block placement, such as placing one to the left, right, front, and then back of the structure. Children will seek out necessary materials to facilitate their building, such as returning to the block storage shelf or bargaining with other children for blocks. Children may or may not name their structures at this stage, and the structures are not used in their play. The structure is made for the sake of building, not as a basis for imaginative, dramatic play. Stages 2 through 5 are examples of children constructing their own knowledge through block building. At each stage, children are making gains in understanding spatial relationships in the manipulation of blocks.

Figure 3–11   *Much attention has been given to pattern and symmetry in this structure.*

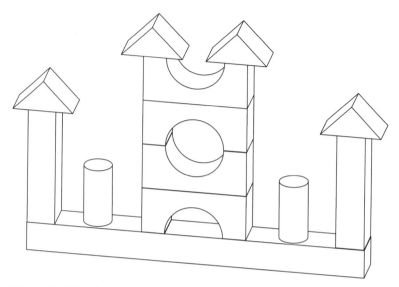

Figure 3–12 *Stage 5: Patterns and symmetry.*

Block Scenario 5

Evan (male, 5 years, 6 months) enters the block corner and watches Lauren (female, 5 years, 3 months) build for almost 1 minute. He then asks, "Can I play?" She responds, "Okay, but don't knock any blocks down." Lauren sends Evan to the shelf to get "some more blocks." He carries a variety of block shapes in his arms and drops them near the structure knocking over several blocks on one side. "Hey! Don't knock them down!" says Lauren. Evan replies, "Sorry." Evan sits next to Lauren and hands her blocks as she asks for them by name. She carefully adds each to her structure. Lauren decides she needs three small triangles, but there are no more on the shelf. She directs Evan to retrieve the needed triangles from another pair of children building nearby. He asks the other children and they say, "No. We need all our blocks." He gathers three unit blocks and a pillar from Lauren's stock and asks if they will trade. The pair agrees, and Evan returns with three small triangles. Lauren directs Evan as they place the blocks along the top of the structure (see Figure 3–12).

Comments

Lauren demonstrates symmetry and pattern in her structure (stage 5) by placing identical blocks on either side and at the top of the block structure. She has strong ideas about the exact blocks needed to create the pattern. Evan shows negotiation skills by bargaining with other children for blocks needed. However, because Lauren instructs Evan almost every step of the way, it is difficult to determine his stage of block building.

Figure 3–13   *Mychael declares her block structure is MacDonald's® and dusts off the final product.*

Stage 6: Early Representational   At this stage, the building techniques learned previously are obvious in children's block structures as a greater number of blocks are used and towers, rows, bridges, enclosures, and patterns are repeatedly used in the same structure. Children have mastered the basics of block construction and design, and begin to take control of their play using blocks as a medium. Children name their products at this stage, even though the structure may not resemble its name (see Figure 3–13). Structures are often named during or after construction, but not prior to construction. It is believed that naming at this stage may be the result of teacher questioning or probing, similar to that which occurs with children's drawings. As adults question, "What are you building?" or "Is that your house?" children believe they need to answer accordingly, even though they had not previously thought of naming the structure. Another explanation for naming at this stage is due to children observing or interacting with children in stage 7 who readily name block structures. Whatever their motivation, this stage is characterized by children's play with completed structures and their firsts attempts to name structures (see Figure 3–14).

Block Scenario 6

Marvin (male, 6 years, 3 months) is sitting near a wall in the block center and begins stacking blocks vertically. Marvin tells Gregory (male, 6 years, 9 months) who is standing nearby, "I'm going to make something 'Neat!' " Gregory sits down by Marvin and begins to pass him blocks. Sometimes Marvin takes a block from Gregory and other times he says, "No, not that one." Marvin continues to build vertically and Gregory joins him by placing a few blocks around the perimeter of the structure. They talk to each other about the structure, and then stand up and look at it. Marvin says, "Isn't it cool?" and Gregory says, "Yeah, we built it." Marvin says, "Hey! This is a robot," then pauses and corrects himself, "No, this is a space robot." Gregory says it needs a longer neck for it to be a space robot so they add a pillar and a small triangle on the top (see Figure 3–14). They both look at it again when suddenly Marvin gives the robot a karate chop with his hand and Gregory gives the structure a second one. Both boys laugh. Together, they finish taking the rest of it apart one block at a time. While doing this, Marvin says, "Let's talk robot language," and they make inaudible sounds in a conversational pattern. They both start laughing as they put the blocks away on a shelf.

Comments

Gregory and Marvin use building strategies from stage 2 (stacking) to create their structure. After completion, they identify it as a robot and then make changes to it to make a space robot. Naming the structure after completion is typical of stage 5. The boys show early signs of using built structures for dramatic play purposes as they destroy the space robot with a karate chop.

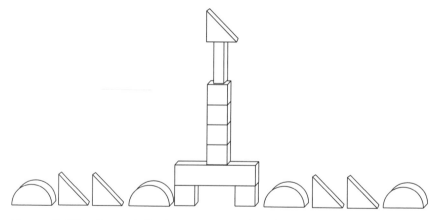

Figure 3–14 *Stage 6: Early representational.*

Stage 7: Later Representational   Dramatic play with the block structures as the center of the scene begins to dominate play at this stage. Naming structures becomes more common, and children will begin to announce what they intend to build before construction begins. This demonstrates that children have an advance plan for their play and blocks are used to set the stage (see Figure 3–15). Buildings are created to symbolize familiar structures so children can reenact their experiences. As a result, the design elements are more intricate and represent actual details of an authentic structure (see Figure 3–16). For example, children will invent ways to make the structure have the same features as the building they hold in memory, such as removing blocks from a solid wall to create "windows."

Figure 3–15   *Primary grade children build and label a replica of their school.*

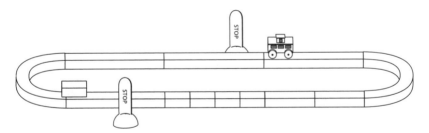

Figure 3–16   *Stage 7: Later representational.*

Johnson did not describe in her writings the role of children's use of accessory equipment that today is widely available in most classrooms that value block play. Accessories such as microfigure dolls and animals and transportation vehicles are often used to support children's dramatic play at this stage. Children will also create their own accessories as needed to support their play, such as drawing symbols for traffic signs, using recycled materials such as milk jug caps, or items from nature such as pebbles and straw. Children's play with blocks during stages 6 and 7 demonstrates the integration of social-arbitrary knowledge (learning that occurs through interactions with other people) into their play. They use language and demonstrate their understanding of typical behaviors in a variety of real-life situations. Observing children as they engage in pretend play with block structures offers insight into the child's interpretation of how his world works.

Block Scenario 7

After discussing yesterday's field trip, a ride on the streetcar, Ms. Landry asks children to select a learning center from the choice board. Kendra (female, 5 years, 11 months) immediately announces, "I'm going to blocks!" and attaches her name card with Velcro® next to the corresponding picture. As Kendra walks to the block center, Damion (male, 5 years, 8 months) asks, "Can I build with you?" Kendra replies, "Sure, I'm making a streetcar line." Together, the two quickly take several quadruple unit blocks and line them up end to end. They place an elliptical curve at each end and fill in the space with one quadruple unit, four unit blocks, and two double unit blocks to form an oval enclosure.

Kendra picks up a unit block and identifies it as a streetcar. She moves it around the track made of blocks. Damion finds a train caboose from the accessory shelf and moves it along the track ahead of Kendra. They make "clunka-clunka-clunka" and "ding-ding" sounds as they move the blocks along.

After a few minutes, they bring family figurines to the area and stand them around the outside of the track. As their "streetcars" go around the track, they stop and pick up passengers. After three times around the track picking up and depositing figurines, Damion says, "The streetcar only stops at the sign." He locates the needed materials in a nearby basket and writes "s-t-o-p" with a marker along the side of three craft sticks. He pushes one end into clay and places them around the streetcar track.

The two play intently with the streetcar line made of blocks until the teacher signals time for clean-up. They place an index card folded in half and labeled "SAVE" on their structure and make plans to build restaurants and gas stations along the track tomorrow (see Figure 3–16).

Comments

Kendra and Damion use blocks specifically to build a streetcar track (a familiar structure) to reenact aspects of their field trip. They used building elements seen in stage 4 (enclosures) as well as accessories such as a caboose and family figures to supplement their play (stage 7). Damion also created props and streetcar signs needed to make the play more realistic. The children showed a desire to continue and elaborate on their play in the future by "saving" their structure.

Block Play Today

Harriet Johnson's research on stages of block play was first published in 1933 and has often been cited and reprinted since then (Johnson, 1933/1996; Provenzo & Brett, 1983). Even though society and education have changed significantly since her first observations of children at play with blocks, researchers still consider the stages to be accurate (Gura, 1992).

The seven stages of block play identified by Johnson are valid and useful to early childhood teachers. However, changes in society and education should be taken into consideration when observing children as they interact with blocks today. Children's personal experiences become evident as they engage in block building, and teachers should be prepared for what they may observe. For example, children who have witnessed violence as a means for solving disputes may use blocks to symbolize weapons for use in aggressive play rather than to build a restaurant or airport. Other children may find violent destruction of their block buildings more satisfying than the building experience or related, subsequent play. Children who have had limited building materials available to them may spend time hoarding blocks or finding ways to take them home. These are just a few examples of situations for which teachers must be prepared when working with children in today's society.

There are other factors that interfere with children's opportunities to play with blocks and other similar materials. One is an increase in standardized testing of young children and the subsequent drill-and-practice curriculum. As a result, young children today may have had fewer experiences with blocks in early childhood programs. Also, lack of funding for appropriate materials in early childhood classrooms may have affected the type, quality, or number of blocks available for children's building. Each of these factors as well and the individual characteristics of each child must be considered when observing and analyzing children's block building.

Conclusion

The seminal work of Harriet Johnson makes it possible to better understand children and their abilities through observing and documenting their block play. As children progress through each of the seven stages, they use more sophisticated building strategies based on skills used in previous stages. By thoroughly understanding these stages and developing the ability to identify each, teachers can facilitate children's play in a way that fosters learning in many areas.

Theory into Practice

1. Observe a group of children as they play with blocks. Determine which characteristics of building, as identified by Johnson, are evident. Do they simply carry blocks around as typical of stage 1? Do they attempt to build enclosures as in stage 4? Do they develop a dramatic play scene with their structure as in stage 7?
2. Observe children of different ages as they engage in block building. What similarities and differences are evident?
3. As you observe children in stage 7 of block play, reflect on how their play scenes may differ from those Johnson observed in the 1930s.

4. Identify factors that might affect individual children's progression through these seven stages.

Related Readings

Johnson, H. (1972). *Children in the nursery school.* New York: Agathon.

Pratt, C. (1924). *Experimental practice in the City and Country School.* New York: E. P. Dutton.

Pratt, C, (1948). *I learn from children.* New York: Simon & Schuster.

References

Gura, P. (1992). *Exploring learning: Young children and blockplay.* London: The Froebel Blockplay Research Group.

Hirsch, E. S. (1996). Block building: Practical considerations for the classroom teacher. In E. Hirsch (Ed.), *The block book* (pp. 117–132). Washington, DC: National Association for the Education of Young Children.

Johnson, H. (1933/1996). The art of blockbuilding. In E. Hirsch (Ed.), *The block book* (pp. 9–25). Washington, DC: National Association for the Education of Young Children.

Kellogg, R. (1970). *Analyzing children's art.* Palo Alto, CA: National Press Books.

Lowenfeld, V., & Brittain, L. (1982). *Creative and mental growth.* New York: Macmillan.

Provenzo, E. F., & Brett, A. (1983). *The complete block book.* Syracuse, NY: Syracuse University Press.

Learning Through Block Play

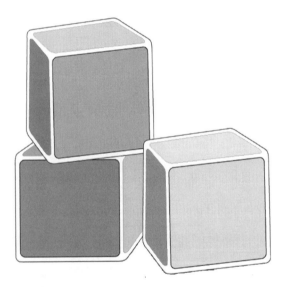

Block Play in Infancy and Toddlerhood

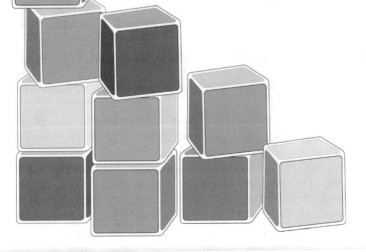

Guiding Questions

- *How do infants and toddlers come to discover and learn about their world through exploration and play?*

- *How can the block play of infants and toddlers facilitate physical, cognitive, language, social, and emotional growth and development?*

- *How can adults interact with infants and toddlers during block play to foster strong emotional attachments?*

There is probably no other period in the life of a child that is as developmentally rich and exciting to watch as infancy and toddlerhood. In a relatively short span, 3 years, the human infant changes from a seemingly helpless and dependent sleepy bundle of sweet-smelling joy to an alert, responsive, active, social, creeping, crawling, walking, running, jumping, talking, singing child. This development results largely from interactions babies and toddlers have with the people and objects they encounter in their environments (Piaget, 1952, 1959, 1962), and represents only the outward development we see as children grow. However, we cannot see the growth and development of the neural network occurring within the child's brain.

Overview of Brain Development During Infancy and Toddlerhood

As babies begin to hear, see, taste, and touch objects and/or people in their environments, the neural network within their brains grows and develops steadily. Dendrites may develop second-, third-, fourth-, fifth-, and even sixth-level branches that relay sensory information among different regions of the brain. This brain growth allows children to experience their environments in different ways, and each new experience, in turn, leads to further brain growth. This phenomenon, called **cognitive bootstrapping**, is the idea that children's development in one area activates development in other areas because it provides new opportunities for exploration and problem solving. For example, when an infant discovers a brightly colored block in her crib she might stare at it for an extended period of time, taking in information only through her sense of sight. If the block is interesting to the baby and the baby is secure in this environment, she may reach out for the block. When she grasps the block in her hand, she will not only learn more about the block, but also about her own abilities. Soon the baby will be able to put the block in her mouth, look at it from all sides, and even hand the block to a trusted adult. As the adult talks to the baby, the baby builds an understanding of language and communication. The adult's involvement in the block play extends the interest of the baby and signals that her efforts are valued. With each new experience, infants and toddlers not only expand their knowledge of objects, people, and their own abilities, but they also create for themselves new opportunities for learning and development. The presence and involvement of caring adults both supports and facilitates this learning process, further demonstrating the reciprocal relationship that exists between the emotional, social, cognitive, language, and motor development of young children.

In fact, the period between birth and age 3 represents a critical period for emotional development. Diamond and Hopson (1998) stated, "the parts of the brain that process emotion grow and mature relatively early in a child and are very sensitive to parental feedback and handling" (p. 124). They also explained that proper nurturing during the first 3 years is a "priceless form of mental enrichment that lasts a lifetime" (p. 125). One of the most critical elements of emotional development is the attachment that forms between children and their parents, family members, and caregivers. When infants and toddlers are in the presence of adults they trust, they feel safe and are able to expend the energy necessary to move about and explore their world through their senses. Therefore, strong attachments enable children to interact with the people and objects in ways that facilitate both brain development and learning.

Exploration and Play in Infancy and Toddlerhood

Initially, infants and toddlers learn about their world through **exploration** and functional, or practice, play. There is a subtle difference between these two activities. Piaget (1962) stated that exploration is a process of getting information that generally precedes play. For example, a baby might spend a long period of time studying a block. As she does this, she takes in all aspects of the toy. She might grasp it, hold it, and study her hand holding it. She might drop the block and watch carefully to see what happens when it hits the floor. She might continue to stare at the block as it lies on the floor. The baby is intent on gathering information about the block and learning what she can do with it or to it.

At some point during her exploration, the baby begins to play with the block by repeating a particular action just for pure pleasure. Much of the functional play infants and toddlers engage in stems from a sensory-motor response. The child receives information through her senses as she explores an object. She responds to this information by repeating a particular action, thereby learning a **sensory-motor schema,** or action pattern, that will be helpful in the future. She might bang two blocks together just to feel the vibrations or to hear the sound they make when they come together. In doing so, she practices the action of banging. Eventually, she will apply that action to other objects and materials. Through a combination of exploration and practice play, the child learns how to make things happen in her world. Therefore, because young children take great delight in their own accomplishments, both exploration and play are intrinsically motivating experiences that foster emotional development.

Exploration and play are similar, but there are subtle differences. Caregivers need to distinguish between the two activities because they each require different responses. When a child is exploring, there is often a look of puzzlement or seriousness on the child's face and even some tension in her body or movements. Most children become very quiet when they are exploring because all their attention is focused on the object. This is a time for the caregiver to maintain vigilance but not, in most cases, to interrupt this important process. Children should be given every opportunity to fully engage in exploration (Trawick-Smith, 1997) (see Figure 4–1).

When infants and toddlers have moved beyond exploration and are fully engaged in play, their bodies are much more relaxed. They smile and laugh

Figure 4–1 *When children explore, they are totally engrossed in the activity and seem very serious.*

out loud as they repeat actions. They are happy to share the joy of their new accomplishments with significant adults or older siblings. This is an excellent opportunity for caregivers to interact with children in ways that reinforce positive attachments. Adults can join in the fun by laughing with the child, clapping to show appreciation for the accomplishments, or just joining in. Often, it is possible for the caregiver to extend the play by introducing a new action schema. But do not be surprised if the child again begins to explore the infinite possibilities presented by any object.

Pretense, or pretend play, emerges during the infant and toddler years and provides children with many opportunities to develop thinking and language skills. Pretense begins when the child is able to represent what she is thinking through her actions. She may pretend to be sleepy by yawning and placing her cheek on her hands. When you comment on how sleepy she is, she opens her eyes wide and laughs. She is delighted that she has fooled you. A more sophisticated form of pretense play occurs when a child uses one object to stand for another. For example, she might pick up a block and put it to her ear, pretending it is a telephone. Adults interacting with children as they engage in pretense have excellent opportunities to extend and expand children's understanding of language and concepts, as well as to foster positive attachments.

Benefits of Block Play in Infancy and Toddlerhood   Exploration, practice play, and pretense are important activities that enrich the environments of young children and foster learning and development. Of course, there are many different toys and materials that support learning and development through exploration and play, and infants and toddlers need to encounter a variety of responsive toys and open-ended materials as they learn about their world. Blocks provide great potential for fostering learning and development. They come in a variety of shapes, sizes, colors, textures, and materials, and can be relatively inexpensive. Blocks are interesting for infants to look at, grasp, hold, and manipulate. They are responsive to infants' and toddlers' emerging fine and gross motor abilities. They can be pushed, pulled, squeezed, held, and carried. They are wonderful objects to use when filling sacks and boxes, and they make interesting sounds when dumped onto the floor. Infants and toddlers also derive great pleasure in stacking or watching others stack blocks and are always pleased with the noise and confusion when block towers come tumbling down.

Because blocks are so versatile, children use them repeatedly, and this familiarity leads to experimentation and the use of blocks in new ways and in different contexts. How a child plays with blocks will change as the child's abilities and imagination grow and develop. At first, she might just look at a block, hold it, or cover the floor with blocks placed end to end. Then she might transfer blocks from the floor to the couch and sweep them off the couch with one big movement of her arm. At another time, she might fill a truck with blocks and scoot it across the floor, then pretend she is the truck driver and the blocks are a load of hay she must deliver. Block play transcends all forms of infant–toddler play and supports all domains of development. Children use blocks as they explore, practice action schema, engage in trial-and-error problem solving, and pretend. As they gain power over their environment through block play, children develop a strong sense of accomplishment that fosters self-esteem.

Block play also provides opportunities to develop strong attachments between young children and their family members and caregivers by providing multiple opportunities for interactive play. Because blocks have been available for many years, the experience of playing with blocks spans generations. Most siblings, mothers, fathers, aunts, uncles, grandparents, and caregivers have memories of playing with blocks and feel at ease with them. Therefore, the familiarity of blocks provides an easy way for adults and older siblings to get involved with a young baby or an active toddler. Many interactive games develop spontaneously as adults and babies sit together sharing a set of blocks. These spontaneous, simple games not only provide pleasure for all involved, but also help to create a warm nurturing environment that, in turn, creates more opportunities for children to learn about themselves, others, and the world in which they live.

Developmental Expectations of Infants and Toddlers During Block Play

An infant's interest and ability to play with people and objects grows and changes in predictable ways as she learns about her world. Piaget (1952, 1959) described the first few years of an infant's life as the sensory-motor period and outlined six distinct substages. Adults who understand the physical, motor, cognitive, language, social, and emotional development that occurs during these substages will be able to offer infants and toddlers many opportunities for development through block play.

Block Play of Infants: 0–12 Months   The first substage of the sensory-motor period is called the **reflexive period** and occurs during the baby's first month. During this stage, a baby reacts to her environment mainly through an internal and involuntary system of reflexes. These reflexes include sucking, blinking, rooting, or grasping an object placed in her hand. Inborn reflexes provide babies with the ability to survive, adapt to their environment, and learn about their world. Sucking is a reflex newborns use when something is placed on their lips. Sometimes, babies get milk when they suck and sometimes they do not. In either case, they get information that helps them develop sensory-motor schema and **circular reaction patterns.** A circular reaction pattern is a learned chain of activities that provides opportunities for learning and development. If you place a block in the palm of a baby's hand, she will grasp that block. Her initial action is a reflex, but because she finds it interesting, she is likely to repeat the grasping action the next time something is placed in her hand. Eventually, the reflex of grasping is replaced by the learned reaction pattern of grasping; that is, the baby learns to use grasping and holding on to things as a means of exploring her environment.

Infants are not generally interested in play during the reflexive period. They sleep a lot, and this sleep is important because it provides the baby's brain time to synchronize vital body systems, such as breathing, digestion, and temperature control. When the baby is awake, she is bombarded by many sensations in her environment and can easily be overwhelmed by the sights, sounds, smells, and textures around her. When this happens, she generally falls back to sleep, giving neurons in the brain needed downtime to process information, thus developing the neural circuitry system necessary for further learning and development. Enriching environments for the neonate are nurturing environments in which caregivers anticipate and respond to baby's signals in warm, caring ways. Figure 4–2 provides a brief overview of development during the neonatal period, as well as suggestions regarding activities and environments that support positive attachments.

At about 1 month of age, the baby stays awake and alert for longer periods of time. During their alert time, babies explore their environments with all their senses and develop an understanding of the capabilities of their own bodies by building sensory-motor schema. Piaget (1952) referred to these initial discoveries as **primary circular reactions** because they involve the child's own

The reflexive period is a transition time between the prenatal and postnatal periods when babies refine and organize their body systems and begin to develop strong attachments with family and caregivers. During the reflexive period, babies will sleep much of the time and show little interest in playing, but they will explore their environments with all of their senses when they are alert.

Emerging Skills

Uses all senses to receive information about the world.

Develops attachments to significant people.

Playing with Baby

- This is a time when caregivers can prepare for the coming months by reading about infant development. When the baby is alert, let her study your face while you speak or sing softly to her.
- Observe the baby carefully, note sleep cycles, and begin to predict her schedule.
- Learn to differentiate between the baby's cries.

Enriching the Environment

Respond to the baby's needs in warm, caring, and consistent ways.

Provide interesting things for the baby to see and hear when she is alert and awake.

Figure 4–2 *Reflexive Period: 0–1 Month—Let sleeping babies lie.*

body. For example, a breeze floats across the room and causes a 3-month-old baby to shiver, a reflex action. As the child squirms, the cloth block on her blanket moves. She is delighted by the movement and purposefully squirms again and again, causing the block to bounce gently on the blanket. Soon the baby learns that squirming and wiggling make interesting things happen, and she employs this newly learned skill repeatedly. At this age, one of baby's most interesting toys is her own body (White, 1981).

During the first 4 months, babies begin to coordinate sensory input by following an object with their eyes or locating sounds. They explore with all their senses and particularly like to look at faces, but they also enjoy bright-colored objects. They begin to notice their hands and will stare at them for long periods of time. When lying on their stomachs, they learn to lift their chest and look at objects that are placed in front of them. Babies become quite social during this period, smile at anyone who appears friendly, and often imitate facial expression.

Even though the 1- to 4-month-old baby is learning mostly about her own capabilities, blocks are interesting toys for babies and promote their exploration and play. Caregivers can provide blocks that are bright colored with interesting designs. Figure 4–3 provides a brief overview of development and additional

Babies discover their bodies and what they can do. They begin to learn action patterns and use them to respond to stimuli in their environment. They continue to build strong attachments.

Emerging Skills

Lifts head and chest off blanket

Follows moving object with eyes

Bats at objects with hand

Imitates facial expressions of others

Grasps object when placed in her hand

Anticipates another's action by shaking whole body

Kicks feet wildly

Studies hand

Locates sounds

Coos, gurgles, and smiles

Playing with Baby

- Allow the infant time to explore her environment.
- Put a large, soft, bright-colored block in the corner of the crib. When the baby notices the block and begins to study it, talk softly to her and tell her all about it. "That is a big block! Isn't it pretty?"
- At some point, the baby might wiggle and the block might shake and move a bit. If the baby notices this, tell her what she is doing. "Look, you made the block move! Can you do it again?"
- Hold a brightly colored block within the baby's sight and move it slowly in an arch. If the baby follows it with her eyes, continue this tracking game. Talk to the baby softly as she tracks the block with her eyes. "Do you see the block? Where is it going? You are following the block with your eyes!"
- Place blocks and other toys on shelves near the baby's crib. When the baby looks at any of the toys for any length of time, bring the toy to the baby and say, "Did you want this? Here it is."
- Notice if your talking interrupts or extends the baby's concentration. Adjust your conversation so it supports the baby's ability to focus and attend.
- Put blocks slightly out of the baby's reach so she will extend her arm and hand. Encourage her with conversation. "You want the block, don't you? Reach for it! There, now you've got it!"
- Place blocks in the baby's hands and let her feel the texture of the block. Now replace the block with one that has a different texture.

Enriching the Environment

Provide interesting things for the baby to see, hear, and touch. Don't forget, you are also interesting for the baby to see, hear, and touch. Notice the baby's signals and respond to them in warm, caring, and consistent ways. Map your language onto the baby's actions and encourage interaction, but be careful not to distract the baby from her own explorations.

Figure 4–3 *Primary Circular Reactions: 1–4 Months—"See what I can do!"*

ideas that caregivers can use to interact with the baby through play, extend the infant's learning, and enrich her environment.

From 4 to 8 months of age, the baby begins to develop **secondary circular reactions** that involve objects and toys. Babies begin to use their eyes and hands together to reach, pat, grasp, hold, squeeze, and release toys. They are interested in detail and the texture of their toys. They are learning to hold objects in both hands and transfer an object from one hand to another. As babies develop the ability to sit, they will spend greater amounts of time repeating actions that are pleasurable. They learn that banging objects together produces very interesting sounds and vibrations. They try out this new action pattern on every object they encounter. Babies enjoy dropping blocks from a high chair, filling a bucket with blocks, and then dumping them out. Blocks are important toys at this stage of development because children can easily move them from place to place, providing multiple opportunities for sensory exploration.

Babies learn new action patterns in several ways: by accident, by trial and error, and by watching others. As they experiment, they begin to develop an understanding of cause and effect. For example, dropping a block from the high chair causes it to be out of reach. However, they soon learn that if they use their voice, they can signal someone nearby to get their block for them. Therefore, block play provides many opportunities for babies and their caregivers to interact and develop warm attachments. Figure 4–4 provides an overview of development at this stage and suggests opportunities for caregivers and babies to engage in block play.

From 8 to 12 months of age, babies enter the fourth substage of the sensory-motor period known as the **coordination of secondary circular reactions** and refine their understanding of cause and effect, combine action schemas,

---

Babies are now awake and alert for extended periods of time. They are very interested in people and toys, and develop many ways of responding and interacting. When they learn a new action pattern, they will repeat it over and over, just for pleasure.

Emerging Skills

Uses eyes and hands together to reach, pat, grasp, bang, squeeze, and release

Sits, first with support and then independently

Imitates actions of others

Recognizes familiar people and things

Babbles, strings together syllables, and accompanies "talking" with gestures

Begins to move through space; rolls, creeps, crawls

Purposefully uses smiles and laughter to engage others

Begins to develop concept of object permanence

Figure 4–4 *Secondary Circular Reactions: 4–8 Months—"Bring on the toys!" (continues)*

Playing with Baby

- Continue to play games that you and the baby know and enjoy playing together.
- Allow the baby time to explore her environment and objects in her environment.
- Give the baby a photo block with pictures of her favorite people. This is a large, soft block with vinyl pockets on each side for pictures.
- When the baby is in her high chair, place several blocks on the tray. Give her time to experiment with the blocks. If one falls, pick it up and place it back on the tray. Eventually the baby will create a game of drop and pick up. Besides being fun, this game shows her she has some control over her environment.
- Place a crib mirror in the baby's bed and put a soft block in front of it so she can see both the block and the image of the block. Let her study this. From time to time, move the block so she gets different views.
- Give the baby a pile of blocks (none smaller than 1 inch) to play with when she is sitting on a blanket. Watch to see what she does with them. Sit beside her with your own set of blocks and imitate her actions. She might bang them together. She might move then all around by moving her hand back and forth quickly. After she finishes an action, imitate it, pause, and wait until she initiates another action. You are modeling turn taking. Laugh together and have fun.
- Let the baby see you hide a block under the blanket. Ask her, "Where is that block? Where did I put it?" Give her any help or cues she needs to find it. Over time, as she develops object permanence, you won't need to give any cues at all. You will even have to find tougher hiding places.
- Place blocks just out of the baby's reach, and use your words to encourage her to get the blocks. "Here are the blocks you wanted. Come over here and get them."
- When you and the baby have invented a game that you both enjoy, invite another adult who baby doesn't know to play with you.
- When the baby is lying on her tummy, place blocks within her sight. When they have her attention, move the block with your hand and pretend it is a car, truck, train, or boat. Make the appropriate sounds as you move the block. If the baby smiles and watches, continue this game.

Enriching the Environment

Provide interesting things for the baby to touch and manipulate. Keep familiar blocks handy when you play together. Occasionally, introduce new blocks. Sit with the baby and a pile of blocks, and give her time to initiate a game. It might be one you have already played together, or it might be a new one. If the baby doesn't initiate a game, read the baby's signals to see if she is interested in continuing.

Figure 4–4 *Secondary Circular Reactions: 4–8 Months—"Bring on the toys!" (continued)*

and invent new ways to solve problems they encounter. When an 11-month-old baby wants to move a pile of blocks from one place to another, she might find a bucket. If the bucket is full of other toys, she will just dump them out. If her bucket is within her sight but not her reach, she might use language and gestures to signal to a nearby adult that she needs the bucket. If the bucket is not in sight, she may go look for it because she is developing **object permanence,** the idea that objects exist even when she cannot see them. Or she might just pile a few blocks on a nearby truck and *zoom* them to the new location.

The versatility of blocks makes them important additions to the learning environment. Babies can play with blocks independently by filling containers with them, dumping them out, carrying blocks from place to place, or banging them together. Blocks can also become the centerpiece of interactive play that fosters strong attachments between family members, attentive adults, caregivers, and babies. Figure 4–5 provides a brief overview of development during this stage and examples of how blocks can be used to foster growth and development.

Babies are busy combining all action patterns they have previously learned to solve problems and make things happen. They are intent on satisfying their own curiosity. Their days are filled with trial-and-error experimentation and practice play activities as they develop a greater sense of cause and effect and object permanence.

Emerging Skills

Increased skill in using hands together; can hold object in both hands; will drop one object to pick up a third; clasps hands together; uses a pincer grasp (thumb and forefinger together) to pick up small objects

Rolls and throws objects

Fits things together and takes things apart, but not necessarily in that order

Increased ability to communicate ideas and needs through sounds and gestures

Increased ability to take turns in conversation and in actions

Increased mobility: crawls with speed and determination, climbs, pulls to stand, steps around while holding on to something, may walk independently

Carries objects in hand as she moves about

Crawls inside of things

Anticipates actions of others

Playing with Baby

■ Allow the baby time to explore and play with blocks on her own.

Figure 4–5 *Coordination of Secondary Circular Reactions: 8–12 Months—"Problems, problems, let me solve the problems!" (continues)*

- Continue to play the games that you and the baby know and enjoy playing together.
- Hide blocks in places where the baby has to move some distance to get them. Encourage her to hide blocks for you to find. Show joy, pride, and surprise when she finds your hidden objects and when you find hers.
- Work together to fill buckets and other containers with blocks. Add language to your game by saying, "I will add one, now you add one." If she pauses and waits for you to add the next, say, "Thank you. It is my turn. Now it is yours." Some days, the baby will respond to this turn-taking game; on other days, she won't. Follow the child's lead and let her control the "rules."
- Play some of the old block games with new or different blocks. This adds variety and gives the baby the opportunity to use skills in new ways.
- Clap rhythms with blocks, then play music. Sway and dance to the rhythm of the music while clapping blocks together. Imitate the baby's movements, and laugh and dance together.
- Build a tower of blocks within the baby's reach. Count the blocks as you place them on top of each other. "Here is one. Here is two. Here is three. Now let's knock them down!" If she doesn't knock them down, you can. She will do so eventually. As the blocks fall down, show surprise, laugh, and clap. If the baby is interested, repeat the game. After the tower is built, pause and show some anticipation before you knock it down.

Enriching the Environment

Balance new objects and activities with familiar objects and activities. Babies need lots of time to repeat actions and practice skills. This is a time when babies begin to exercise their will by pushing away objects they do not want. If the baby has the opportunity to do this during playtime, she will eventually learn that there are times she can control her environment and times she can't. It is important to continue to interpret and respond to the baby's signals and map words onto her actions.

Figure 4–5   *Coordination of Secondary Circular Reactions: 8–12 Months— "Problems, problems, let me solve the problems!" (continued)*

Block Play of Toddlers: 12–24 Months   The toddler years begin when a baby becomes mobile and easily moves from place to place on her feet. It often seems, to parents and caregivers, that infants become toddlers quite suddenly. One day, you can put the baby on her blanket in the living room and she will stay in the living room until you move her to another area of the house. She may scoot around the room and play with items within reach, but you are assured that she will stay in the general area. The next day, you may put the same baby in the living room, but before you know it she is down the hall, in the bedroom, out of the bedroom, in the bathroom, through the living room, and into the kitchen. She has become a toddler, and moves rapidly from one place to another experimenting and trying out new ideas to solve problems and overcome barriers. The toddler years also bring new uses for blocks and an interest in constructive play.

The fifth substage of the sensory-motor period, **tertiary circular reactions,** is characterized by experimentation. Toddlers often use toys and other objects as tools, and through trial and error, try out previously mastered strategies and create new action patterns to solve problems and meet their goals. For example, a toddler might find it necessary to move a pile of small blocks from one side of the room to another. In the past, she has used a bucket, but there is no bucket in sight. She has also used trucks to carry blocks, but again, there are no trucks in sight. Finally, she spreads the blocks onto a blanket and begins pulling the blanket across the room. Many of the blocks fall off the blanket, so she pushes them to the center of the blanket and continues across the room. This child has never seen anyone transport blocks via blanket, but at this age, *where there is a will there is a way!* Toddlers use trial-and-error experimentation to accomplish their goals and, in doing so, develop a sense of autonomy and independence.

This sense of independence extends to all areas of development. The language skills of 12- to 18-month-old toddlers grow steadily during this period. They learn to express their ideas not only through actions, but also through words. As their ability to express their ideas through words increases, toddlers begin to engage in pretend play. During play, a simple block could become, in the child's mind, either a sandwich or a car. This newfound ability to express ideas through pretense enables toddlers to interact with others in increasingly complex ways. Figure 4–6 provides an overview of development for this stage and suggests ways caregivers can use blocks and block play to encourage growth and development.

The last stage of the sensory-motor period is characterized by the toddler's growing ability to use **mental combinations** to solve problems and accomplish goals. For example, a toddler may see a plate of cookies sitting on a table. She walks over to the table, but because it is slightly taller than she is, she can no longer see the cookies. However, she knows they are there. She stretches her arm up and out to reach the plate of cookies, but she still cannot reach them. She pauses, looks around, and studies the room for inspiration. She sees a long block on the floor, picks it up, puts it on the table, and pushes it forward, somewhat haphazardly. She feels the block touch the plate and moves it forward carefully. She then goes to the far side of the table and reaches up and out for the cookie plate. She can feel it on the tips of her fingers, but again she cannot quite grasp it. She returns to the block and again pushes it forward. Finally, she runs to where the cookie plate sits at the far side of the table and helps herself. This child has never seen anyone push a plate of cookies with a block, but by thinking ahead and using a series of premeditated trial-and-error experimentations, she put together a string of actions and satisfies her goal of getting a cookie. As with previous stages,

The infant becomes a toddler and moves quickly throughout her environment. She experiments with toys and other objects, and often invents new and novel actions not seen before. She begins to use words along with gestures to express her ideas and feelings. These new language skills enable her to use pretense to enrich and enhance her play episodes.

Emerging Skills

Understands and use words to express ideas and needs

Walks and runs everywhere

Pushes, pulls, and carries things

Imitates actions she has seen before

Playing with Toddlers

- Allow the child time to explore and play with blocks on her own.
- Continue to play the games you and your toddler know and enjoy playing together.
- Make a game out of putting things away. Enlist toddler's help by asking her to bring you things as you place them on the shelf.
- Invite the child to pretend with you. Build a simple structure, and use animal or people figures to enact simple scenes.
- Invent a game of demolition. Stack several blocks into a tower. Count to five and knock them down. Enlist the toddler's help in stacking and knocking down the towers, or take turns.
- Make two parallel rows of long blocks on the floor. Roll a ball between the rows. Enlist the toddler's help and take turns rolling the ball. Experiment with different sizes and weights of balls.
- Add push toys, for example, a wheelbarrow or shopping cart, to the toddler's play materials. Help her move blocks from one area to another with these toys.
- Create a book for your toddler. Use photos of you, your child, other family members, and friends playing together with blocks. Paste the photos on colorful construction paper, and write a short sentence under each.

Enriching the Environment

Provide things for the toddler to push and pull, for example, toy wheelbarrows and shopping carts.

Figure 4–6 *Tertiary Circular Reactions: 12–18 Months—"Look out world, here I come!"*

blocks and block play offer children many opportunities to expand and extend their abilities. Figure 4–7 outlines the highpoints of development at this stage, and offers suggestions to caregivers for using blocks and block play to foster learning and development.

Toddlers use all of their skills together to solve problems and overcome barriers. When confronted with a problem or a barrier to something she wants, she makes a plan, and then sets about to make it work.

Emerging Skills

Walks and runs with greater control and purpose

Refinement of small motor skills leads to greater control

Uses language, words, and short phrases to get needs met and express emotion

Uses adults as resources to get things done or to solve problems

Expands use of pretense and imagination, and brings fantasy to play activities

Playing with Toddlers

- Allow the child time to explore and play with blocks on her own.
- Continue to play the games you and your toddler know and enjoy playing together. Modify those games to challenge the toddler's developing abilities.
- Make two parallel rows of long blocks and take turns rolling balls in between them. Add to this game by standing one or two blocks on end at one end of the horizontal row. Now you have a bowling alley and can take turns bowling.
- Extend child's pretense by playing with her and following her lead during play. Add ideas and use accessories that spark the child's imagination while letting her stay in control of her play.
- Invent a game called "Copy Me." Arrange two or three blocks in some way and invite the child to copy your formation. Give her whatever help she needs. Then let her make a structure or block arrangement for you to copy. Ask for help, even if you don't need it.
- Invent matching games. For example, pull a red square block out of a pile of colored blocks. Ask your child to find one that matches yours. Give the child all the help she needs to be successful. Take turns.

Enriching the Environment

Provide objects the child can ride such as toy cars and tricycles with wagons that can be hooked on like trailers to carry blocks.

Figure 4–7 *Mental Combinations: 18–24 Months—Necessity is the toddler's reason to invent.*

Block Play of Toddlers: 24–36 Months   The time between a child's second and third birthdays marks the transition between the sensory-motor stage and the preoperational stage of development and is known as the **preconceptual stage.** With time and experience, the toddler becomes less and less dependent on perceptions and sensory-motor experiences to understand and affect her environment. She becomes more able to think about ideas and actions mentally and then use these actions to solve problems (Wilson, Douville-Watson, & Watson, 1995). For example, on Tuesday, a child spontaneously makes a simple circular enclosure with blocks. She puts several toy cars and trucks into the center. As she is playing, her caregiver walks by and remarks, "Oh, I see you made a garage for your cars and trucks." The child continues to play. On Wednesday, she decides to make the garage again, goes to the block shelf, and picks out just the blocks she needs. She carries them to where she will build the garage, then goes to the toy shelf and picks out the trucks and cars that she used yesterday. When she has assembled everything she needs, she begins to build. As she plays, she thinks of other objects she needs for her play and goes to find them. Even though there is still much spontaneity in her play, a good deal of mental planning preceded the activity and continues throughout.

As children in this transitional phase of development play with blocks, they develop a greater understanding of spatial concepts, quantity, weight, and sequence. They also refine their understanding of cause and effect. For example, a child might pick up a long rectangular unit block and carry it across the floor. As she walks, she will feel the weight of the block and make adjustments in the way she carries it. Because the block is long, she will need to make additional adjustments in the way she carries it so that she does not bump into anything. No one would be able to tell the child how to carry the block. She must figure that out for herself. Later, she reaches over to pick up a cardboard block, thinking she will need to use the same strength to carry it, but when she feels how much lighter it is, she makes the necessary adjustments in the way she carries it. She may even refer to one block as heavy and the other as light. Therefore, while playing with blocks, she not only learns about the quality of weight, but also develops concepts of heavy and light. Figure 4–8 outlines the highpoints of development at this stage and offers suggestions to caregivers for using blocks and block play to foster learning and development.

The young child represents objects and actions in her thinking without having to actualize sensory-motor experience. She uses all her skills together and creates new ways of working with materials. Pretend play becomes an important tool for engaging others in play.

Emerging Skills

Refines both gross- and fine-motor skills and uses them to solve problems or overcome barriers

Improves the ability to express ideas and emotions through words and phrases

Answers yes and no questions

Begins to identify colors by pointing to a named color

Understands the quantities of one, two, and many

Builds a tower of 6–9 blocks

Builds horizontally to make an enclosure

Plays in the company of others

Engages others in pretend play

Playing with Very Young Children

- Allow the child time to explore and play with blocks on her own.
- Continue to play the games you and your toddler know and enjoy playing together. Modify the games to challenge the toddler's emerging skills and abilities.
- Invent a game called, "What's Missing?" Place three toys on the floor in front of the child. You could start with a block, a car, and a doll. Cover the toys with a cloth, tray, or piece of cardboard. As the child closes her eyes, take away one of the toys. As the child opens her eyes, remove the cloth and ask, "What is missing?" Keep playing as long as the child is interested. This game can change with time and experience. For example, you might take turns and let the child set up the toys and hide them from you. As the child gains experience, choose toys that are similar, for example, three different shapes of blocks.
- Continue to play the games you and your toddler know and enjoy playing together.
- Invent a game called, "Is this . . . ." Ask the child yes or no questions about concepts she understands. For example, when she has learned the names of the shapes of the blocks, ask her, "Is this the square block?" She will be delighted at being right, and it will boost her confidence. You could apply this game to other concepts such as color names or the numbers 1, 2, and 3.
- Extend the "Is this . . . ." game to a "Which one . . . " game. For example, pull out a red block and a green block, and ask the child, "Which one is red?" Give the child as much help as she needs, and be sure to keep the game a game. That is, keep it fun. These games should be used to interact with the child and to give the child an opportunity to practice what she knows.
- Use blocks to develop an obstacle course. This game can be played outside or inside. Outside, the child might run or ride a wheel toy through the obstacle course. Inside, she might crawl, tiptoe, or drive a toy truck through the course.
- Extend the child's pretend play by playing with the child, following her lead. For example, while driving a truck through the obstacle course, ask the child where she is going. If she gives you an answer, ask her if she needs any help. If she doesn't give you an answer, then she is probably concentrating on moving the truck and needs to focus her attention on that action.
- Admire the child's constructions. Take photographs and display them.

Enriching the Environment

Add sets of animals or other toys to enrich pretense play.

Figure 4–8 *Preconceptual Stage: 24–36 Months—Putting it all together.*

Maintaining Clean and Safe Environments for Infants and Toddlers

Infants will play with blocks or other construction toys wherever they are. This might be in their crib or playpen, on a blanket on the floor, in their car seat, or in the lap of a parent or other caregiver. Block play is an activity that can occur inside or outside. However, there are safety factors to consider when selecting play materials and creating an environment conducive to exploration and play. Consider the following when choosing blocks or construction toys for infants:

- Blocks or construction toys should not have strings or ribbons that are longer than 10 inches. Strings or ribbons should not be used around the baby's neck or to tie toys to the crib. Entanglement and possible choking can occur.
- Blocks or construction toys should be made of sturdy nontoxic materials that will not break easily or disintegrate when washed. Wood, metal, dense foam, or high-impact plastics are good choices.
- Blocks or construction toys should be nonflammable or made from flame-retardant materials, splinter free, with rounded edges to prevent injuries.
- Blocks or construction toys should be larger than 1 inch in diameter so they can not be lodged in the baby's nose or mouth and cause the baby to choke or suffocate. There should not be any small pieces on the toy that could become detached and create a choking hazard.
- The squeaker in any block or construction toy should be built into the toy in such a way that it cannot become detached and choke the child. These toys should be removed from the crib or playpen when the baby is asleep.

Figure 4–9 provides descriptions of blocks and block accessories that are appropriate for infants.

If blocks come wrapped in plastic bags, these bags should be discarded immediately and not used for storage or for transporting blocks from place to place. Baby blocks and other toys should be stored in small baskets that can be easily moved to wherever the baby is playing. Having several toys together in one basket allows caregivers to stay with the baby and provide uninterrupted exploration or playtime.

If babies are playing inside on the floor, they should be placed with their blocks on a clean blanket. The floor on which the blanket is placed should be away from the major traffic patterns in the room, and outlet covers should be placed on all electrical outlets in the area. The blanket and the area around the blanket should be inspected frequently and crumbs, dust, dirt, or small items removed. In many child care centers or family child care homes, parents or other adults are asked to cover street shoes with surgical slippers or large socks when they enter babies' indoor play areas. This helps to maintain a clean environment.

Soft Stacking Blocks	Cloth-covered foam cubes that range in size from 5 $\frac{1}{2}$ to 3 inches. They are bright colored, many have pictures on them, and others are squeezable and make jingly sounds when they are shaken or moved.
Soft Sensory Block	A colorful cloth hollow block. Each side is covered with different textured cloth.
Peek-A-Boo Soft Blocks	Squeezable soft vinyl blocks that fit comfortably in a baby's hand. When they are squeezed, they squeak or rattle. On two of them, a little bear pops out. They interlock and, therefore, are easily stacked.
Stacking or Nesting Cups	These usually come in a set of 10 cups that fit inside each other or stack on top of each other to make a tower.
Stacking Rings	Plastic rings that are graduated in size and fit on a form.
Animal Sound Cube	Six-inch foam blocks that have battery-operated sound mechanisms safely enclosed within. When an adult activates the sound mechanism, it will emit a realistic animal sound when moved. The sound matches the colorful picture on the cube.
Baby Mirror	Double-sided, unbreakable, acrylic mirror. Many have plastic frames with finger holes so they are easy for babies to hold.
Photo Cube	A 6-inch foam cube covered in bright fabric. Each side has a pocket where a photo can be inserted.

Figure 4–9   *Blocks and constructive toys for infants.*

It is important to keep blocks and other construction toys sanitized and clean. Toys that spend a lot of time on the floor or in a baby's mouth or that are shared among children should be cleaned after each use. Some blocks can be easily washed in the washing machine or dishwasher, whereas others will need to be cleaned and sanitized by hand. Bassett (1996) suggested a method to hand wash toys: use warm water with a mild detergent, rinse well, disinfect by dipping the toy into a solution of 1 tablespoon chlorine bleach to 1 quart of water, and let the toy air-dry. When cleaning hollow toys that have a hole in them, wipe the surface with a clean cloth that has been dipped in the disinfecting solution. This will prevent the toy from becoming filled with the cleaning solution. Use fresh solution each day and store it in a child-safe container out of children's reach. Inspect toys as you clean them, and repair or discard broken toys immediately.

Most babies enjoy being outside during nice weather, and playing outside gives them an opportunity to see, feel, and smell different things. It is important to find an area protected from the sun and the wind, and away from streets or parking lots where there might be car exhaust or fumes. Babies might enjoy playing in infant chairs or on blankets. Plastic swimming pools (without water) keep babies off the ground and, because they provide a boundary, give babies a sense of security. Again, it is important to keep the play area clean and have a variety of toys available. Baby blocks and construction toys are portable and babies will enjoy playing with these familiar toys in new surroundings.

Two important things to keep in mind when creating safe play environments for toddlers is that they can and do move quickly from one place to another and are extremely curious. In short, the old adage that toddlers *"get into everything"* is true. When choosing toys and blocks for toddlers, all the guidelines for selecting toys for infants still apply. However, because of the toddler's expanding gross and fine motor, cognitive, and social skills, a greater variety of toys and blocks are needed to provide expanded experiences in play. As children progress through the toddler years, they become increasingly able to build and construct. Large, lightweight blocks will be easier for toddlers to handle, and they will find multiple uses for these blocks. Unit blocks are available in a dense foam material and provide older toddlers with many opportunities to build. Accessories such as animal sets, shopping carts, and wheelbarrows will encourage toddlers to combine constructive and pretense play. Figure 4–10 describes block and construction toys that are appropriate and challenge toddlers' curiosity and growing motor abilities.

The guidelines suggested for developing safe play spaces for infants, reviewed earlier in this chapter, are also appropriate for creating and maintaining safe environments for toddler play. However, because toddlers are continually refining their ability to move from place to place and to act on objects in their environment, several additional considerations are necessary. The following is a composite list of guidelines to use when developing and maintaining safe environments for toddler block and constructive play, either indoors or outdoors:

- The play area should be located away from the major traffic patterns in the room and free of electrical cords. Outdoor areas should be partially shaded and separated from streets or parking areas by a fence.
- Inspect floors frequently and remove dirt, crumbs, and tiny objects. All small objects are stored out of reach of children. If adults accidentally drop small items they are carrying as they walk through this area, they should pick them up immediately.

Soft Unit Blocks	These blocks are built to the same scale as hardwood unit blocks but are made from rugged, dense foam. These are lightweight, colorful, and safe for toddlers.
Large Soft Interlocking Blocks	Colorful interlocking blocks. Bendable pieces come in four shapes and are made of flexible plastic. The rectangular piece is $4^1/_2$ by 9 inches. They are both durable and washable.
Foam Cubes	These are made of soft foam and covered with washable vinyl. Each cube is $5^1/_2$ inches square. They are lightweight but durable enough for toddlers to stack, sit on, or crawl over.
Giant Soft Blocks	Large, lightweight foam blocks. Some are covered with a tough, tight-fitting plastic "skin" that can be wiped clean. Others are laminated sheets of colorful foam. They are similar to foam cubes; however, sets consist of blocks of different sizes, shapes, and colors.
Cardboard Blocks	Shaped and painted to look like bricks, these cardboard blocks are lightweight and easy to stack. They are crush resistant, colorful, and come in several sizes.
Soft Play Forms	These durable, vinyl-covered foam shapes are light enough for toddlers to push around and arrange, then climb on. Set includes rectangles, squares, triangles, and cylinders.
DUPLO Baby Builders®	Jumbo-size DUPLO® blocks that are easy to grasp and stack.
Bunny Links®	Large $5^1/_4$- by 5-inch plastic bunnies that come in five bright colors. They are easy for toddlers to connect and pull apart.
Giant Soft Vehicles	Huggable, soft, vinyl vehicles; fire truck, police car, airplane, bus, ambulance, and car.
Thistle Blocks®	Colorful squares and rectangles. Their sides stick together and come apart easily.
Push Toys	Shopping carts, wheelbarrows, dump trucks. Toys can be filled with blocks and moved around.

Figure 4–10 *Blocks and constructive toys for toddlers.*

- Remove area rugs or fasten them securely to the floor so children will not trip over them. Secure children's long or loose clothing and shoe strings so they will not get caught in spokes or under wheel toys or cause children to trip as they move and carry blocks around.
- Frequently check to see if tables, shelves, and other furniture in the play area are sturdy and will not topple over if a child uses them to pull herself to a stand. Tall shelves should be anchored to the wall.
- Use safety devices such as gates, outlet guards, childproof locks on cabinet doors, and corner guards for low tables throughout the home or center.
- Use only lead-free paint on wooden blocks and all surfaces in the play area.
- If a toy chest is used to store toys, the lid should be lightweight and have a catch that holds the lid open.

When safe play areas are maintained, toddlers can be allowed to explore the environment freely. Blocks and other toys should be stored on shelves so children are able to choose what they need or with what they want to play. Therefore, safe, well-maintained environments promote exploratory and interactive play as well as foster growth and development.

Responding to Infants and Toddlers During Block Play

Strong attachments between babies and significant adults in their lives provide a secure base from which children can explore and learn about their world (Bowlby, 1969). Warm, caring, responsive interactions between young children and their caregivers are important elements of attachment (Greenspan, 1989). The caregiver's ability to read each baby's or toddler's unique signals; interpret the child's mood, intention, and motivation correctly; and respond in a consistent, nurturing manner is crucial. Infants and toddlers have not yet developed fluid language to clearly express their interests and emotions, so they use facial expressions, gestures, and their whole bodies to express themselves. For example, when babies become interested in an object, their eyes get very large and they seems to stare for long periods of time. A responsive caregiver will notice when the child is displaying an interest and follow the child's eyes to the object of interest. When both the child and the caregiver are focused on the same object, there will be many opportunities for them to interact. The caregiver could talk to the baby about what she is looking at or suggest an action they could do together. For example, "Oh, I see you have spotted the photo block. Do you want me to bring it to you? Here it is. Let's look at it. Whose picture do you see on the block?" The baby responds with her eyes and her attention. She is certainly a part of this conversation. During this interchange, the baby not only receives information about the block, but she also gets the message that she is a competent communicator. Each child signals her interests, needs, and emotions in a different way, and caregivers need to take the time to learn each child's individual communication system so they can foster responsive relationships.

A second component of responsive interactions with infants and toddlers is the adult's willingness and ability to follow the child's lead as she plays (Greenspan, 1989), that is, to let the child set the theme, action, and mood of the play. When infants and toddlers explore or play, they learn they have some control over themselves and their environments. This sense of empowerment fosters the development of autonomy and self-esteem, both important aspects of emotional development. When an adult follows a child's lead in play, the adult becomes a **supportive play partner** and shares the power inherent in the play episode with the child, thus extending and enriching the child's play experience. This signals to the child that the adult values her ideas, actions, and sense of power (see Figure 4–11).

Supportive play partners know the children they play with well and interpret their moods and intentions carefully. They also take time to observe the child before initiating play or entering into an ongoing play episode. As the caregiver observes the child's activities, she determines what kind of interaction

Figure 4–11 *Supportive play partners follow a child's lead while enriching the play experience.*

will best support the child's power and control and extend the child's pleasure and attention. There are times when a caregiver could extend the child's power and control by offering a suggestion or modeling a solution to a problem. There are other times when the very same actions and suggestions would cause the power inherent in the play situation to shift from the child to the caregiver. When this happens, the child has lost an opportunity to learn about her own personal power.

Supportive play partners, who follow the child's lead during play, carefully select interaction strategies that both extend the play episode and provide infants and toddlers the opportunity to share their enjoyment with others. Therefore, when infants and toddlers have the opportunity to share their play power, they develop autonomy and independence, as well as develop a sense of **interdependence,** that is, an appreciation for what they can do with others. Here are guidelines for developing supportive play partnerships and for responding to infants and toddlers during block play:

1. *Follow the child's eyes to determine in what she is interested. Find a way to help the child get closer to the object.* Julian (at 3 months) is looking at a block that is sitting on a nearby shelf, his mother notices, brings the block to the blanket where Julian is lying, and describes the block as she hands it to him. Cynthia (at 8 months) seems interested in nesting cups that are out of reach, her father moves the cups within the child's reach so she can pick them up.

2. *Sit close to the child and notice her facial expression, tone of voice, gestures, and body language. Match your mood and enthusiasm to the child's, being careful not to overpower the situation. Ask the child questions about the object and, if the child is not verbal, provide the answers.* Sharon (a 2-year-old) is busy making towers by stacking blocks. When she has placed the fourth or fifth block on the tower, she becomes tense with excitement, pauses for a moment, and then laughs as she knocks the tower down. Her mother sits close by and watches the action. She laughs with Sharon and shows surprise when the blocks come tumbling down. She claps to show her appreciation for Sharon's efforts. Raymond, also 2, is quietly stacking blocks. He studies each block, then carefully places it on top of the stack. He watches carefully to see what will happen. When the block stays put, he smiles slightly and reaches for another and, with great care, places it on the stack. His mother also sits close. She shares Raymond's mood and quietly studies each block as it is placed on the stack.

3. *Respect the child's need to explore and give her the time and opportunity to experiment and try out action schemes with the object. Being nearby and acknowledging the child's actions shows the child you value her efforts.* Theresa (at 18 months) fills a bucket with blocks. When the bucket is full, she dumps it out and starts over again.

Theresa occasionally looks to her mother who is sitting nearby. When Theresa does look at her mother, her mother smiles, nods, or says, "You are really having fun with those blocks!"

4. *Engage in parallel play with the child. Sit near the child and use the same play materials in the same way as the child.* Joseph (at 32 months) sits on the floor with a pile of small, colorful, wooden blocks. He places them on their sides and creates an enclosure. Christina, Joseph's caregiver, sits near Joseph and creates an enclosure similar to his.

5. *Introduce a new toy only when the infant or toddler has lost interest in an activity in which he is engaged.* Jeremy's mother has just bought a new set of blocks and is anxious to show them to her 2-year-old son. When she arrives home from shopping, Jeremy is quite absorbed in looking at books with his older sister. Jeremy's mother decides to save the new blocks for another time.

6. *Ask open-ended questions and make supportive comments about the child's play. Talk softly and notice if your talking disrupts or extends the child's attentiveness. If your talk seems to interrupt her attention, just sit quietly and watch.* Terry (at 30 months) is building a tower with large cardboard blocks. Terry's caregiver is watching quietly from a distance. She moves closer to Terry and comments, "Such a tall tower! How high are you going to build?" Terry looks quickly at her caregiver and smiles, but returns her focus to the building process. The caregiver remains close by quietly watching.

7. *Take turns.* Tommy (at 16 months) and his dad are playing a hiding game with a cloth and a block. Tommy's dad covers the block with the cloth and asks, "Where is the block?" Tommy looks intently at the cloth-covered block, then back at his dad. "Is it here?" asked the dad. Tommy smiles brightly as his dad pulls the cloth off the block. They both laugh. Tommy's dad remarks, "Now it is your turn," as he hands the cloth to Tommy. Certainly, Tommy is not expected to be able to take turns independently, but this early interactive play with his dad provides a great model for fostering the development of this ability.

8. *Maintain the child's intrinsic motivation to explore and play. When you talk to an infant or toddler about her play, focus your attention on helping the child learn about her feelings and her accomplishments. Use words that give children information about themselves as learners, thinkers, players, and companions. Avoid words such as good, bad, great, and best. These words put a certain value on children's actions and create an expectation that they might not be able to live up to the next time they play.* Carlos (at 14 months) is moving a set of blocks from one place to another. He picks up a block, puts it into his other hand, picks up another block, walks across the room, sets the blocks down, and returns to the original pile for two more blocks. Carlos

repeatedly performs this action. His mother notices the activity and appreciates Carlos's persistence by saying, "Wow! You are working so hard, and you are really getting the job done."

9. *Keep a sense of play in your interactions with the child. Do not think of yourself as "the teacher" but as a play partner. There are, of course, many things you will teach the infant or toddler as you play, but trust the child to learn from her play and playful interactions with you.* Carlos' mother (in the previous example) thinks this situation provides a good opportunity to teach Carlos to use a toy wheelbarrow to move his blocks from place to place. She does not want to interrupt or interfere with his play, but she does want to show him she values his initiative. So, after watching Carlos for a few minutes, she joins the fun and picks up one block, puts it in her other hand, picks up another block, walks across the room, sits them down, and returns to the original pile for two more blocks. They laugh together. The mother understands there will be plenty of opportunities later for Carlos to learn about transportation.

Choosing the right interactive strategy in any play situation is an important decision. Adults who know an infant or toddler well will be able to match strategies and situations, as well as build and maintain a strong attachment. When choosing strategies, it is important to be flexible, allowing the child to explore her own ideas and create her own action schemas, while also being available to extend the play and expand the child's understanding of her power and abilities. This shows true appreciation for infants' and toddlers' unique but effective problem-solving abilities.

Conclusion

The first three years of life represent a time of tremendous growth, development, and learning. Infants and toddlers learn as they explore their environments, engage in functional play, and interact with supportive play partners. The open-ended nature of blocks and other constructive toys provides infants and toddlers with multiple opportunities to develop skills and abilities that cross all domains.

Theory into Practice

1. Observe and make anecdotal records of several infants and toddlers as they interact with their environment. Review your records, and note when children are exploring and when they are playing. Explain how these two actions are reciprocal and how they further learning and development.

2. Using a video camera, record your interactions with infants and toddlers who are playing. As you watch the video, compare your actions with the guidelines for responding to infants and toddlers presented in this chapter. What are your strengths? Develop two goals aimed at strengthening your response skills.
3. Design a newsletter for family members that fosters the idea of interactive play between adults and infants and toddlers.

Websites

www.users.sgi.net/~cokids/

Early Childhood Educators' and Family Web Corner provides articles, teacher pages, family pages, online courses, and list serves aimed at creating healthy environments for children and their families.

www.nccic.org/

National Child Care Information Center has been established to complement, enhance, and promote child care linkages and to serve as a mechanism for supporting quality, comprehensive services for children and families.

Related Readings

Brazelton, T. B. (1992). *Touchpoints: Your child's emotional and behavioral development*. Reading, MA: Perseus Books.

Chamberlin, D. (1998). *The mind of your newborn baby*. Berkeley, CA: North Atlantic Books.

Segal, M. (1998). *Your child at play: Birth to one year* (2nd ed.). New York: New Market Press.

References

Bassett, M. (1996). *Infant and child care skills*. Boston: Delmar.

Bowlby, J. (1969). *Attachment and loss. Volume 2: Separation, anxiety, and anger*. New York: Basic Books.

Diamond, M., & Hopson, J. (1998). *Magic trees of the mind: How to nurture your child's intelligence, creativity, and healthy emotions from birth through adolescence*. New York: Plume.

Greenspan, S. (1989). *First feelings*. New York: Penguin.

Piaget, J. (1952). *The origins of intelligence*. New York: International Universities Press.

Piaget, J. (1959). *Language and thought of the child.* London: Routledge and Kagan Paul.

Piaget, J. (1962). *Play, dreams, and imitation in childhood.* New York: Norton.

Trawick-Smith, J. (1997). *Early childhood development: A multicultural perspective.* Upper Saddle River, NJ: Merrill.

White, B. L. (1981). *The first year of life.* New York: American Baby Books.

Wilson, L. C., Douville-Watson, L., & Watson, M. (1995). *Infants and toddlers: Curriculum and teaching* (3rd ed.). Albany, NY: Delmar.

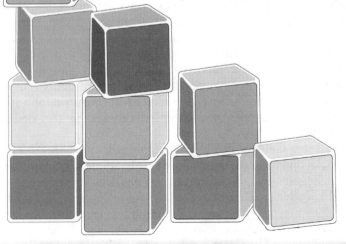

C H A P T E R 5

Block Play for Preschool and Kindergarten Children

Guiding Questions

- *What are typical expectations of children ages 3, 4, and 5 in each developmental domain: cognitive, language and literacy, social, emotional, and motor?*

- *How does a learning center system facilitate block play?*

- *How does block play indoors differ from block play outdoors?*

- *What are the three recommended basic block systems for preschool/kindergarten?*

89

The developmental nature of children ages 3 to 5 is significantly different from that of infants and toddlers. They have more cognitive capabilities, yet their logic is still very different from adult-like ways of thinking. Language skills are more developed, and early signs of literacy learning become evident. Preschool/kindergarten children try out different ways to get along with others as they are beginning to enjoy the company of peers. They are more cognizant of their emotions and new motor skills provide a sense of greater independence.

Due to the active nature of preschool- and kindergarten-age children, teachers must carefully plan each day, organize the learning environment, and prepare materials and activities that provide successes and challenges. This chapter helps to prepare preschool and kindergarten teachers as they make decisions regarding block play.

Cognitive Development

You only have to spend a few hours with preschool children to understand they think differently than adults and older children. Piaget (1952) provided a rich description of the qualitative differences between preoperational thought, the thinking qualities of very young children, and the more logical thought processes of older children and adults. Definitions of preoperational thinking and examples are summarized in Figure 5–1.

The definitions and examples of preoperational thinking show that, generally speaking, the thought processes of preschool/kindergarten children are based mainly on their perceptions, not on logic. Perceptions are interpretations of information received from the senses. The perceptions of young children are often based solely on sensory information, what they see, hear, smell, touch, or taste, to tell them about their world. Unfortunately, sensory information alone, without logic, can be deceiving and lead to false conclusions.

As children continue to work with materials and with each other, they gradually learn to use both their perceptions and their prior knowledge to build logical thinking and problem-solving ability. It is easy to see how block play can provide a wealth of opportunities for children to expand their thinking and problem-solving skills. As children handle blocks, moving them around to create different forms and structures, they become mentally active, interpret sensory information more accurately, combine that interpretation with prior knowledge, and learn strategies needed to produce the effect they desire (Williams & Kamii, 1986).

In addition to helping children develop logical thought processes, block play provides multiple opportunities for children to handle and manipulate blocks and other materials, and to construct both **physical knowledge** and **logicomathematical knowledge**. (Refer to Chapter 9 for a complete discussion of these terms.) With this increased understanding, children are able to master early academic skills such as counting, sorting, classifying, identifying shapes, and understanding equivalencies and part-to-whole relationships. When children

Centration—the tendency to focus on only one characteristic of an object or aspect of a problem at a time. *Stephanie, in deep concentration, is putting double unit blocks end to end across the floor of her classroom. She is not taking into account that she has left the block area and that with just one more block she will be out of the classroom and into the hall. She does not appear cognizant of this because her thinking is **centered** on the task of placing the blocks end to end.*

Irreversibility—the inability to reverse the direction of one's thinking or actions. *Keisha and Sonja have spent almost an hour building in the block area. They have pulled every block off the shelves and are sitting among the large piles. Their teacher signals that it is time to clean up, and asks them to put the blocks away. The girls sit still for a few moments and survey the seemingly endless piles of blocks around them. The amazed look on their faces shows clearly that they are not being lazy or defiant, but they simply do not know how to begin the process of putting the block center back the way it was when they began their play.*

Egocentrism—the inability to understand that different people see things in different ways. *Raymond and Jake have been stacking large hollow blocks in a single tower-like structure for about 10 minutes. They work together easily and are intent on the process of building the tower. Raymond declares, "Man, this is going to be some space shuttle!" Jake studies the situation for a few moments, obviously confused by Raymond's comment. He replies, "What do you mean space shuttle? We've been building a skyscraper."*

Animism—attaching lifelike qualities and feelings to inanimate objects. *Rachel and Evan have built a corral and are playing with several plastic horse models. Jamie enters the block area and accidentally steps on one of the horse models. Evan becomes very upset because he believes the horse is physically injured.*

Inability to conserve—results from children's misjudgments that are based on perception rather than logic. Preoperational thinkers do not understand that a quantity is fixed even when its physical appearance has changed. *Julian and Robert have trouble sharing unit blocks. They decided to count out equal shares of the pillars and agreed they each had six. The boys were satisfied with the arrangement, and each set out to build their own structure. After a short time, Robert looked around to see what Julian was doing. Julian had placed each pillar on end in a long row on top of a quadruple unit. Robert's pillars were spaced closer together on a double unit. To Robert, it appeared that he had fewer pillars and he insisted that the division of pillars had not been accurate after all.*

Transductive reasoning—the inability to link cause and effect. *Susan and Cynthia are building towers side by side on the playground with blocks made from corrugated board. Susan stands up to get more blocks from the wagon. Suddenly, a strong gust of wind causes Cynthia's tower to fall. Cynthia becomes upset with Susan, blaming her for knocking down the tower.*

Figure 5–1 *Preoperational thinking typical of preschool/kindergarten children.*

are allowed to choose to play in the block area, they repeatedly practice these newfound skills and abilities, and through this consistent repetition, they are able to transfer the thinking processes and the skills they learn in block play to other contexts. Teachers can encourage children to develop these thinking processes and early academic skills by asking open-ended questions that encourage the child to discuss their actions, reconsider their ideas, or describe the effect they are trying to achieve.

Language and Literacy Development

Block play provides a basic foundation for promoting language and literacy learning. Interacting with others while building encourages oral language development in three specific ways (Stroud, 1995). First, children playing together with blocks need to *communicate* with one another and sometimes with an adult. They may discuss plans for building, barter with others for blocks needed, or explain the process of building the structure to an interested teacher. Second, children *expand their vocabulary* during block play. As new scenes are created and buildings erected, children learn new terminology from one another, resourceful adults, books, displays, and other sources. Finally, dramatizing, which occurs as children incorporate imaginative play into their structures, provides opportunities for using *rich language*. As children take on roles such as parking attendant, pilot, or firefighter, they adopt new words and terminology.

The value of oral language learning through dramatic play in the block center is supported by Isbell and Raines (1991). A research study compared children's language in the block center versus the housekeeping center and found the block center elicited more and higher-quality oral language than the housekeeping center (which is traditionally recognized for promoting language development). Children playing with blocks had greater **verbal fluency** (total number of words spoken), used significantly more **communication units** (complete sentences), and produced more **vocabulary diversity** (number of different words) than children in the housekeeping center. The explanation for these results is children have more freedom to improvise settings and roles in the block center and, therefore, have more opportunities for greater oral language production. The researchers concluded that block centers should be considered a prominent means for fostering children's oral language development.

Block play is equally valuable for teaching early literacy concepts. Because blocks are representational in nature, they serve as an introduction to symbols (Cuffaro, 1995; Stroud, 1995). A child sliding a single unit block under a bridge is pretending the block is a car. A group of children constructing and sitting in the middle of a building made of hollow blocks, understands the structure is a representation of a real building. Learning that one object can be used to represent another helps prepare children to understand abstract symbols used in reading and writing. These dramatic play experiences are an important step toward using and processing written symbols (Vygotsky, 1966).

Drawing pictures has long been considered an appropriate scaffold for beginning readers and writers (Sulzby, 1990). Through random markings on paper or realistic drawings, children tell stories. Oken-Wright (1998) noted the importance of avoiding certain questions as well as the need to ask the right ones when encouraging young children to tell stories from their pictures. Asking inappropriate questions, such as, "What is it?", may offend the child who thinks the representation is obvious. Also, this question elicits minimal language as he can give a one-word answer. Declaring the quality of the work, such as "What a pretty picture," requires no response from the child. The often recommended comment, "Tell me about your picture," may produce only static language as he points to the drawing and names the pictures, such as "My dog. My mom. Me." Instead, Oken-Wright (1998) suggested asking, "What's happening here?" when looking at a child's drawing. This question sets an expectation that something is occurring in the drawing and that there is a beginning to a story. This questioning technique is equally beneficial for encouraging oral language production and providing a scaffold from storyteller to storywriter when children are deeply involved in block play. By asking, "What's happening here?" as children are building, the floor is open to a myriad of responses. Children may narrate the drama being carried out within a structure, explain building plans, relate future play intentions, or recount how a specific structure was made. This simple question asked at the right time has great potential for promoting storytelling, a necessary skill for young readers and writers.

Blocks promote early literacy by providing experiences for visual discrimination, a skill necessary for deciphering new words and recognizing familiar ones. As children select specific blocks needed for building, later returning materials to the shelf labeled with an outline of the shape, a picture, or written word, children are exercising necessary visual discrimination skills (Stroud, 1995).

Early literacy concepts can further be encouraged by stocking the block center with appropriate writing materials (Morrow, 1995; Morrow & Rand, 1991). Stroud (1995) found when writing materials were included as props in the block center, children created labels to name or identify the structure, wrote their name and attached it to their product, made signs warning others not to demolish their building, and drew doors, windows, and other architectural embellishments. Appropriate teacher responses to this writing behavior are vital (Morrow & Rand, 1991). When children produce writing samples to support their play in centers, it is important for teachers to accept all writing samples regardless of whether they are drawings, scribblings, direct copying, or invented spellings (Rybczynski & Troy, 1995). Teachers need to give as much time to listening to children talk about their writing during center time as they do in daily writing routines such as journaling. Accepting and acknowledging children's writing in play situations reinforces literacy concepts and encourages children to continue writing.

Literacy props selected to promote early literacy in learning centers should be "appropriate, authentic, and functional" (Neuman & Roskos, 1990). Appropriate props refer to materials that are safe and interesting for children of a particular age and stage of development. Authentic materials are those that may typically be found in a similar adult setting. Functional props are practical and useful for both the child and the learning center. Stroud (1995) found the following literacy props in the block center meet these three criteria: various sizes and colors of paper, notecards, invoices, order forms, envelopes, self-sticking notes, adding machine tape, pencils, markers, crayons, masking tape, and scissors. In addition to materials that encourage children to write, environmental print should be available as a model for writing. These materials include reference books, magazines, house plans, blueprints, and children's books. Teachers can creatively devise other pertinent materials, such as organizing interesting pictures of buildings in a three-ring binder or taking sequential photographs of a construction site over time so children can see significant changes.

Social Development

Observation is crucial to understanding children's social development, and the block center provides an excellent arena for watching children's interactions with peers. Teachers who spend time in areas where block play is occurring can see how children communicate and cooperate with others. Block play is an ideal representation of social living as children work in close physical proximity and share available materials (Weiss, 1997). During the preschool/kindergarten years, children have some of their first experiences working cooperatively with others and discovering that playing with others is enjoyable. Although it is important to be readily available to assist children working in groups, Rybczynski and Troy (1995) advised teachers to let peers help and support each other when possible. They should even have the opportunity to resolve disputes, which are inevitable when children with different developmental viewpoints are in close physical proximity and sharing resources for an extended period of time.

Opportunities for development of social skills occur in environments that have been carefully planned and prepared with this goal in mind. Cartwright (1995) suggested the following parameters for the block center when helping children develop effective group learning skills:

1. An open floor area of 10 × 12 feet can accommodate up to eight preschool/kindergarten children at one time. Unrelated traffic is routed around the block area.
2. An adequate number of blocks are sorted and stored by size and shape on low, open shelves bordering the building area.
3. Accessory materials are visible but stored separately from blocks. The best accessories are kept simple to allow children to use their imaginations.
4. Adults assist with clean-up by occasionally putting away stray blocks to keep the area neat while children are building and to minimize the large undertaking of replacing blocks on shelves.

5. Blocks are treated with care, and rules such as "no swinging, throwing, dropping, stepping, or marking on blocks" are enforced.
6. Adults should be knowledgeable of young children's developmental patterns and treat them with respect and trust.

The result of setting these parameters in the block center is a community atmosphere of concern and support when interactions between children run smoothly as well as when they are settling disputes.

Emotional Development

For healthy emotional development to occur, preschoolers and kindergartners need opportunities to explore their environment and be creative using concrete materials, their imagination, or a combination of the two. They need to be allowed to participate in making plans and decisions for themselves and their peer group to feel emotionally satisfied (Hendrick, 1990). Teachers should recognize that 4- and 5-year-olds will often make elaborate plans and begin the activity but abandon a project before it is completed. For example, three children playing with hollow blocks outlined a detailed plan for constructing a hangar where they could take on the role of mechanics working on planes. They spent a significant period of time with the construction of the hangar, but once it was completed decided to dismantle it and build an airport with unit blocks instead. Teachers of young children need to recognize this as typical behavior because the planning stage is often more emotionally satisfying than actually seeing the project through to the end.

Teachers who work closely with young children and their parents will inevitably witness hardships and crises within families. Ideally, families will inform the teacher of the situation so that he will be prepared if a change in behavior or emotional stance occurs within the child. However, some families are not comfortable sharing personal problems with others, so teachers should be aware of signs that indicate a child is experiencing stress. Signs of stress that are observable in a child's play include development of play themes that are inappropriate for the age of the child, a fixation with one play theme or role, extremely atypical play themes, or excessive preoccupation with one object (Curry & Arnaud, 1982). If these signs become evident, the teacher can sensitively approach a family member to discuss his observations as well as make allowances for the child's behavior and keep the group environment as stable as possible.

Teachers can help children to satisfy the emotional need to plan and make decisions as well as deal with crises in their lives by providing an environment in which play is the vehicle for supporting emotional development. A play-oriented curriculum helps children act out and deal with negative emotions such as sadness or confusion, as well as positive feelings such as delight and excitement, when their play reflects their personal interests.

Blocks promote children's emotional development in a number of different ways. First, the simple act of building and knocking down structures gives children a feeling of being in control (Church & Miller, 1990). Second, blocks enhance self-esteem because they are an open-ended material and there is no right or wrong way to play with them. Finally, blocks allow children to translate their personal ideas and experiences into three-dimensional concrete representations. They can develop scenes that enable them to express feelings by acting out personal experiences or make-believe stories. These actions can then be discussed with a sensitive, understanding adult.

Motor Development

Blocks provide children with opportunities to develop large motor and fine motor skills. As children work in a defined space with delicately balanced block structures, they become aware of how much space their bodies occupy and how their bodies change as they sit, stand up, crouch down, or reach across. With experience, they learn to carefully maneuver themselves around their own and other children's block structures. Teachers can observe and watch for children who lack the coordination and control necessary to work successfully in the block area. These children may need a larger area or special place to build so they do not accidentally disturb others' constructions. Additional opportunities to develop large muscles and motor coordination should be provided.

During the preschool and kindergarten years, children's fine motor ability rapidly becomes more refined. Santrock (1993) used children's block building as an illustration of the development of fine motor skills. Three-year-olds build block towers with great concentration but blocks are stacked haphazardly, rather than in a straight line. By age 4, fine motor coordination becomes much more precise and children attempt to perfectly straighten each block in a stacked tower. At 5 years of age, fine motor coordination has improved so that the hand, arm, and body move easily together, which enables children to build more intricate structures. The repetitive process of balancing and moving blocks is great practice for fine motor and coordination skills.

Arranging the Environment

Appropriate organization of the classroom requires attention to time schedules, room arrangement, materials, and activities. Indoor spaces best suited for 3- to 5-year-olds use a **learning center system** for major portions of the day. A learning center system coordinates time and space to facilitate various small group or individual activities, such as water and sand play, block building, library, art area, dramatic play, and so on (Bredenkamp & Copple, 1997; Kieff & Casbergue, 1999). When making initial plans for learning centers, teachers should look for functional relationships between spaces in the classroom. Learning centers should be planned around noise levels with quieter centers, such as the library corner, writing table, and computer, in a separate area from noisier centers, such as blocks, sand table, and dramatic play. Brewer (1998) suggested teachers look for multiple uses of a single space. Tables that serve children snacks can be used at center time when children are playing with table blocks and other smaller building materials. A carpeted area used for group meetings and storytimes can be transformed into a gross motor center by adding a floor beam for balancing and barrels for crawling.

Traffic patterns in the classroom should be considered to facilitate smooth transitions between centers. Creating useful traffic patterns requires determining the most obvious route children will take on their way from one area of the classroom to another. Plan clear, direct routes to often traveled spaces, such as the restroom or water fountain, and think about how children will enter and leave each learning center. Consider the needs of individual children and make sure there is enough space for every child to move about easily, regardless of adaptive equipment in use. Careful planning of traffic patterns is crucial for promoting harmony in the classroom and eliminating unnecessary disruptions.

Learning center systems also dictate the degree of choice in how children will spend their time in centers. Children should be allowed enough time to develop their play. The exact amount of time will depend on a variety of factors, such as age, interest, and previous experience. The best way to ensure children have the time they need is to allow them to select a play area and stay as long as they choose. If children "overuse" a particular center, teachers can intervene by encouraging them to try a different center, to ensure they are receiving a healthy balance of experiences. Limits on time that must be set to accommodate the group or school setting should be kept to a minimum. Be cautious of learning center routines that require children to spend a specific amount of time in each center before each small group "rotates" to another assigned area. Such routines do not allow children the important task of planning and making choices about where they will spend their time. Also, it does not allow enough time for play to develop. Envision a group of children working diligently to build a car wash with hollow blocks. Just as they finish the structure and assign roles for their dramatic play, the teacher tells them to clean up and move to the next area. Children whose play time is cut short before it has had a chance to develop to some level of satisfaction become frustrated. If children's play is constantly interrupted in this manner, it prevents them from becoming involved in more sophisticated play and stifles their creative ability.

Isbell (1995) recommended asking a series of questions about each center, such as "Is the center attractive and appealing to the young children in this classroom? Is the center organized and labeled so materials are easy for the children to locate and return when play is complete? Are the activities and materials flexible and open-ended to allow children to work at different levels and with diverse ideas?" Specific questions for evaluating the block center include:

1. Are children working on block constructions for a focused period of time?
2. Do children value their constructions?
3. Is coordination improving as children build block structures?
4. Are children discussing their ideas and creations during the building process?
5. Are block constructions becoming more complex, and is the activity involving dramatic play?

These questions can help guide teachers as they design and make necessary changes to learning centers.

Block Play Indoors   The block play area is ideally set in a spacious area that can be bordered on three sides by sturdy cabinets for storing blocks and accessories or an adjacent wall. A semisecluded space away from high traffic areas eliminates problems with block structures being accidentally knocked down. The block center is active; therefore, it should be grouped with other noisier centers and away from quieter play areas. Many classrooms with limited space assign block play to the same area where the whole class meets for circle time. This may be necessary in some situations, but ideally block play should have its own reserved space (Church & Miller, 1990). This capitalizes on the importance of this activity, plus provides a space for children to preserve intact structures or buildings in progress. If space will not allow block structures to be left intact for an extended period of time, they can still be preserved by leaving them up for a day with a label for others to view, taking photographs that are put on display, making a sketch of the construction, or taking dictation as children describe the process or product of their block play.

Different types of blocks may be integrated into other learning centers to provide more opportunities for block play and to encourage children who typically shy away from the block center. Smaller table blocks or connecting blocks can be stored in separate containers in the manipulative area. Also, blocks may be incorporated into a theme study, such as a unit on homes. Teachers should be alert for new and novel ways to promote block play. Figure 5–2 illustrates an ideal set-up for a block center.

Block Play Outdoors   Outdoor play spaces provide additional valuable experiences not always possible in an indoor environment. The same system of analyzing space and deciding on traffic patterns should be used. Teachers can sketch the permanent features, such as climbing and sliding areas, sandboxes, and cargo nets, and plan from there. Because most playground equipment is permanently fixed and secured, teachers must improvise to provide an appropriate outdoor play area for specific age groups. One of the most cost-effective and time-efficient ways to make changes to a play yard is through the introduction of loose parts. The term *loose parts* refers to a variety of materials introduced to the environment to promote discovery and ingenuity. Loose parts enable children to physically change the environment to suit their play (Rivkin, 1995). Three of the suggested categories for loose parts include:

- large moveable pieces (large blocks and tires)
- building materials (milk crates, boards, blocks, and cardboard boxes)
- natural items (rocks, logs, leaves, and sticks)

In addition to introducing new building materials and providing more time for play, new interest in traditional indoor materials, such as unit blocks, can be provoked simply be bringing them outdoors. Guidelines for using, transporting, and caring for materials must be established and enforced, but the extra effort of providing loose parts to children outdoors will magnify the pleasure of their play and learning.

Block Selection and Accessories

The types of blocks recommended for preschool and kindergarten children have been divided into two categories: basic blocks and supplementary building materials. Basic blocks are considered a necessity for providing preschool and kindergarten children the experiences needed for growth in the cognitive, language-literacy, social-emotional, and physical domains. Basic blocks needed for the preschool-/kindergarten-age child include unit blocks, hollow blocks, and table blocks. These sets of blocks will provide a multitude of valuable learning experiences. Supplementary building materials are recommended to extend, supplement, and enhance the concepts and skills learned from the recommended basic block sets. Although these supplementary building materials are beneficial and enjoyable to children, they cannot replace the experiences provided by playing with unit, hollow, and table blocks.

When making decisions about types and number of blocks to make available, teachers should keep in mind that quantity is more important than variety. That is, it is better to have a sufficient amount of one block set than a few pieces of various types of blocks.

Unit Blocks and Accessories   In 1914, unit blocks were designed by Caroline Pratt and are still widely used in early childhood settings that value block play. The basic unit is $1\frac{3}{8} \times 3\frac{3}{4} \times 5\frac{1}{2}$ inches. Other blocks in the set are multiples or divisions of the basic unit length and are based on the proportions of 1 : 2 : 4. For example, the half unit is the same thickness and width but exactly half the length of the unit, whereas the double unit is twice as long as the basic unit block. The relationship in size between the blocks was deliberate to provide an early understanding of mathematical concepts.

Church and Miller (1990) provided guidelines for the number and shapes of blocks appropriate for groups of 7 to 10 children playing in a block center

The illustration shows some simple and safe ways to set up a block area. The numbers in the illustration coincide with these suggestions.

1. Develop a storage arrangement with matching "puzzle bases" for easy cleanup.
2. Display larger accessories on shelves with matching outlines for easy access and to facilitate cleanup.
3. Display smaller accessories in clear plastic boxes, labeled with simple outlines, for easy identification.

Figure 5–2 *An ideal set-up for block play.*
Reprinted with permission of Scholastic, Inc.

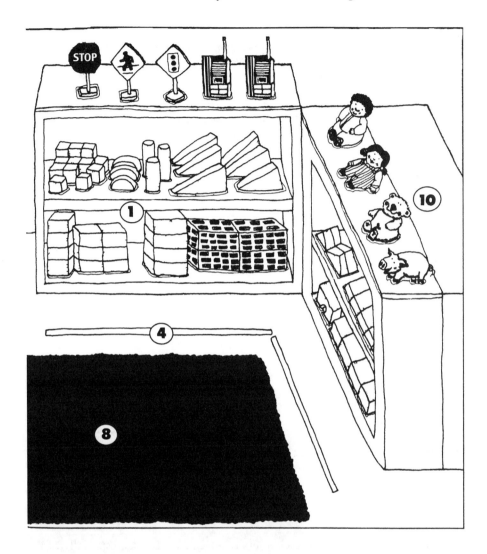

4. Use colored plastic tape to mark off building boundaries.
5. Mark off "parking areas" for large vehicles with colored tape.
6. Display posters and photographs of city scenes to inspire children's play and constructions.
7. Hang a bulletin board at children's eye level to display their drawings, dictated stories, and photographs of their work.
8. Use low-pile carpet to muffle the sound of falling blocks.
9. Provide a sign-up system to play in the area.
10. Back storage shelves with other shelf units for added stability.

The following chart has been adapted from *Play Equipment for the Nursery School* by Jessie Stanton and Alma Weisberg (Bank Street). Keep in mind that these are guidelines for 7 to 10 children and make adjustments for your group.

Block Recommendations for Three- to Five-Year-Olds (for 7 to 10 children)

Block Type	3 years	4 years	5 years
Half units	24	24	30
Units	54	96	110
Double units	48	70	95
Quadruple units	24	24	36
Pillars	12	24	36
Small cylinders	10	16	20
Large cylinders	10	12	16
Circular curves	6	8	10
Elliptical curves	4	8	10
Pairs of small triangles	4	8	9
Pairs of large triangles	4	8	12
Floor boards—11"	6	15	30
Ramps	6	16	20
Right-angle switches	0	4	8
Y Switches	2	2	4
Roofboards	0	6	10
X-switches	0	4	8
Half pillars	0	6	8
Total	214	351	472

Figure 5–3 *How many blocks are enough?*
From *Play Equipment for the Nursery School* by Jessie Stanton, Alma Weisberg, and the faculty of the Bank Street School for Children. Reprinted with permission from Scholastic, Inc.

(see Figure 5–3). Younger preschoolers require fewer blocks, especially of the larger type, whereas kindergartners need more blocks, plus unique shapes such as roof boards, large switches, and intersections to encourage more complicated building.

There are several manufacturers of unit blocks but Community Playthings claims to make the most accurate blocks, precise to within $\frac{1}{100}$ of an inch. A good starting set for classrooms with few or no blocks is the Community Playthings Half School Set, which includes 360 blocks in 20 shapes. It corresponds closely with the recommended number and shapes of blocks appropriate for 4-year-olds, and adaptations can be made for other age groups. Programs serving 3-year-olds can use the block recommendation guide (Church & Miller, 1990) to decide which blocks to retain from the Half School Set until the children are ready for them. Kindergarten classrooms will need to order additional block sets such as the Supplementary Set with 57 blocks in 14 shapes, additional sets of 48 units or 24 double units, and individual block shapes. When budgets dictate limiting materials, remember it is more important to have multiples of the basic unit, half unit, double unit, and quadruple unit to make building easier and facilitate mathematical understanding than to sacrifice the number of blocks needed for basic building to have one of each unique shape. Unit blocks are expensive when compared with other materials in the preschool/kindergarten classroom; however, because they are so versatile and beneficial to children's development and learning, and with care will survive many generations of children, they should be considered a wise investment.

An important part of playing with unit blocks is knowing and using the correct name for each shape. Rather than asking a peer for the long block, a child can more specifically learn to request a "double unit" or "quadruple unit." This terminology provides a foundation for learning fractions and other mathematical concepts. To facilitate the understanding that a written word is a symbol for a spoken word, teachers can trace around each block shape on a posterboard and label each shape with the appropriate name. Displaying this poster in the block center will also be helpful to student teachers and parent volunteers who are learning the names of the blocks.

Accessories are a necessary ingredient for productive, enjoyable block play. They add to the experience, "stimulation, variety, beauty, and dramatic play content" (Hirsch, 1996, p. 122). The number, type, and variety of accessories need to be tailored to the group of children using them. For example, young preschoolers would be overwhelmed by too much variety in accessories offered, as might kindergartners, during the first days of school. Teachers may introduce new accessories throughout the year if interest in the block center lags, if they see a particular accessory might be useful, or if children request specific accessories to support or extend their play. Block accessories may be added to support a theme or project the class is exploring. Children's structures will naturally reflect places they have visited on field trips, stories that have been read to them, and information received from specialists who have visited their classroom. Some block accessories can expand children's understanding of people different from themselves. Incorporating people figures of various ethnic groups, age ranges, and ability levels contribute to antibias attitudes.

Accessories should include *well-defined pieces* that relate to children's most recurrent themes and *ordinary, nondescript materials,* which suggest many uses rather than a single function. Well-defined pieces include human figures to scale (adult figures will be about 5 inches high), which represent families of different ethnicities and community workers, and animals that are familiar, such as pets, zoo, or farm animals. Transportation vehicles, including cars, trucks, tractors, planes and trains, and familiar road signs should also be offered on a daily basis. These well-defined pieces designed specifically for block centers can be purchased through school supply catalogs or can be made. Road signs can be drawn, cut out, laminated, and attached to wide craft sticks. Teachers can make human figures by cutting and laminating full-length pictures from magazines, mounting them on foam board, and placing them in a clay base so they will stand independently. This same technique can be used with full-length pictures of the children that have been scanned into a computer and printed. Using representations of themselves in their play allows for a different perspective on children's dramatic play.

There is no end to the number and variety of *ordinary, nondescript materials* that can be made available to children at block play. A traditional material of this nature is 1-inch colored cubes that have been used to embellish block structures since unit blocks were designed and made available to children. Other examples are lumber scraps and samples of floor coverings such as tile and carpet. For children who have outgrown the tendency to put small objects in their mouths, shells, pebbles, and small stones are inexpensive and versatile enough to be used with most block structures (Stanton & Weisberg, 1996). Figure 5–4 provides a comprehensive list of accessories.

Storing and Caring for Unit Blocks and Accessories   Children learn important classification and mathematical skills when blocks are stored properly. Sturdy block cabinets with cubicles of various sizes are needed to store blocks so children can see the size relationships and be able to easily return blocks to shelves. When half units, units, double units, and quadruple units are stored next to each other, children can visually see the increased gradations of length. Early number concepts are learned when teachers instruct children to place blocks in stacks of a particular quantity such as six. Consistently stacking six blocks during clean-up provides a concrete example of the number six. As children remove blocks one by one from the stack, they are exploring the processes of addition and subtraction in a concrete way. Blocks of the same size and shape should be stored together, longest side facing out from shelf. Unit blocks should not be stored in tubs because it makes it difficult for children to find a specific shape, blocks can become damaged, and bins do not give the visual presentation of the relationship between sizes. To help children put blocks away properly, outlines of block shapes can be drawn on shelves or silhouettes of block shapes can be cut, laminated, and taped on shelves for a less permanent arrangement (Iceberg & Along, 1997), and word labels can be added for authentic environmental print. Block pattern adhesives can also be purchased commercially or made with solid color contact paper. Spaces for larger accessories, such as trucks, cars, and figurines, can be indicated by taping to the shelf laminated photos taken by the teacher, or pictures cut from the catalogs through which the item was purchased. A word label should be made to correspond to the photograph. Smaller accessories, such as 1-inch cubes, shells, and stones, can be stored in separate bins. Storage of literacy-related accessories must also be taken into

This extensive list of accessories provides teachers with ideas for adding interest or supporting children's block play. Ideally, accessories should be provided when requested by children. Accessories introduced by the teacher should be added one at a time and must be relatively limited in number. The main focus should always be on the blocks.

acorns	Easter basket grass	pictures from catalogs
aluminum wrap	film canisters	pine cones
animal figures	firefighter hats	plastic surgical tubing
bed sheets	flashlights	plastic table cloth
blankets	hardhats	PVC pipe
bottle caps	headphones without	rocks
boxes	cord	rulers
buttons	insulation for copper	shells
car wash sponges	tubing	shower curtain
cardboard tubes	keys	shredded paper
ceramic tiles (1")	margarine tubs	spools
clay	measuring tape	spoons, plastic
clothespins	milk jug caps	spray paint can caps
coffee can lids	modeling materials	straws
cosmetic bottles filled	paper towel tube	string
with sand, with	pegs	tape
people figures	people figures (repre-	toy tools
glued on	sentative of various	trays of different
cotton	ethnicities, ages,	shapes/sizes
craft sticks	and abilities)	vehicles
crib sheet	photographs of	wood scraps
dollhouse furniture	children	yogurt containers

Figure 5–4 *Accessories for block play.*

consideration. Writing utensils can be sorted and stored in clear shoebox-size containers, boxes, or cans covered with contact paper and labeled with a word and picture describing the contents. Paper and tagboard can be placed in a storage tray obtained from an office supply store. Miscellaneous pieces can be sorted and stored into clean, 5-gallon plastic ice cream containers with lids. Cleaning up can be an overwhelming task for young children. Adults in the classroom should voluntarily assist and encourage children who are putting blocks away. Although the materials should be returned to the proper place, do not overemphasize the need for neatness because this may discourage children from playing with blocks at all.

New blocks should be waxed with a heavy-duty paste wax to keep them clean over the years. If blocks become dirty, they can be washed with a mild dishwashing soap using a stiff brush. Blocks should be exposed to water only briefly (never soaked) and must dry completely before they are used again. With a brief demonstration and a little adult assistance, children can help keep blocks clean. In addition to learning a new skill, they will develop a heightened sense of ownership for play equipment.

Unit blocks were designed for play on the floor, and an area rug is needed to protect tumbling blocks and to cut down on noise. A low pile and tight weave is best and the rug should be large enough to accommodate the number of children building in the area. It is important that the rug be kept clean. It should be vacuumed daily and children should remove their shoes before entering the play area (this also protects blocks that may be stepped on accidentally by children). In recent years, area rugs with printed city and road designs have become popular. These rugs should be considered an accessory that children can use if it suits their play. It should not be the primary rug because the detailed scene may interfere with their own creative ideas, dictating what and how they play.

Guidelines for Unit Block Play

1. Building away from shelves reduces problems when children reach for blocks. Church and Miller (1990) suggested applying masking tape 1 foot from block shelves, with the rule that children cannot build between the line and the shelf.
2. Provide enough blocks for the age and number of children in the group to keep them interested in block play (see Figure 5–3).
3. Keep accessories simple and austere so children can use their imaginations and apply their own meaning. Allow children to suggest and add their own accessories as their play dictates.
4. Be thoroughly familiar with Johnson's stages of block play.
5. Allow time for play as well as cleaning up, an important benefit of unit blocks.

Large Hollow Blocks   Large, hollow blocks, also designed by Caroline Pratt, offer a different type of building experience than smaller blocks. These large blocks require large motor manipulation for picking up, carrying, stacking, and building. Hollow blocks are used to make child-size buildings and structures that can be used for role playing. The children themselves replace the family figures used with smaller block sets as they crawl through houses and sit in the driver's seat of a bus made from hollow blocks. Hollow blocks require children to solve real-life construction problems and fantasy play disputes simultaneously (Cartwright, 1995). These larger, durable blocks are ideal for both outdoor and indoor play. They allow for larger groups of children to get involved in building because it may take cooperative effort to lift, stack, or arrange hollow blocks (see Figure 5–5).

There are five different sizes and shapes of hollow blocks and two lengths of boards. Most commercially manufactured hollow blocks are left open on

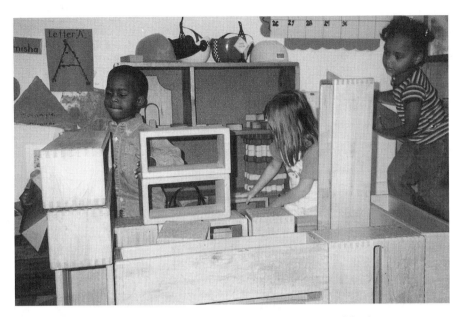

Figure 5–5 *Preschoolers build together using hollow blocks.*

two sides to make them easier for children to hold and carry, although original hollow blocks were completely enclosed.

Square	5½″ × 11″ × 11″
Half square	5½″ × 5½″ × 11″
Double square	5½″ × 11″ × 22″
Half double square	5½″ × 5½″ × 22″
Ramp	5½″ × 11″ × 22″
Long board	5½″ × 44″ × ¾″
Short board	5½″ × 22″ × ¾″

Cartwright (1990) recommended about 20 hollow blocks for indoor play, supplemented with 10 boards. Outdoor play can accommodate approximately twice as many blocks and boards, along with accompanying pieces such as packing boxes (30″ × 30″ × 40″) and small ladders, wagons, and sawhorses (Cartwright, 1996).

Hollow blocks can be purchased commercially from several manufacturers of school equipment. The Half School Set from Community Playthings provides enough hollow blocks to be used indoors or outdoors. Cartwright (1990) recommended enlisting the help of parents and devising a set of homemade blocks from #2 grade white pine (see Figure 5–6). According to

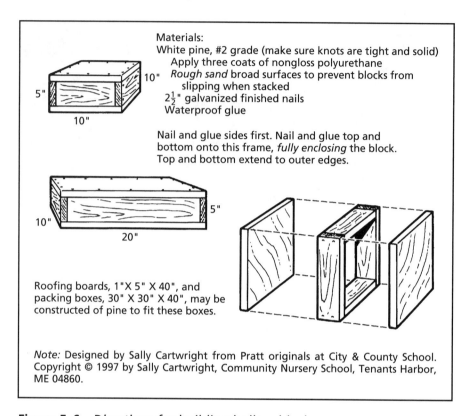

Materials:
White pine, #2 grade (make sure knots are tight and solid)
Apply three coats of nongloss polyurethane
Rough sand broad surfaces to prevent blocks from
slipping when stacked
$2\frac{1}{2}$" galvanized finished nails
Waterproof glue

Nail and glue sides first. Nail and glue top and bottom onto this frame, *fully enclosing* the block. Top and bottom extend to outer edges.

Roofing boards, 1"X 5" X 40", and packing boxes, 30" X 30" X 40", may be constructed of pine to fit these boxes.

Note: Designed by Sally Cartwright from Pratt originals at City & County School. Copyright © 1997 by Sally Cartwright, Community Nursery School, Tenants Harbor, ME 04860.

Figure 5–6 *Directions for building hollow blocks.*

Reprinted with permission of Sally Cartwright, Education Consultant, Tenants Harbor, ME.

S. Cartwright (personal communication, August 12, 1999), involving parents in building is an ideal way to develop a sense of community within a school setting. Most important, building homemade hollow blocks will ensure they are completely enclosed, as first designed by Pratt. Enclosed hollow blocks are much more for beneficial building strength, coordination, and necessary motor skills.

Due to the large size of hollow blocks, children take on various dramatic roles to accommodate their structures, rather than using people figurines. Therefore, accessories needed are similar to those found in dramatic play areas. Accessory materials may include lengths of hose or rope, buckets, wagons, stuffed animals, carpet squares, community worker hats, plastic tools, steering wheel, pots, empty food containers, sheets, and child-size furniture. A variety of materials that can be improvised should be on hand to accommodate impromptu themes created with hollow blocks.

Care and Storage of Hollow Blocks   Hollow blocks used outdoors should be lightly sanded with fine-grade paper and lacquered once per year with a good quality boiled linseed oil to extend the life of the blocks (Hendrick, 1990). Whether blocks are played with indoors or out, a protective surface such as carpet, grass, or artificial turf should be used to prevent blocks from cracking or breaking. Smooth, round pebbles are an ideal surface for outdoor play because blocks can be pushed down into the pebbles for extra stability (S. Cartwright, personal communication, May 19, 1999). A 10 × 12-foot rug can accommodate up to eight builders indoors, whereas a level, protected surface of 30 × 40 feet is needed outdoors (Cartwright, 1990). Artificial grass is an ideal outdoor surface because it provides protection for falling blocks and can withstand the elements.

Because hollow blocks are large, heavy, and durable, they can be stored on the floor rather than on shelves. Children can take responsibility for carefully loading blocks onto a cart or wagon and moving them indoors and outdoors. For safety purposes, stored hollow blocks should not be stacked higher than the height of the children, and cots or mats should not be placed in the area during naptime.

Guidelines for Hollow Block Play

1. Traditionally, it has been recommended not to mix hollow blocks with other types of block sets such as unit blocks. Each style of block has different purposes. When playing with hollow blocks, the children become part of the drama. Unit blocks are representational and move children into a microworld. Therefore, integrating the two styles is at cross purposes.
2. When hollow blocks are used indoors and outdoors, store them in a protected area away from natural elements and provide a synthetic protective surface or an organic ground cover such as grass or sand.
3. Maintain blocks annually to extend their life.
4. Encourage children to integrate familiar materials from their environment as accessories to support their play.
5. Document cooperative efforts among children that are necessary for successful play with hollow blocks.

Table Blocks   The third basic block set that should be provided for preschool and kindergarten children is table blocks, also called Kinder Blocks®. These are similar in shape and proportion to unit blocks but are scaled down to two-thirds the size, thus making them convenient for play in smaller areas such as on a table. Table blocks may have a natural maple finish, but many are painted in bright shades of blue, green, red, yellow, and orange. Table blocks are typically sold in groups of 30 to 60 pieces, so even a small set contains enough blocks for a pair of children working together. These smaller blocks require more fine motor control for building, balancing, and keeping structures standing for dramatic play. Many children will have previous experience playing with these blocks because they are affordable and sold commercially at toy and discount stores. Teachers can ask parents to donate table blocks no longer used at home and purchase used sets from garage sales or flea markets.

Accessories should always be to scale with the blocks being used; therefore, figures 1 to 3 inches in size, such as small animal figures, Hot Wheels® cars, Fisher-Price® Little People, or doll house families, can be used to accommodate play. Interlocking wooden train sets, such as Brio®, can add a new dimension to play with table blocks because children can add tunnels and bridges to the existing railway system. Recyclable materials, such as film canisters, clothespins, cone-shape drink cups, and small paper milk cartons, can be available for children to use as they see fit. Recycled containers, such as large, plastic peanut butter jars; clear, disposable food storage containers; and margarine tubs with a picture of the contents taped to the outside, can also be used to hold smaller accessories.

Because table blocks are relatively small, they can be stored together in a box or a bin. It is recommended that table blocks be stored in a clear container so children can easily find a specific block for which they are looking. Also, commercial packaging often sends a message that the contents are more appropriate for one gender than another, which may discourage children's participation with the materials. These small wood blocks are extremely durable and will hold up to years of use. Additional sets can affordably be purchased to replenish lost pieces.

Guidelines for Table Block Play

1. Table blocks are more beneficial for older preschoolers' motor skills.
2. Encourage children to use their imaginations to embellish their play with table blocks by making various accessories available.
3. Be available to assist children as they begin experimenting with the table blocks to balance frustration with success.
4. Because they are affordable, table blocks should be plentiful and replenished often.

Supplementary Building Materials

There are many possible supplementary building materials available for 3-to-6-year-old children. These materials can be purchased at toy and discount stores, ordered from school supply catalogs, or made by adults. They can be manipulated on the floor or at a table. Coverings for tables should be used to minimize noise, provide boundaries for individual or partner play areas, and protect materials (see Figure 5–7). Inexpensive table coverings include plastic placemats (preferably in solid colors); shelf liner, which can be cut to a specific size; trays without dividers; and tile or low-pile carpet samples. Supplementary blocks may be stored in separate bins within the same play center so children may choose materials, carry the container of like blocks to the table, and then easily clean up and return the blocks when finished. This area should remain separate from the unit block and hollow block centers; however, table blocks could easily be incorporated into this area.

Duplos® Duplos® are made by the same manufacturer of Legos® and are based on the same interlocking system. However, Duplos® are much larger and easier for small hands to manipulate. The Basic Set provides a variety of Duplos® shapes and can be supplemented with other interlocking pieces such as Duplos® World People, Community Workers, Transportation Vehicles, and Community Vehicles. Duplos® building plates can be purchased separately or attached to building tables. Using building plates is more appropriate for kindergarten-age children who will exhibit a stronger interest in saving a structure to display or making changes at a later time. Duplos® offer children the experience of playing with semipermanent locking pieces, and they are challenged to devise new ways to connect blocks in

Figure 5–7 *Kindergartners building with Duplos® foam pattern blocks, Waffle Blocks®, and Bristle Blocks®.*

desired shapes and structures. Microdramatic play occurs when accessories, such as animals, people, and vehicles, are offered. Playing with Duplos® provides a strong foundation for later Legos® play, which is valuable to young builders.

Bristle Blocks®   Bristle Blocks®, also sold under the names Krinkles® and Thistle Blocks®, connect with soft, flexible, interlocking bristles. Sets of Bristle Blocks® are sold with or without family figures and accessories, such as wheels used to create vehicles. Interlocking building plates, approximately 7 × 6 inches, are also covered in the bristles and can be used as a building surface. Blocks come in bright colors, and the texture of the bristles plus their pliability make them attractive to young children.

Snap Blocks®   Snap Blocks® are brightly painted, hardwood blocks in a variety of shapes, each with numerous snaps firmly attached. Children create and build by snapping blocks together to form structures, vehicles, and animals. Some sets include Snap Block® characters, which can be mounted to structures. A building base approximately 8 × 8 inches is available with 16 snaps attached. In addition to challenging children's creative thinking, these blocks teach an important self-help skill.

Magnet Blocks®   Magnet Blocks® will add a new twist for experienced preschool block builders and kindergarten children. These smooth-surfaced plastic blocks in shapes and sizes similar to Duplos® are joined by magnetic points. They introduce the concept of magnets and encourage discovery of positive and negative poles. After experimental play, children can use magnet Blocks® to build houses, vehicles, and other constructions.

Waffle Blocks®   Square Waffle Blocks® connect together easily to form flat "floors," tracks, or roads on which to park and drive vehicles. Children enjoy making three-dimensional shapes such as boxes that can be opened by lifting one hinged block. They come in a variety of sizes and are usually made in bright primary colors. Waffle Blocks® are versatile enough to accommodate children with varied experiences in block building.

Homemade Blocks   Homemade blocks can be used to temporarily add variety and interest to children's block play but should never be used in place of unit, hollow, or table blocks. Blocks can be made using clean milk cartons in half-gallon, quart, pint, and half-pint sizes. The tops of the cartons are cut off and the cartons are stuffed with newspaper. A second empty carton is slid over the top to form an enclosed block. The block should be taped securely and covered with a self-sticking shelf liner in a solid color. Larger blocks can be made by simply taping empty cardboard boxes of similar size so that all sides are closed. They are light enough for young preschoolers to lift and stack

(Church & Miller, 1990). Another suggestion for homemade large blocks is using L-shaped plastic pieces designed to connect flat pieces of cardboard to create triangles, squares, and other shapes that will stand up independently. Harris (1994) observed children successfully using this device to create a lemonade stand, which they used in their dramatic play.

Conclusion

There are many decisions to be made when planning for young children. To plan effectively, teachers must be familiar with the developmental characteristics of the children in their care. Scheduling and classroom arrangement should reflect the teacher's understanding of young children and their particular needs. Variety and availability of appropriate materials will help ensure that children have many opportunities to learn through their play.

Theory into Practice

1. Draw a diagram of the classroom and design a learning center system with special attention to:
   a. functional relationships between spaces in the classroom
   b. traffic patterns
   c. routines for center selection that maximize student choice
   d. questions for evaluating the center.
2. Plan an outdoor block center with rules for use and guidelines on caring for materials.
3. Develop an inventory of blocks and accessories currently available to children. Begin to collect and organize additional materials as needed.

Websites

www.perpetualpreschool.com

This website offers ideas and activities for young children in a variety of play areas, including blocks.

Related Readings

Driscoll, A. (1995). *Cases in early childhood education: Stories of programs and practices.* Boston: Allyn & Bacon.

Fisher, B. (1998). *Joyful learning in kindergarten.* Portsmouth, NH: Heinemann.

Walmsley, B. B., Camp, A. M., & Walmsley, S. A. (1992). *Teaching kindergarten; A developmentally appropriate approach.* Portsmouth, NH: Heinemann.

References

Bredenkamp, S., & Copple, C. (1997). *Developmentally appropriate practices in early childhood programs.* Washington, DC: National Association for the Education of Young Children.

Brewer, J. (1998). *Introduction to early childhood education: Preschool through primary grades.* Boston, MA: Allyn & Bacon.

Cartwright, S. (1990). Learning with large blocks. *Young Children, 45*(3), 38–41.

Cartwright, S. (1995, May). Block play: Experiences in cooperative learning and living. *Child Care Information Exchange,* 39–41.

Cartwright, S. (1996). Learning with large blocks. In E. Hirsch (Ed.), *The block book* (3rd ed., pp. 133–141). Washington, DC: National Association for the Education of Young Children.

Church, E., & Miller, K. (1990). *Learning through play: Blocks. A practical guide for teaching young children.* New York: Scholastic.

Cuffaro, H. (1995, May). Block building: Opportunities for learning. *Child Care Information Exchange,* 36–38.

Curry, N., & Arnaud, S. (1982). Dramatic play as a diagnostic aid in the preschool. *Journal of Children in Contemporary Society, 14*(4), 37–46.

Harris, T. (1994). The snack shop: Block play in a primary classroom. *Dimensions, 22*(4), 22–23.

Hendrick, J. (1990). *Total learning: Developmental curriculum for the young child.* Columbus, OH: Merrill.

Hirsch, E. (1996). Block building: Practical considerations for the classroom teacher. In E. Hirsch (Ed.), *The block book* (3rd ed., pp. 117–132). Washington, DC: National Association for the Education of Young Children.

Isbell, R. (1995). *The complete learning center book.* Beltsville, MD: Gryphon House.

Isbell, R., & Raines, S. (1991). Young children's oral language production in three types of play centers. *Journal of Research in Childhood Education, 5*(2), 140–146.

Isenberg, J., & Jalongo, M. (1997). *Creative expression and play in early childhood.* Columbus, OH: Merrill.

Kieff, J., & Casbergue, R. (1999). *Playful teaching and learning.* Boston: Allyn & Bacon.

Morrow, L. (1995, January). Literacy all around. *Early Childhood Today,* 34–41.

Morrow, L., & Rand, M. (1991). Preparing the classroom environment to promote literacy during play. In J. F. Christie (Ed.), *Play and early literacy development* (pp. 141–165). Albany: State University of New York Press.

Neuman, S., & Roskos, K. (1990). Play, print, and purpose: Enriching play environments for literacy development. *The Reading Teacher, 44*(3), 214–221.

Oken-Wright, P. (1998). Transition to writing: Drawing as a scaffold for emergent writers. *Young Children, 53*(2), 76–81.

Piaget, J. (1952). *The origins of intelligence.* New York: International Universities Press.

Rivkin, M. S. (1995). *The great outdoors: Restoring children's right to play outside.* Washington, DC: National Association for the Education of Young Children.

Rybczynski, M., & Troy, A. (1995). Literacy-enriched play centers: Trying them out in "The Real World." *Childhood Education, 72*(1), 7–12.

Santrock, J. (1993). *Children.* Dubuque, IA: Brown and Benchmark.

Stanton, J., & Weisberg, A. (1996). Suggested equipment for block building. In E. Hirsch (Ed.), *The block book* (3rd ed., pp. 149–152). Washington, DC: National Association for the Education of Young Children.

Stroud, J. (1995). Block play: Building a foundation for literacy. *Early Childhood Education Journal, 23*(1), 9–13.

Sulzby, E. (1990). Assessment of emergent writing and children's language while writing. In L. M. Morrow & J. K. Smith (Eds.), *Assessment for instruction in early literacy* (pp. 83–109). Englewood Cliffs, NJ: Prentice Hall.

Weiss, K. (1997). Let's build! *Scholastic Early Childhood Today, 12*(2), 31–39.

Williams, C., & Kamii, C. (1986). How do children learn by handling objects? *Young Children, 42*(1), 23–26.

Vygotsky, L. (1966). Play and its role in the mental development of the child. *Soviet Psychology, 12*(6), 62–76.

CHAPTER 6

Block Play
in the Primary Grades

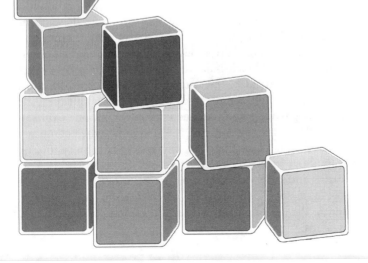

Guiding Questions

- *How does block play benefit the cognitive, language, literacy, social, and emotional development of primary-age children?*

- *How does block play in the primary grades contribute to an enriched environment that supports brain development?*

- *How can block play be incorporated into the ongoing curriculum of primary-age classrooms?*

In the United States, the primary grades are seen as the beginning of the formal education of children. Therefore, the use of play as a teaching strategy is often controversial (Driscoll & Nagel, 1999; Johnson, Christie, & Yawkey, 1999; Klugman, 1990). However, as Bronson (1995) stated,

> *"Beginning school does not signal the end of children's need for 'play' in learning. Concrete experiences are the basis of learning throughout early childhood, and play continues to be important for supporting and nourishing both cognitive and social development during the school years." (p. 109)*

Block play activities in the primary classroom offer children many opportunities to develop, strengthen, and use concepts related to physical and logical-mathematical knowledge, as well as to develop language, thinking skills, and social competence while planning and collaborating with others. When learning is linked to enjoyable, relevant activities, children develop positive attitudes and dispositions and, therefore, are able to successfully make the transition to formal and abstract learning strategies used in the intermediate grades.

Block play also offers primary-grade teachers opportunities to develop rich, child-centered, and meaningful contexts for learning. Wassermann (1990) pointed out, "The richer the play, the more potential it has for concept development, creative and investigative opportunities, and examination of issues of substance" (p. 27). Block building in primary classrooms provides a forum where novice and expert builders can work together comfortably and create a shared experience from which all can learn. Therefore, block play is a developmentally appropriate activity that meets the diverse needs of all children in primary classrooms.

Learning Across Domains Through Block Play

During the years children are in the primary grades, their thinking abilities change considerably. Due to the effect of cognitive bootstrapping, these cognitive changes foster growth in language and social skills as well as emotional development. Developmental changes are reflected in primary-age children's approach to constructive play and block-building activities. During these years, children grow in their ability to regulate their attention and delay gratification. As they do, they are able to sustain activities for longer periods of time. As a result, their interest in any particular building activity may continue over several days or even weeks. Perlmutter and Burrell (1995) found, when compared with preschool children, the play of primary-grade children was more focused and resulted in complex story lines that lasted over several weeks. Children become capable of creating intricate structures that promote rich, complex dramatic play. Complex play creates opportunities for children to study concepts in depth, while fostering the development of literacy, numeric understanding, and problem-solving skills.

Cognitive, Language, and Literacy Development   Children's growing ability to think abstractly and separate reality from fantasy is reflected both in the themes they choose and in the building projects themselves. During the primary years, children begin to develop interests in events that take place in other times and other places. They also become keenly aware of activities and events in their own community (Bronson, 1995). Children fuse aspects they know as fantasy and aspects they know as reality together to develop creative and imaginative play scenarios. For example, a group of third-grade children construct a microworld depicting a sheep ranch in Australia. In doing so, they consult many different resources, including books, articles, and Internet postings. Their construction and the role play that evolves from it reflect aspects drawn from fictional depictions in movies and books, and factual information they discover during their investigation.

The constructive play of children from 6 to 8 years of age is quite different than the play of younger children because older children refine their ability to think through their ideas and the way they express their ideas before they act. Therefore, they will often revise their ideas before actually engaging in construction activities. This process of reevaluation and revision stems from children's growing ability to understand and monitor their own thinking and use of language. The abilities to self-monitor thinking and language are known as **metacognition** and **metalanguage** and are important aspects of self-directed learning because they enable a person to recognize mistakes or faults in logic or language and make necessary corrections.

Because primary-age children have mastered the physical skills involved in the process of building, they devote their mental energy and concentration to creating a product that includes not only the construction, but also the whole scenario of the play surrounding the construction (Bronson, 1995; Johnson et al., 1999). For instance, while building the model of a space station, third-grade children develop a narrative description of life on that station. As they learn more about life in space, they recognize mistakes in their thinking and revise their narrative. They develop costumes and props that carry out the theme in their play. Therefore, the products they produce during their play become as important as the play itself.

Social Development   Negotiation, problem solving, and collaboration are characteristic of the social constructive play of primary-age children. During this stage of development, children refine their ability to take the perspective of others. That is, they begin to understand how others think and feel, as well as their intentions. They also develop the skills necessary to regulate their emotions and exercise impulse control. As a result, both the construction and the role play that occurs during play are more complex and reflect the group's understanding of a particular theme or phenomena. For example, first-grade children begin constructing a replica of a grocery store in their classroom by talking together and exchanging ideas. As each child expresses an idea, other children expand on that idea and incorporate it into the ongoing role play associated with the construction of the grocery store. During this process of negotiation, children reconstruct their ideas about the grocery store so the play that results represents both a collective group understanding, as well as a change in the way individuals understand the grocery store.

Emotional Development   As children develop abstract thinking and the ability to express their ideas and negotiate differences, they are able to form lasting friendships based on mutual interests and shared experiences. Constructive play fosters the development of friendships by providing children with the opportunity to share interests and ideas with others, and use their imaginations to create a common experience. For example, a second-grade class is involved in creating a replica of their school from LEGOS®. One group decides to re-create the library because it is their favorite place. Another group decides to construct a model of the gym because it is their favorite part of the school. Each group comes together through mutual interests; however, as they work and play together, they discover they share other common interests. This fosters the development of long-term friendships.

These friendships help children understand their own abilities and capabilities and, therefore, foster the development of social competence and positive self-images (Katz & McClellan, 1997). When engaged in constructive play, children are able to externalize their feelings in positive ways and gain a sense of control over their environment. They begin to see themselves as learners and doers, and are able to exercise their imaginations in constructive adventures. Figure 6–1 summarizes the benefits of block play for children in the primary grades.

Enriching Classroom Environments Through Block Play

The changes that take place in the neural circuitry of the brain during the years children are in the primary grades, generally ages 6 to 8, are less dramatic than during infancy and the preschool years but are nonetheless crucial to development and life-long learning. Diamond and Hopson (1998) stated,

> *"The abilities we develop in middle to late childhood—proficiency in soccer or tennis or ice-skating, or in self-expression, in constructing things, in working math problems, or all of these—tend to become the framework upon which we hang our later vocations and avocations." (pp. 191–192)*

Therefore, it is important to pay attention to aspects of the classroom environment that support brain development and learning. These aspects include the continued need for stimulation, avoidance of the negative aspects of stress, the brain's need for neural rest, and the encouragement of the effect of cognitive bootstrapping.

Block play provides primary school children opportunities

TO DEVELOP:

- abstract thinking
- aesthetics
- creativity
- dispositions for learning
- flexibility
- initiative
- positive attitudes
- a sense of personal accomplishment
- sensitivity
- three-dimensional thinking

TO EXPRESS:

- feelings
- ideas

TO ENGAGE IN:

- creative endeavors
- collaborations
- negotiations
- planning
- problem solving
- the execution of plans
- visual representation

TO EXPERIENCE:

- cognitive conflict
- competence
- fulfillment
- a state of flow
- success

TO PRACTICE:

- language and literacy skills
- math skills
- metacognitive skills
- metalinguistic skills
- social skills

TO UNDERSTAND:

- the perspective of others

Figure 6–1 *The benefits of block play for children in the primary grades.*

Providing Stimulation   One form of stimulation, **cognitive conflict,** occurs when children are asked to rethink previously held ideas or opinions. This challenges the child to extend prior knowledge and think in new ways. Children who have had many opportunities to build with blocks when they were in preschool and kindergarten will approach block building with preconceived ideas as to how to form different structures. However, when they encounter the ideas of other children, they will have to rethink—or reconstruct—their knowledge about how to best represent a particular structure with blocks. Teachers can also introduce cognitive conflict into block-building activities by suggesting new ways to work with familiar materials, introducing new materials, and asking questions during the building process that cause children to extend and reconstruct their ideas.

Another form of stimulation that leads to brain development and learning occurs when children work or play in a state of attentiveness psychologists refer to as **flow** (Csikszentmihalyi, 1990). This occurs when the child's own internal drive to work at an activity is in balance with her skill level and the challenge of the task (Diamond & Hopson, 1998). For example, a group of second-grade children build a replica of the hospital emergency room (ER) they recently visited. They use a variety of blocks to form the structures and accessories. As they work, they concentrate on making realistic models. They consistently reevaluate elements of their structures and revise them. They check notes they made while at the ER and again revise their models. Their work and play continues over several days. It is easy to spot children in this state of flow because they seem to be totally involved in what they are doing. That is, they are completely wrapped up in the activity.

When children are engrossed in an activity, in the state of flow, it often seems they are playing. As mentioned previously, the introduction of play as a teaching strategy in the primary classroom is often controversial. However, work and play are not opposing concepts in regard to learning, even though many adults see them as dichotomous. John Dewey (1916) developed a continuum of experience that ranged from drudgery on one end to foolery on the other. He placed work and play side by side in the center of this continuum, illustrating the reciprocal function of work and play in regard to children's learning. The important issue related to learning is engagement. Because children can reach their peak learning potential when intrinsic motivation is linked with concentrated attention, the state of flow, children should be encouraged to enjoy activities fully. This might look like play to some, but it is the kind of play that supports learning and development. Furthermore, when children work and play in the challenging, self-absorbed state of flow, they strengthen their ability to concentrate and maintain attention and these abilities will transfer to other tasks that might not be as intrinsically motivating.

Avoiding Stress   Not all activities that children engage in during their years in elementary school are designed to help children reach this state of flow. Children in the primary grades are exposed to more formality in their learning environment than in kindergarten and preschool. That is, they are asked to concentrate for longer periods of time, learn more by listening and less by doing, think abstractly, refine skills, and memorize facts and ideas. This high expectation for refinement of skills and memorization that characterizes primary education increases children's need for practice. Children are often asked to complete a series of worksheets or seatwork activities designed to provide practice for refining their skills and memorizing facts. However, for a child to achieve a state of flow, the activity in which she is engaged should require high attention and be intrinsically motivating. Generally, worksheets or seatwork assignments do not provide this combination of attention and motivation. A worksheet or assignment that requires a child to repeat something over and over, such as writing spelling words 15 times, can be completed without full concentration, and may not be intrinsically motivating. If the child does not understand the meanings of the words, there is even more reason to believe she will not find the activity rewarding. Most of us can recall a time when we invented a game of copying our spelling words by creating columns for each letter in the word. The game itself was challenging and intrinsically motivating, but we probably learned more about creating straight columns than spelling words. However, the children engaged in building the miniature ER are highly motivated to correctly spell the words they need on the signs and narratives that will accompany their replica, and have a great sense of pride and accomplishment when it is done.

Some worksheets or seatwork assignments may be too difficult for a particular child to understand or complete on her own. This often happens when concepts or ideas covered in the assignment are abstract or have no real meaning to the child. Therefore, the assignment requires high attention, but the child may become frustrated and have a low level of motivation to continue working. What was intended to be practice actually becomes drill because it is meaningless for the child, and over time, meaningless drill can create stress. It is important that teachers understand that high levels of stress can have a negative effect on brain development (Diamond & Hopson, 1998).

There are several ways to reduce stress while providing children opportunities to practice and memorize facts or refine skills. One way is to offer children interesting and authentic ways to practice and give them freedom to choose. Finding activities that allow children to reach a state of flow will increase their attention and support their learning. In the National Association for the Education of Young Children's (NAEYC's) position statement regarding developmentally appropriate practice for primary-age children Bredekamp and Copple (1997), pointed out:

> *"The line between challenging children and inducing stress in them can be difficult to determine and will vary for individuals. But research increasingly supports the need to provide intellectually challenging curriculum within the context of supportive, positive human relationships." (p. 144)*

Block-building activities provide children meaningful practice related to the development of physical and logical-mathematical knowledge, literacy, thinking, and social skills.

Providing Neural Rest   Challenge and engagement are certainly important factors when developing environments that foster brain development and learning. However, neural rest or downtime is equally important because a break from challenge is needed to process information and strengthen synapse formation and neural circuitry. Jensen (1998) stated the brain is at its most efficient when challenging activities that require high concentration are followed by activities that demand lower levels of attention. Neural rest also provides a source of stress reduction in a primary classroom. A 10- to 15-minute break from direct instruction or challenging activity will give the brain time to process information and ideas, and make meaningful connections. Block building can provide neural rest while also providing children opportunities to explore concepts in a self-directed way. For example, after a lesson on angle and shadow, several third-grade children build block structures and experiment with flashlights to create different shadow effects. They decide to maintain their structures and return to their experimentation during their lunch recess.

Maintaining the Effects of Cognitive Bootstrapping   One way to foster cognitive bootstrapping is to provide an integrated curriculum in which children are encouraged to use knowledge and skills in a variety of learning contexts. Block-building activities provide interesting ways to integrate curriculum goals in primary classrooms. For example, a group of third-graders are involved in tower building with a group of kindergarten children. The third-graders act as assistants to the kindergarten children as they build many towers. As the play period ends, the third-graders count the towers and develop a graph that depicts the number of blocks used in each of the structures. They also write a narrative for the kindergarten newsletter that explains the outcome of this experience. It is easy to see how many different skills the third-graders engaged in during this experience. Not only did they count towers, graph sums, and write narratives, but they also engaged in a great deal of perspective taking as they worked with kindergarten children and wrote for their families.

Incorporating Block Play into Curriculum

Unfortunately, block play is an underutilized teaching strategy in many primary classrooms. This is due, in part, to the fact that adults seem to have less tolerance for play as a teaching strategy in primary and elementary school than in preschool and kindergarten (Driscoll & Nagel, 1999; Klugman, 1990). However, King (1987) found three specific types of play that do exist in many elementary classrooms: **curriculum-generated play, recreational play,** and **illicit play.** Curriculum-generated play is play that is designed to foster the development of concepts and skills drawn from content areas such as literacy, math, science, and social studies (Johnson et al., 1999; Van Hoorn, Nourot, Scales, & Alward, 1993). Recreational play is free play that generally occurs outside the classroom during recess or before or after school play periods (Johnson et al., 1999). Illicit play is the play that occurs when the teacher is not looking and provides children with a sense of autonomy and control over teacher-centered curriculum (King, 1987). Everhart (1987) stated that when children are engaged in meaningful curriculum-generated play, and when they have consistent opportunities for recreational play, they may be less inclined to engage in illicit play.

There are other advantages to providing children in the primary grades multiple opportunities to engage in recreational and curriculum-generated play. These activities can provide neural rest and stress relief to children. They also provide a source for integrating curriculum goals and activities. The interest and intensity generated by such play provides children with countless opportunities to engage in meaningful practice of literacy and numeric skills, and opportunities for social interaction and collaboration (Hall & Abbot, 1991; Stone & Christie, 1996). Therefore, curriculum-generated and recreational play not only provide a source for integrated curriculum, but also create opportunities for children to develop the state of flow as they work and play. We will now take a closer look at how block play supports learning in primary grades through both curriculum-generated play and recreational play.

Curriculum-Generated Play   Johnson and his colleagues (1999) explained that curriculum-generated play can serve two separate functions, depending on when it occurs in relationship to formal instruction. If children are given the opportunity to play with materials or ideas before instruction, they have the opportunity to use their prior knowledge and experience as they act on these materials and ideas. Teachers can use this opportunity to assess children's prior knowledge and plan for further instruction. For example, a third-grade teacher, Mr. Gaston, is about to introduce the concept of symmetry. Before he develops his lesson plans, he observes the block constructions of children in his class. He takes note of who has created symmetrical constructions and who has created asymmetrical constructions. He asks each child to describe their work and takes note that no one used the terms symmetrical or asymmetrical, even though their work represents those qualities. Mr. Gaston asks students to save their work and provides a space to display it. He then introduces the concept by using the children's own work as examples of both symmetry and asymmetry. He takes children on an observational walk around the school and grounds where they observe and record, through drawings, examples of both concepts. Finally, he sets up peer coaching sessions where students teach other students how to achieve symmetry and asymmetry, using various sets of construction materials.

When play occurs after instruction, children have the opportunity to practice skills and consolidate knowledge in meaningful ways. **Consolidation of knowledge and skills** refers to the ability to make connections between ideas and contexts and is an important part of learning for primary-age children. For example, Byron, a third-grade student, has enjoyed building since he was an infant. Therefore, he instinctively understood the concepts of symmetry and asymmetry when Mr. Gaston introduced them, even though he had never heard the words before. As the children walked through the school and grounds,

Byron was not only aware of the examples he was seeing, but also was able to connect the terms with other examples he had seen in the past. He remembered the fireplace mantle in his home and the porch columns in his grandmother's house. While he worked with a group of children to construct an asymmetrical building, he consolidated—or pulled together—and applied many ideas concerning symmetry, gravity, and spatial relationships.

An advantage of using curriculum-generated play as an instructional strategy is its flexibility. One activity can serve different purposes for different children, thus allowing the teacher to meet the diverse needs of her class (Johnson et al., 1999). For instance, in the previous example, Byron was consolidating knowledge concerning symmetry as he engaged in peer coaching. However, Jamal was quite unfamiliar with the concept and, therefore, the peer coaching experience served as part of his initial instruction regarding the concept. Deana had intuitively built symmetrical designs, but during the peer coaching group work, she developed her ability to construct asymmetrical forms. Therefore, through just one activity, the teacher was able to facilitate the learning of three children who had diverse levels of understanding and experience. During the peer coaching activity, the teacher circulated among the students and offered help and support individually to each child on an as-needed basis. Johnson and his colleagues (1999) emphasized the importance of teacher assessment and interaction as the keys to the learning process regarding curriculum-generated play. Even though children learn through play, teachers can maximize and focus learning when they become keenly involved through observation and interaction.

Recreational Play   Recreational play refers to what children choose to do with their unstructured time. This might occur during recess, transitional time between activities, or during free-choice center time. Opportunities for recreational play in the primary years offer students many advantages. As mentioned previously, it provides neural rest and can act to reduce environmental or performance-based stress. Engagement in recreational play can also foster the development of positive self-esteem because it gives children a chance to engage in activities in which they see themselves as highly competent. This, in turn, fosters social development and friendship because children have opportunities to see each other in highly competent situations (Katz & McClellan, 1997).

The use of recreational play in the primary grades provides teachers opportunities to observe the spontaneous interests of children expressed through their play and incorporate these interests into curriculum designed to meet the mandated goals of their program. Van Hoorn and her colleagues (1993) referred to this as **play-generated curriculum** and described it not as the opposite of curriculum-generated play but as a point of reference and balance from which meaningful and authentic learning experiences can be developed. For example, in October, a group of first-graders spend every recess period building a set and developing role-play scenarios that closely resemble what the teacher recognizes as a popular, prime-time, crime-and-punishment television program. As the teacher observes the children's patterns of building and play, she takes note of many misconceptions they have regarding police work. She becomes concerned about the violence expressed in their play. Her district mandates a unit on community helpers that is generally taught during the spring; however, because of the interest shown by these children through their recreational block play, she decides to begin a theme-study project focusing on the work of police officers. She initiates the study by asking the children what they know about police work, what they would like to know, and how they would like to learn about this topic. During the course of the study, which spreads over several weeks, children visit police stations and interview officers. They talk about the effects that crime has in their own lives. As the study continues, they are able to see the many different facets of police work. Throughout their study, block building serves to help children express their ideas. At one point, the children built a replica of a police station and developed a role-play scenario that depicted a lost child coming to the station for help.

Block Play as an Instructional Strategy

We now turn our attention to the development of curriculum-generated and recreational block-building activities that incorporate curriculum goals and foster learning and development among primary-age children. Four specific strategies are discussed: investigative play, microworld construction, model building, and the project approach.

Investigative Play   The play of primary-age children becomes increasingly scientific and experimental as they develop the ability to engage in the process of inquiry, that is, observing, comparing, classifying, predicting, and interpreting. Through open-ended **investigative play,** children are encouraged to solve problems by generating multiple hypotheses and evaluating each based on logic and reasoning. What results from investigative play is more than finite answers or random facts, but a greater understanding of the important issues and concepts embedded in a learning activity. Wassermann (1990) referred to these concepts and issues as **big ideas** and suggests that "curriculum that reflects big ideas will enrich classroom life and promote deeper and more sophisticated understanding of the world we live in" (p. 96).

Wassermann (1990) suggested that a sequence of play–debrief–replay activities helps children formulate big ideas. The teacher designs problems or dilemmas that challenge children to conduct investigations involving substantive concepts. The investigative play stage begins as children experiment with materials, generating and testing a hypothesis aimed at resolving the dilemma. During the debriefing phase of investigative play, the teacher invites students to express their ideas. As she listens, she encourages them to consider the ideas of others, reflects children's understanding, and fosters vocabulary development. The teacher does not declare ideas to be right or wrong but poses additional questions that challenge children's thinking and inspire additional investigation. During the replay phase of investigation, children use the same materials but carry out more sophisticated investigations that lead to a broader understanding.

The study of any one substantive concept often leads to the development of related concepts that could also be considered big ideas. Determining which concept is the big idea is somewhat arbitrary as it is related to the context of the investigation and the prior knowledge of each student involved. Gravity itself is a big idea, but an investigation of gravity will lead students to consider other substantive concepts, such as mass, force, and horizontal or vertical direction. For example, three first-grade students develop two separate marble runs (see Figure 6–2). One is tall with many long vertical drops, and the other is wide with several long horizontal paths. The children drop marbles from the top of each pathway and time their decent. They repeat the trials several times and notice a consistent pattern. The marbles dropped into the wider pathway take longer to move through the pathway than the marbles dropped through the tall pathways. One student has had little prior experience with the concept of gravity, so for this student the investigation centers on the big idea of gravity. However, another student has a good understanding of the downward pull of gravity and expected a rapid decent of the marble through the vertical paths but is surprised by the rapid reduction of its speed as it moves through horizontal paths. For this

Figure 6–2 *First-grade children investigate gravity using a marble run.*

student, the big idea of the study shifts from gravity to force, velocity, and horizontal paths. All concepts are substantive, but investigative play provides children with differing levels of understanding opportunities to work together in a way that promotes learning for all. Figure 6–3 suggests big ideas that can be investigated through block play. Note how the concepts are interrelated.

Note the interrelationship of concepts. Investigative play activities can lead children to many discoveries.

Big Ideas	Related Concepts
Architectural Features	Curves, patterns, height, ramps, tunnels, bridges, towers
Aesthetics	Form, symmetry, asymmetry
Attributes	Size, shape, color, material
Balance	Stability
Cause and Effect	Velocity, force
Classification	Sorting, attributes, serration
Comparisons	Size, weight, color
Counting	Number concepts, sets
Descriptions	Written, graphic, oral
Dimensions	Height, length, depth, area
Estimation	Size, stability, number, height
Fractions	Joining, separating, whole, part, proportion
Geometric Solids	Cube, cone, sphere, volume
Gravity	Force, velocity, horizontal, vertical
Mapping	Scale, grids
Measuring	Length, width, volume, weight, scale, perimeter
Mazes	Barriers, paths
Perspective	Location
Predictions	Estimation, percentage
Properties of Matter	Size, shape, weight, dimension, thickness, length, width
Proportions	Fractions
Serration	Classification, order, comparison
Shadows	Perspective, time
Simple Machines	Ramps, fulcrums, levers
Tessellation	Repetition, pattern, multiplication
Topological Concepts	Exterior, interior, open, closed, near, far, proximity (on, under, by, beside), separation (near and far), enclosure (inside and outside)

Figure 6–3   *Big ideas to investigate through block play.*

The use of blocks in investigative play provides children with opportunities to use concrete materials and actively engage in the formulation of big ideas that will be useful as they construct an understanding of science and math. *Tessellation* is the repeated application of one or more shapes to cover a particular surface. This concept, or big idea, relates directly to multiplication. Therefore, children's early experience in constructing patterns with blocks, which is a form of tessellation, lays the groundwork for understanding addition, subtraction, multiplication, and division.

Continuing with the example of tessellation, let us look at how a third-grade teacher uses investigative block play to encourage the development of the concept.

Dilemma	Determine the number of 4-inch square blocks you would need to cover the surface of a table that is 3 feet wide and 4 feet long.
Materials	Twenty 4-inch square blocks, a table that measures 3 × 4 feet, pencils, paper, rulers, scissors.
Investigative Play	In groups of four, children set about to generate ideas useful in resolving the dilemma. Most groups begin by spreading blocks end to end across the width of the table, and soon run out of blocks. Various methods of resolving the solution are generated. One group marks with a member's finger where additional blocks would begin and end, while another member keeps track of the total. Another group decides to make replicas of blocks with paper, lay all the papers out, and then count all that were used.
Debrief	The teacher encourages children to share ideas and demonstrate the methods they used in solving the dilemma. She asks questions that help children reflect their understanding and clarify their ideas. She encourages the children to think of coverage in rows, and consider the number needed in one horizontal row and in one vertical row. She challenges them to find a shortcut in determining the number of blocks it will take to cover other surfaces.
Replay	Children return to their investigations with new ideas and set about to find a shortcut.

The cycle may continue over several days. Eventually, the teacher will lead the students to investigate big ideas such as area, perimeter, and surface. Through investigative play, students begin to make important connections and form an understanding of the relationships that exist in their world. For a detailed discussion of investigative play, see Wassermann (1990).

Microworld Construction **Microworlds** are miniature recreations of a total environment. As children recreate this environment, they clarify their ideas about various relationships that exist in the environment (Provenzo & Brett, 1983). For example, third-graders who live in a community where the dairy industry is prominent decide to build a replica of a dairy farm. They use small blocks to build the buildings, create fencing and fields from other materials, and add animal and people figures to complete the scene. Because primary-age children generally have clear ideas of what they are building before they build, they go about the process systematically, and engage in negotiation and problem-solving activities as they build. When they complete the scene, they begin to play and create elaborate, complex scenarios and dialogue. Each day they modify the scene and play scenario, so the play that emerges is dynamic and increasingly complex.

As with all forms of constructive play, it is easy to incorporate many curricular goals into the children's play activities. One such goal is the development of spatial awareness, that is, the ability to reposition objects in one's mind and determine how to fit one object into another. For example, when children build a miniature zoo with blocks, they will need to create some openings large enough for elephants and tall enough for giraffes. A novice builder would do this physically by trial and error, using blocks and animal models. However, as children develop spatial awareness, they are able to imagine how to position the blocks in their mind. They cognitively slide, rotate, or flip over different blocks before putting them together on the floor. When children develop this skill, they change from being two-dimensional to three-dimensional thinkers (Diamond & Hopson, 1998; Reifel, 1984) and gain the ability to solve problems through mental action rather than physical action.

Constructing microworlds also creates opportunities for teachers to support children's social and emotional development. Many of the themes children use when building microworlds come from their own life and their struggle to understand what is happening around them. As children work together, they develop not only a greater understanding of their world, but also a greater ability to take the perspective of others. For instance, second-grade children begin to build a replica of the neighborhood that surrounds their school. They take walks around the neighborhood, plot buildings on a grid, and interview home and business owners they encounter. During the process of building the microworld, a public controversy arises in the neighborhood concerning the location of a group home. This controversy is discussed both on television and in the newspaper. The teacher brings the articles and media coverage to the attention of her students. Much discussion takes place regarding whether the group home should be included both in the neighborhood and in the replica they are building. The teacher gives the children the opportunity to express their feelings and their fears. She provides factual information that helps them clarify their ideas and see the issue from many perspectives. In the end, the children decide not to include the group home in their replica. However, their decision is not based on any bias against the group home but on an interesting discussion concerning the concepts of past, present, and future.

It is easy to see the possibilities of enriching literacy development through microworld building. The development of vocabulary, reading, writing, and research skills are encouraged as children work to make their microworlds represent their ideas and feelings. Children often create stories, puppet plays, or scripts for dramatic productions based on their microworld constructions. Children's literature can inspire the development of microworlds that depict the settings of a favorite book or scene from a book. For example, the Laura Ingalls Wilder *Little House* series offers multiple opportunities for primary-age children to combine their interest in the books with a historical study of settler life on the prairie and the migration to the West.

Model Building   Model building refers to the recreation of a specific structure or form. Children may become interested in building a model that has particular interest to them, such as a car, school bus, or airplane. Replicas are often built from a two-dimensional blueprint, sketch, or diagram and provide children opportunities to transfer a two-dimensional design into a three-dimensional model, thus developing skills related to visual representation. A good example of model building can be seen when children work with LEGO®, K'NEX®, or No Ends Building Sets® and the instruction sheets that accompany them (see Figure 6–3 for a description of these materials). Children concentrate on the diagrams, match pieces with the pieces pictured in the diagram, and experiment with different positions until they are able to re-create the airplane or motorcycle pictured in the plans. With experience, children begin to visualize the way pieces fit together and spend less on time trial-and-error experimentation.

Model building also serves to integrate many of the curricular goals generally held for primary-grade students. For example, when building models, children count, compare, and categorize the blocks they are using. Because many models are developed according to some specific scale, children gain experience in measuring and representing length, width, height, and depth through the use of proportions. They also work with angles and surfaces, and figure how to form angles from the blocks available. As they work, they read instructions, descriptions, and background information that come with the blueprints (see Figure 6–4). When they finish a model, they may write a narrative description for the class newsletter or a reflective narrative to accompany a picture of the model for their portfolio.

Models can be built on a large scale using hollow blocks and boards or No Ends Building Sets®, or on a smaller scale using LEGO® or Flexiblocks™. Children may choose to use their imagination to create a certain structure or design and then draw a blueprint, sketch, or diagram for others to re-create. Or a child might see a building she finds particularly pleasing, draw a diagram, either by hand or with the aid of a computer and appropriate software, and then create a model from blocks or other construction materials.

Figure 6–4 *Shawn built a model rocket ship using a no ends building set® and blueprints.*

In all cases, model building is an exciting and rich form of block play that provides primary-age children with many opportunities to practice and consolidate skills.

The Project Approach   When block play inspires or becomes a part of the in-depth study of a phenomenon, the study itself becomes a project. Katz and Chard (1989) defined a **project** as "an in-depth study of a particular topic that one or more children undertake" (p. 2). They explained that the **project approach** "refers to a way of teaching and learning as well as the content of what is taught and learned" (p. 3). The first-grade study of police work and the second-grade study of the neighborhood previously described in this chapter are both good examples of project work. Block building served as a way for children to represent their knowledge and understanding throughout the course of these projects.

There are three distinct phases of a project (Chard, 1994; Katz & Chard, 1989), and recreational block play, model building, and the construction of microworlds can supplement children's learning at each stage. During the first phase of a project, teachers determine a topic of interest and develop an understanding of what children know about a particular topic (Chard, 1994; Katz & Chard, 1989). One way children represent both their interest and prior knowledge is through block building. For example, the teacher of a multiage (kindergarten/first grade) classroom observes that much of the free-choice block activity is focused on planes and air travel. Through discussion, she discovers that only 6 children in the class of 21 have traveled by plane, but 5 children will be taking their first plane trips during an upcoming vacation. As she observes their block play, she notices that the airport models the children build are simplistic, having only one runway. Often one plane would be landing as another was taking off. This, of course, leads to many midair collisions. She also notices that children do not represent an understanding of the complexity of actions and services related to air travel. In their replicas of airports, there are no passenger waiting areas, no control tower, no ticketing agents, and no service vehicles. When questioned, the children display little understanding of ticketing, luggage collection, or air traffic control. The teacher determines there certainly is sufficient interest in the topic and begins to implement the project. She asks students to represent and share their experience with air travel through stories, models built from blocks, and drawings. She also helps children formulate their questions concerning airports and air travel.

The second phase of a project involves children in many activities designed to increase their knowledge and understanding of the topic (Chard, 1994; Katz & Chard, 1989). In the air travel study, students visit the airport on two occasions, read books about air travel, view videos, and visit websites related to air travel. In addition, different members of the class interview a pilot, traffic control personnel, luggage handler, ticket agent, and passengers. As the study continues, one group of children decides to build a replica of an airport. They use a large piece of poster board as a foundation and small blocks for buildings. As their understanding of air travel develops, their replica becomes more and more elaborate. A second group of children become very interested in the conveyer belts they saw transporting luggage in the airport. This group works together to find additional information about conveyer belts and actually build a model using small blocks, bits of canvas, and rubber bands. Therefore, in the second phase of the project, children used blocks and other constructive materials to both formulate and represent their new learning.

During the third phase of a project, children consolidate their understanding of the topic and concepts related to the topic studied and bring the study to a close (Chard, 1994; Katz & Chard, 1989). Generally, teachers will arrange a culminating event where students share what they learned with families and classmates. Block play and constructions can serve as a means for children to display their knowledge. In the air travel study, one group of children display their replica of the airport and explain the relationship between the terminal, the control tower, and the runways. Another group demonstrates their conveyer belt, and another group puts on a play that depicts the process of checking in and boarding a plane. For an extended discussion of the implementation of the project approach, see Chard (1994), Hendrick (1997), or Katz and Chard (1989).

Setting the Stage for Block Play in Primary Classrooms

As we have seen, both recreational and curriculum-generated block play enrich curriculum and learning opportunities for children in the primary grades. Teachers encourage block play by providing time, space, and materials. Time for block play comes when teachers incorporate aforementioned strategies, such as model building, microworld development, projects, and investigative play into ongoing curricular activities, and when blocks are available for use when practicing related concepts and during free time. Now we turn our attention to providing space and materials for block play.

Creating Space   Ideally, first-, second-, and third-grade classrooms resemble kindergarten classrooms, where space is appropriated for a learning center system in which children are encouraged to work and play together. This arrangement is more developmentally appropriate than traditional intermediate or middle-school classrooms, where space is dedicated to desks and students are encouraged to work in isolation and listen to lectures. The lack of adequate space is often cited by teachers as a barrier for making provisions for recreational or curriculum-generated play in elementary schools (Goldhaber, 1994). When a lack of space prevents teachers from developing many single-purpose learning centers, such as a block center, dramatic play center, and manipulative center, they can instead create a few multipurpose centers. These centers would house materials that can be used in a variety of ways and provide space for work, play, and the display of products resulting from play and investigations. A literacy center and an investigation center would be two important multipurpose centers and would encourage the integration of learning activities in primary classrooms.

Blocks and block activities can be housed in both the literacy center and the investigation center because block play supplements both literacy development and investigative play. Blocks should be stored on low shelves in clear plastic containers that are easily moved from place to place within the classroom, to other classrooms, or outside. When blocks and accessories are visible, accessible, and portable, both teachers and children will find creative ways to incorporate them into learning and play activities.

Work areas, whether within a center or in another area of the classroom, should provide enough space for several children to work together. A table or floor space with tile or low-pile carpet serves as a suitable building surface. Within the classroom or center, there should also be room to display photographs of completed work and to store works in progress, such as models, microworlds, or investigations. Large sheets of posterboard can serve as a building surface for models or microworlds. The whole project can then be moved to a protected area, such as the top of a bookcase, when children are engaged in other activities.

Often teachers work out creative ways to share both space and materials among children in different classrooms. For instance, large hollow blocks are expensive materials and take up a large amount of space. Therefore, it may be impractical to provide sets for all primary classrooms in a building. Teachers can work out a time-share plan for the materials. For example, groups of third-graders could work in the kindergarten room during the kindergarten's music period or lunch recess. Teachers can also form multiage block-building teams composed of students from different classrooms. Novice builders will learn new techniques, whereas experienced builders will have opportunities to share their skills, encourage other children, and cooperate in joint ventures. Another approach would be to have sets of blocks stored in plastic containers on portable carts that could be moved from room to room or to outdoor play areas.

Selecting Materials   There are many different types of blocks available that are suitable in a primary classroom. Decisions about which blocks and which accessories to include should be related to the age, experience with block building, and interest of the children in the classroom. For example, children entering first grade may not have had many opportunities to build with hollow blocks or unit blocks and, therefore, will need access to these materials on a regular basis. Although third-grade children may occasionally want to borrow a set of hollow blocks for a special project, they will probably get more use out of smaller blocks with more intricate accessories.

Because block building becomes more elaborate as children get older, it is important that the block sets in primary classrooms are large enough to afford children the opportunity to build large, complex structures. Teachers may want to invest in one particular kind of block, and collect multiple sets and the various accessories that go with it. For example, a first-grade teacher began collecting LEGOs®. One year, she used money budgeted for materials to buy three sets of regular LEGOs®, two sets of LEGO® wheels, one set of LEGO® doors and windows, and one set of LEGO® people. Over the course of the year, she purchased miscellaneous pieces from garage sales, and several families donated additional pieces. She added to her collection over the next 2 years, and eventually had enough LEGOs® for several groups of children to develop simultaneous microworld constructions. As her collection grew, so did her strategies for incorporating building into all areas of the curriculum. Another first-grade teacher in the same building began a collection of unit blocks. She also acquired a set of windows and doors that fit the unit blocks, architectural unit blocks, castle accessory blocks, several sets of marble runs, see-through unit blocks, and many sets of animal and people figures. Both teachers now have enough blocks to support major building projects, and they trade sets midyear. This provides both classrooms with multiple opportunities to experience rich, complex block play.

The building materials in any classroom should include not only block sets, but also accessories that extend children's play and expand curricular opportunities. Important accessories include highway sign sets, people sets representing many ethnic groups and family constellations, transportation toys, steering wheels, and animal sets. In addition, art materials such as foil, modeling plastic, and pipe cleaners will allow children to use their imagination and create unique and original structures. Figure 6–5 provides examples of blocks and accessories that will enrich curriculum and learning in primary classrooms.

Conclusion

The block play of children in the primary grades is complex, and provides children with multiple opportunities to integrate ideas and skills, make connections that cross disciplines, and study topics in-depth. Block play can be integrated into the ongoing activities and curriculum of primary classrooms through investigative play, the construction of microworlds, model building, and the project approach.

Theory into Practice

1. Observe a primary classroom for a full day. Make note of environmental factors that foster growth and learning across the curriculum. Collect examples depicting cognitive conflict, neural rest, and cognitive bootstrapping. Devise a plan for further enrichment of the environment.
2. Review the mandated curriculum for a specific first-, second-, or third-grade class. Find appropriate places to supplement and enrich the curriculum with different block play strategies.
3. Incorporate block play into an ongoing class project.

Architectural Unit Blocks	Smooth hardwood columns, domes, and spires scaled to use with unit blocks.
Build and Play Tubes	Plastic tubing that fits together in towering structures. Children can pour sand and water through these tubes.
Castle Accessory Blocks	Designed to simulate castles when added to unit blocks.
Colored See-Through Blocks	Hardwood frames with colored panels that are scaled to use with unit blocks.
Clear Plastic Blocks and Climbers	Translucent blocks, discs, and cylinders that stack together and create beautiful designs, particularly when used with a light box or table.
Flexiblocks™ and Flexiswivels™	Plastic blocks and swivels with interlocking pegs and swivel joints. Provides side-to-side or up-and-down motion in constructions.
Gears! Gears! Gears!®	Gears and other pieces that fit together to form constructions that turn when cranked.
K'NEX®	Color-coded rods, connectors, tires, and pulleys that come with diagrams for building 22 different models, including trucks, space ships, and amusement parks.
LEGO®	Building sets in colorful plastic designed to interlock and form stable constructions.
LEGO® Accessories	Sets designed to augment basic LEGO® material. Accessories available include people, vehicles, town sets, doors, and windows.
Marble Runs	Blocks with marble holes, tubes, and ramps children can use to design elaborate pathways for marbles. Runs come in a variety of materials, including wood, plastic, and translucent plastic.
Middle Eastern Block Set	Simulates architecture of seventh through sixteenth centuries in Persia, Syria, and Egypt.
No Ends Building Sets®	Straight and curved beams and connectors that fit together to form large structures.
Pipe Construction Sets	Real plumber's fittings with special theadings for easy screwing and coupling.
Pop Tubes	Plastic tubes that stretch, bend, snap together, twirl, and create a whistling sound as they move.
Skyscraper Blocks	Designed to simulate city scenes.
SPACE-A-MAZE®	Corrugated cardboard panels that fit together with plastic connectors to make large intricate structures.
Tree Blocks®	Handcut blocks made from reclaimed tree pruning. The bark is removed, and blocks are sanded and cut to Unit Block scale and incremental lengths to foster spatial reasoning and problem solving.

Figure 6–5 *Block and constructive materials for children in the primary grades. (continues)*

Unit blocks	Wooden blocks.
Window and Door Blocks	Hardwood doors and windows scaled to use with standard unit blocks.
Wooden Stand-Up	Hardwood figures that are painted to represent people.
People	Sets depict families, community workers, or children who are differently challenged.
ZOOB™	Units that snap, click, and pop together to form joints that rotate, limbs that extend, and axles that spin.

Figure 6–5 *Block and constructive materials for children in the primary grades. (continued)*

Websites

www.project-approach.com

The Project Approach Home Page is maintained by Dr. Sylvia Chard at the University of Alberta, and presents information on conducting projects and examples of successful projects.

Related Readings

Chard, S. C. (1994). *The project approach, book two: Managing successful projects.* New York: Scholastic.

Hendrick, J. (Ed.). (1997). *First steps toward teaching in the Reggio Way.* Upper Saddle River, NJ: Merrill.

Short, K. G., & Burke, C. (1991). *Creating curriculum: Teachers and students as a community of learners.* Portsmouth, NH: Heinemann.

References

Bredekamp, S., & Copple, C. (Eds.). (1997). *Developmentally appropriate practice in early childhood programs* (Rev. ed.). Washington, DC: National Association for the Education of Young Children.

Bronson, M. B. (1995). *The right stuff for children birth to 8: Selecting play materials to support development.* Washington, DC: National Association for the Education of Young Children.

Chard, S. C. (1994). *The project approach, book two: Managing successful projects.* New York: Scholastic.

Csikszentmihalyi, M. (1990). *Flow: The psychology of optimal experiences.* New York: Harper & Row.

Dewey, J. (1916). *Democracy and education.* New York: Macmillan.

Diamond, M., & Hopson, J. (1998). *Magic trees of the mind: How to nurture your child's intelligence, creativity, and healthy emotions from birth through adolescence.* New York: Plume.

Driscoll, A., & Nagel, N. G. (1999). *Early childhood education birth–8: The world of children, families, and educators.* Boston: Allyn & Bacon.

Everhart, R. (1987). Play and the junior high adolescent. In J. Block & N. King (Eds.), *School play* (pp. 167–192). New York: Garland.

Goldhaber, J. (1994). If we call it science, then can we let the children play? *Childhood Education, 71,* 24–27.

Hall, N., & Abbot, L. (Eds.). (1991). *Play in the primary classroom.* London: Hodder & Stoughton.

Hendrick, J. (Ed.). (1997). *First steps toward teaching in the Reggio Way.* Upper Saddle River, NJ: Merrill.

Jensen, E. (1998). How Julie's brain learns. *Educational Leadership, 56*(3), 41–45.

Johnson, J. E., Christie, J. F., & Yawkey, T. D. (1999). *Play and early childhood development* (2nd ed.). New York: Longman.

Katz, L. G., & Chard, S. C. (1989). *Engaging children's minds: The project approach.* Norwood, NJ: Ablex.

Katz, L. G., & McClellan, D. E. (1997). *Fostering children's social competence: The teacher's role.* Washington, DC: National Association for the Education of Young Children.

King, N. (1987). Elementary school play: Theory and research. In J. Block & N. King (Eds.), *School play* (pp. 143–165). New York: Garland.

Klugman, E. (1990). Early childhood moves into public schools: Mix or meld. In E. Klugman & S. Smilansky (Eds.), *Children's play and learning: Perspectives and policy implications* (pp. 188–209). New York: Teachers College Press.

Perlmutter, J., & Burrell, L. (1995). Learning through "play" as well as "work" in the primary grades. *Young Children, 50*(5), 14–21.

Provenzo, E. F., Jr., & Brett, A. (1983). *The complete block book.* Syracuse, New York: Syracuse University Press.

Reifel, S. (1984). Symbolic representation at two ages: Block building of a story. *Discourse Processes, 7,* 11–20.

Stone, S., & Christie, J. (1996). Collaborative literacy learning during sociodramatic play in a multiage (K–2) primary classroom. *Journal of Research in Childhood Education, 10,* 123–133.

Van Hoorn, J., Nourot, P., Scales, B., & Alward, K. (1993). *Play at the center of the curriculum.* New York: Merrill.

Wassermann, S. (1990). *Serious players in the primary classroom: Empowering children through active learning experiences.* New York: Teachers College Press.

Teachers' Role in Fostering Block Play

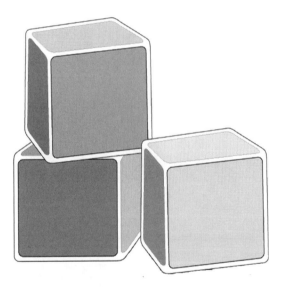

CHAPTER 7

Creating Environments for Block Builders

Guiding Questions

- *How can teachers ensure girls and boys have equal opportunities to benefit from block play?*

- *How should the degree of teacher involvement in children's play be determined?*

- *What role do parents play in facilitating children's block play?*

Knowledge of how children grow and develop is crucial to setting up environments for young children. The individual teacher is the decisive factor in determining the appropriateness of indoor and outdoor environments for children in his care and in making decisions about children's learning experiences. This chapter discusses the role of the teacher in creating a balanced learning environment, determining the degree of involvement with children at block play, and making meaningful connections with parents.

Dimensions of the Environment

Classroom environments will vary greatly, depending on factors such as ages and developmental stages of children; the number of children and adults in the group; children's prior experiences and current interests; and the range of cognitive, language, social, emotional, and motor skills represented. There are, however, five dimensions of the environment that should be taken into consideration regardless of these individual factors. The **dimensions of the environment** (Prescott, 1994) are described in terms of dichotomies to show the need for creating a balance in the physical space and materials in the classroom:

1. *Softness/hardness.* Softness relates to objects and materials that are responsive to touch, such as sand/water, molding dough, sofas, and pillows. Hardness is an element of a material that is permanently shaped and not malleable, therefore providing a challenge for children, such as wooden and plastic blocks.

2. *Open/closed.* Open play materials such as art supplies and dramatic play props, can be used in various ways. Closed play materials, such as puzzles and Montessori materials, can only be manipulated in one way for them to work. Blocks are a good example of a material that registers in between these two dichotomies. The blocks themselves are not pliable but can be manipulated in an endless number of ways.

3. *Simple/complex.* The more complex the material, the longer it holds children's attention, and the more opportunities there are for play. A simple unit of play, such as modeling dough, has one manipulative aspect. A complex unit, such as modeling dough with cookie cutters, offers two kinds of materials. A super complex unit such as modeling dough, a cookie cutter, and a plastic knife, has at least three play components. As more features are added to a unit, it adds greater variety to the play. The complexity of block play grows by providing children with additional blocks, a variety of block types, or accessories to extend their block play.

4. *Intrusion/seclusion.* Children in group settings learn different methods of responding to others who want to join them at play. Although it is important for children to learn to play together, they also need opportunities and space for private play without having to share or worry about interruptions. Teachers can plan for times of the day and areas in which children can build with others or alone if they choose.

5. *High mobility/low mobility.* Mobility is the degree of freedom a child has for moving around. High mobility involves using the whole body, and low mobility relates to activities that require children to sit still. When playing with unit and hollow blocks, children learn to maneuver their bodies around structures and other children as they build. Other types of blocks provide opportunities for sitting at a table while concentrating on building.

These dimensions of the environment should not be viewed as black or white but as a continuum with shades of gray between each end. Thinking about these elements, along with a particular group of children and their needs, is a good beginning to establishing a safe, stimulating classroom environment.

Attention to Gender Differences

In addition to creating a balanced physical environment, teachers must ensure children receive a balance of experiences within that environment regardless of individual differences. Research shows that boys continue to dominate the more active/aggressive play areas in early childhood classrooms, such as areas designated for block play. Girls, however, still spend the majority of their time in language-rich play, which is typically associated with the home living center (Hughes, 1995). Serbin (1980) showed that boys strongly prefer and spend more time with three-dimensional-type toys such as blocks than do girls. This may be because children are drawn to familiar materials (American Association of University Women, 1990) and parents are more likely to provide blocks for their sons at home (Pereira, 1994), or it may suggest males are genetically drawn to materials that require spatial visualization. Regardless, blocks provide experiences that lead to the ability to solve cognitive problems requiring mental rotation and transformation of shape (visualizing how an object will look when it is moved, turned, or altered in some way). These types of visual-spatial skills are crucial to success in higher-level mathematics and in careers that are currently dominated by males, such as pilots, engineers, physicists, and architects (Serbin, 1980). The direct relationship between access to blocks in early childhood and the likelihood of success in a visual-spatial-oriented career is unknown. However, it is clear that providing experiences with blocks enhances a child's ability in this and other cognitive tasks necessary for a strong foundation in mathematics and science (Chaille & Silvern, 1996). Therefore, teachers must ensure all children, regardless of gender, are provided with equal opportunities to play with all classroom materials, including blocks.

Schlank and Metzger (1997), authors of *Together and Equal: Fostering Cooperative Play and Promoting Gender Equity in Early Childhood Programs,* suggested that teachers assess their classroom by devising a chart in which the learning centers available are listed in a column on the left-hand side and time increments are recorded along the top. This evaluation chart enables the teacher to tally the number of boys and/or girls in each center every 5, 10, or 15 minutes. By looking at the overall chart, teachers can see where boys and girls spend the majority of their time while at free play. We suggest these data be further analyzed by dividing the total number of girl tallies in each center by the total number of children who played in that center. This calculation can be repeated using the total tally of boys in the center, divided by the total number of children. This provides the teacher with a percentage of boys versus girls, using each center that can be checked for large disparities to determine if a center is being dominated by one gender. Changes can then be made to encourage equitable participation in all activities and experiences provided to children. Suggestions for encouraging girls *and* boys to play with blocks include:

- Make blocks widely available by expanding the size of the block center to accommodate more children or by setting up a second block center, perhaps with a different selection of blocks.
- Encourage "overusers" in the block center to try new activities available in the classroom, thus giving others more opportunity to enter the block area.
- Use a planning board (Stritzel, 1995) to help children decide where they will spend their time.
- Integrate blocks into other centers. Smaller blocks in a home-dramatic play center may be used to make simple furnishings for dolls, whereas larger blocks can be made into a car for a family outing.
- Place traditionally girl-dominated centers (e.g., dramatic play) next to the block center, which is typically boy-dominated to encourage cross-gender interactions (Schlank & Metzger, 1997). This will encourage children to expand their role play.
- Provide block accessories that have strong appeal to girls, such as micro-figures of animals or families and dollhouse furnishings (Schlank & Metzger, 1997), to encourage their participation in the block center.
- Female adults can model their interest in block play by spending more time in the block center (Henniger, 1999).
- Intervene when gender-biased attitudes of peers prohibit or discourage a child from playing with blocks (Wellhousen, 1996).
- Post pictures of boys and girls building with blocks together and focus on similar characteristics (Burkhardt, 1993).
- Use similar language when discussing boys' and girls' block structures (Weiss, 1997).

Evaluating the Physical Environment

After planning a classroom that is balanced in terms of the physical environment and the opportunities provided to both boys and girls, teachers can refer to formal evaluations for more ideas on creating an appropriate setting for children. Most published classroom environment scales have undergone rigorous procedures that ensure the scale is useful for its stated purpose and results will be consistent when evaluating different environments. Recommended evaluation instruments include the *Early Childhood Environment Rating Scale–Revised*

The *Early Childhood Environment Rating Scale–Revised Edition* (ECERS-R; Harms et al., 1998) has been in use in earlier versions for many years. The ECERS-R is designed for use in programs serving children ages 2½ to 5 years and can be used for supervision, program improvement, self-assessment, and teacher training. The scale consists of 43 items that can be rated on a scale of 1 (inadequate) to 7 (excellent). There are seven different areas that can be evaluated using the ECERS-R, including "space and furnishings." This section specifically looks at space and furnishings; furniture for routine care, play, and learning; furnishings for relaxation and comfort; room arrangement for play; space for privacy; child-related play; space for gross motor play; and gross motor equipment. Variations of the scale are available for evaluating school-age care, family day care, and infant/toddler care.

The *Accreditation Criteria and Procedures* (National Association for the Education of Young Children, 1998) provides guidelines that are used for accrediting early childhood programs in centers and schools. There are 10 general criteria, with multiple, specific descriptions provided for each. The criteria component, "Physical Environment," addresses issues such as safe, clean, attractive, and spacious indoor and outdoor environments; clearly delineated spatial arrangements; space for storing individual belongings; private areas; soft elements; and a variety of activities available from which children can choose. The criteria can be used for self-study when working toward accreditation, or by an individual teacher to evaluate his own classroom space.

The *Playground Rating System* (Frost, 1992) provides a means for evaluating the outdoor play environment. It enables the observer to evaluate in detail an existing playground and provide information for developing a master plan for improvement. The three sections are labeled as follows:

I. What does the playground contain?
II. Is the playground in good repair and relatively safe?
III. What should the playground do?

Each of the 40 items on the scale can be rated from 0 to 5 with a possible rating of 200 points, with all three sections combined.

Figure 7–1   *Evaluation instruments.*

Edition (ECERS-R; Harms, Clifford, & Cryer, 1998), *Accreditation Criteria and Procedures* (National Association for the Education of Young Children, 1998), and the *Playground Rating System* (Frost, 1992; see Figure 7–1).

Teacher Involvement

There are endless opportunities for teacher involvement with children who are involved with block play and construction. This range of choices can leave teachers asking, "When should I intervene in children's play? Should I interrupt if children are building productively? To what degree do I take part in their play?" There is no one right answer to any of these questions because teachers' decisions about when and how to intervene in children's play are influenced by personal values and subsequently their goals for the educational program (Wassermann, 1990). Personal values reveal what matters most to a teacher. When he has reflected on his personal values and is clear about what is important to him as a teacher, it is easier to make quick but sound decisions in the course of a busy classroom day. Program goals reflect his personal values and are evident in the daily workings of the classroom. For example, if a teacher's goal is to encourage children to be autonomous in their thinking and actions while providing direct support when needed, this will be reflected in how he intervenes with children at play.

Reviewing Smilansky's (1968) pioneering research on children's socio-dramatic play provides insight into the need for teacher involvement. This study showed the most effective way to help children learn how to successfully enter and stay in a play situation with peers was to provide direct instruction. The various techniques used included modeling, making suggestions, and giving supportive comments. The type and degree of teacher interaction needed depends on individual children's ability to "read" and negotiate play situations.

Teachers must make many decisions, including those involving teacher intervention, on a case-by-case, minute-by-minute basis. Therefore, a framework has been provided to guide teachers as they think about and discuss this issue with their colleagues. Thinking about the varying degrees of teacher involvement in advance is the best preparation for making split-second decisions in the classroom.

Wolfgang and Wolfgang (1992) placed teacher roles for all aspects of teaching on a behavioral continuum that ranges from "open" with minimal teacher intervention, such as observation of children, to "directive," which requires maximum teacher intervention such as physically intervening in children's play. Labels along the continuum include observing, providing nondirective statements, asking questions or giving directives, modeling a behavior, and physically intervening. For the purpose of teacher involvement with children at block play, the Wolfgang model has been reconfigured into a continuum of teaching strategies ranging from indirect to direct with a range of approaches in between.

Teaching strategies positioned at the left of the continuum demonstrate teacher behaviors that support children's learning in the least intrusive manner. In general, these strategies include initial set-up of the block area, observing and recording children's actions, listening to children's explanations, and making general comments as to what the teacher observes, such as "you used a quadruple unit to make the bridge."

Teaching strategies that require more time and attention to small groups and individuals as they experiment with blocks are located toward the middle of the continuum. Teachers are more actively involved as they ask questions about children's play, such as "Are you using the colored cubes for windows?"; responding to requests for quick assistance, such as "Can you help us find an elliptical curve?"; and providing additional materials as needed, such as "We need a sheet to make a roof for our hollow blocks house." Other strategies that fall in the middle of the continuum are related to helping children find solutions to conflicts. The teacher's physical presence may be reassuring enough for children to resolve minor differences or he may find it necessary to suggest options for working out problems. Church and Miller (1990) offered the following suggestions:

- Help children enter play in progress. "Matthew would like to park his car in the garage you built. Can he join you?"
- Suggest words children can use to initiate play. "If you want to build a town with Allison, say, 'Can I play with you?'"
- Explain to children that materials need to be shared. They can say, "May I play with that truck when you are finished?"
- Inform children that no one is excluded from the block center. Use the reminder, "Everyone will have a chance to play here."
- Assist children with understanding that accidents happen and the victim needs reassurance. "We know you worked for a long time and Stacey is sorry she knocked over the house you built."

Some situations will require more direct involvement, meaning the teacher is physically assisting and verbally directing constructions or taking part in the play by building or taking on a dramatic role. Teachers must become directly involved when a serious disruption occurs that could result in physical or emotional injury and when there is no time for children to resolve a conflict on their own. A common situation in which teachers should be directly involved is during clean up of blocks and accessories. The overwhelming task of returning blocks and accessories to the proper place can discourage some children from entering the block area. Younger children will need the most help, whereas primary-grade students may simply need an adult to help organize clean-up procedures. Figure 7–2 provides six possible solutions.

---

1. Give children at the block center advanced notice to give them more time for cleaning up.
2. As children finish cleaning up other centers, they help assist in the block center.
3. Allow children to choose the block shape, type of block, or accessories for which they want to be responsible.
4. Organize an assembly line in which children pass blocks to two or three children who return them to the shelves.
5. Add a "block manager," who will assist in clean up and maintenance, to the Helper Chart.
6. Give each block and accessory an obvious place where it belongs, and make storage areas easily accessible to children.

Figure 7–2 *Suggestions for cleaning up blocks and accessories.*

Direct involvement is sometimes the most appropriate approach when introducing new concepts. According to Vygotsky's (1978) theory of the zone of proximal development, children who are provided with assistance at crucial points of learning can accomplish slightly more difficult tasks than they could master alone. Over time, with additional practice and gradually less assistance, they successfully accomplish the task independently. Providing this necessary assistance has been labeled *scaffolding* (Wood, Bruner, & Ross, 1976) and is crucial to children attempting block constructions beyond their present ability. Therefore, scaffolding requires direct involvement by the teacher.

Teacher involvement will vary based on the age of the children in the group and their ability levels (see Figure 7–3). It will also be influenced by prior experiences with building materials, individual interests, and level of risk-taking behavior.

Reading books aloud to children daily is a teacher activity that integrates literature with other activities such as block building. When teachers select and read aloud books that relate to building, children develop new ideas and strategies for their play. Making these books available to children in the block center will encourage reference skills. Children's books that relate to block building are listed in Figure 7–4.

Making Home–School Connections

An additional responsibility of the teacher involves informing and including families. Teachers must first recognize the obstacles to communicating with families, such as illiteracy, language barriers, and lack of time due to other responsibilities, including work, children, or aging parents. Disabilities that prevent family participation, such as parents or siblings who are hearing or visually impaired, mentally disabled, or physically disabled, should also be considered. Once these specific situations are recognized, teachers can make special arrangements to ensure all families have the opportunity to take part (Kieff & Wellhousen, 2000).

Teachers must be able to communicate with families to share the experiences children are having with blocks and other classroom activities. This can be accomplished by sending home newsletters that describe classroom events. Letters may be written by hand or computer and sent home with students, sent through electronic mail, or posted on a school website. Some families may need the newsletter translated into their native language or recorded onto a cassette tape recorder.

Family members may also be invited to visit the classroom during the day and observe their children at play. Photographs, a slide show, or a video presented at an evening open house shows the children in action for parents who cannot visit the classroom during the day. An open house also

Teacher Involvement In Infant/Toddler Programs		
Minimum	**Moderate**	**Maximum**
Observe children at play	Sit in close proximity to children playing and offer assistance as needed	Talk about properties of blocks (color, shape, texture)
Select materials	Provide sufficient quantity for number of children	Model stacking, bridging
Clean/disinfect materials often	Provide duplicates to eliminate the need to share	Assume responsibility for clean up

Teacher Involvement In Preschool/Kindergarten		
Minimum	**Moderate**	**Maximum**
Initial set up and materials selection	Respond to requests for assistance	Maintain close physical proximity
Observe and keep records	Introduce new accessories as needed	Model and initiate block building
Document with photos or videos	Ask appropriate questions	Provide verbal suggestions
Provide motivational materials: floor plans, pictures of buildings, blueprints, children's literature	Introduce new vocabulary	Offer assistance
	Assist with clean up and care of materials	Take on a dramatic role
	Plan related field trips	Suggest an accessory
Listen to children's explanations	Read related children's literature	Scaffolding

Teacher Involvement in Primary Grades		
Minimum	**Moderate**	**Maximum**
Observe and conduct assessments	Introduce more challenging materials as children are ready	Use blocks to demonstrate math/science concepts
Integrate interest in building into projects/themes	Encourage cooperation	
Provide time for children to describe block products with peers	Help children make decisions and carry out activities related to project/theme	
Help coordinate clean up as needed		

Figure 7–3 *Teacher involvement continuum.*

Anno, M. (1983). *Anno's USA*. New York: Philomel Books.
Barton, B. (1981). *Building a house*. New York: Viking Penguin.
Begaye, L. S. (1993). *Building a bridge*. Flagstaff, AZ: Northland.
Blos, J. W. (1984). *Martin's hats*. New York: William Morrow.
Buchanan, K. (1991). *This house is made of mud (Esta casa esta hecha de lodo)*. Flagstaff, AZ: Northland.
Burton, V. (1939). *Mike Mulligan and his steam shovel*. Boston: Houghton Mifflin.
Burton, V. (1942). *The little house*. Boston: Houghton Mifflin.
Burton, V. (1943). *Katy and the big snow*. Boston: Houghton/Mifflin.
Cole, J., & Cole, P. (1988). *Hank and Frank fix up the house*. New York: Scholastic.
Curtis, P. (1991). *Animals and the new zoos*. New York: Lodestar Books.
Dale, P. (1987). *Bet you can't*. New York: Lippincott.
Dorros, A. (1992). *This is my house*. New York: Scholastic.
Gibbons, G. (1986). *Up goes the skyscraper*. New York: Macmillan.
Gibbons, G. (1990). *How a house is built*. New York: Holiday House.
Graham, B. (1996). *This is our house*. Cambridge, MA: Candlewick.
Hoban, T. (1975). *Dig, drill, dump, fill*. New York: Greenwillow.
Hoberman, M. A. (1978). *A house is a house for me*. New York: Viking Press.
Hutchins, P. (1971). *Changes, changes*. New York: Macmillan.
Isadora, R. (1983). *City seen from A to Z*. New York: Greenwillow Books.
Jackson, R. C. (1994). *Hammers, nails, planks, and paint*. New York: Scholastic.
Leodhas, S. N. (1965). *Always room for one more*. New York: Holt.
Macaulay, D. (1977). *Castle*. Boston: Houghton Mifflin.
Mayers, P. (1970). *Just one more block*. Chicago: Whitman.
McGraw, S. (1989). *This old new house*. Toronto: Annick Press.
Pomerantz, C. (1987). *How many trucks can a tow truck tow?* Westminster, MD: Random House.
Prater, J. (1985). *The gift*. New York: Viking Penguin.
Provensen, A., & Provensen, M. (1987). *Shaker Lane*. New York: Viking.
Rabe, B. (1981). *The balancing girl*. New York: E. P. Dutton.
Retan, W. (1990). *The big book of real trucks*. Dayton, NJ: B & N Distribution.
Rockwell, A. (1986). *Big wheels*. New York: Dutton.
Slater, T. (1987). *The big book of real fire trucks and fire fighting*. Dayton, NJ: B & N Distribution.
Stevenson, R. L. (1988). *Block city*. Dayton, NJ: B & N Distribution.
Weller, F. W. (1992). *Matthew Wheelock's wall*. New York: Macmillan.

Figure 7–4   *Children's literature for supporting block play.*

gives children the opportunity to lead family members on a tour of the classroom and describe the different activities available. They can even provide demonstrations.

Teachers can enlist families' help in collecting building materials and maintaining the block center and other areas. Previously used toys that are no longer of interest to children at home can find new life in a classroom full of imaginative minds. If families are aware of the types of materials that are appropriate and needed, they can be on the lookout at local garage sales or discount stores. Families can assist in collecting accessory materials and containers needed to enhance and organize block play. They can be made aware of materials needed by posting a list on a classroom bulletin board or including it in a newsletter. Finally, families can be brought together to build blocks, such as large hollow blocks for the classroom. These directions and dimensions are found in Figure 5–6.

There are many ways teachers can include families in classroom events. Some communities may identify committees to assist with different aspects of the classroom or teachers may capitalize on individual talents of family members. The inclusion of *all* families strengthens the home–school connection, which is crucial to learning, achievement, and positive attitudes toward school.

Conclusion

Teachers and parents play the primary roles in promoting children's block play. Attention to the environment and materials made available to children are necessary to ensure equal opportunities to all children. One method for evaluating the environment is to implement a published evaluation instrument. Another important role of the teacher is to determine the appropriate level of involvement with children at play (see Figure 7–5). Considering the different types of involvement for children at each age level will be useful when making quick decisions. Remember to inform families of the educational value of block play and enlist their help in collecting materials.

Theory into Practice

1. Observe boys and girls playing with blocks and note similarities and differences. Choose and implement a strategy suggested in this chapter to make the environment more gender fair.
2. After reviewing the teacher intervention continuums, make yourself available to children to enhance children's block play. Describe your actions and the reasons behind them.
3. Discuss the importance of block play with the parent of an infant, toddler, preschooler/kindergartener, or primary-grade student. Summarize in writing their reactions to your ideas.

Figure 7–5 *A teacher's aide observes and documents children's block play.*

Websites

www.bv.net/~stormie/index.html

A preschool teacher invites visitors to the website to read or contribute good ideas for teaching young children.

www.cyfc.umn.edu/Children/naeyc5.html

Early years are learning years. (Playgrounds: Keeping outdoor learning safe.)

www.scholastic.com

Resources for parents and teachers on improving the home–school connection.

Related Readings

Bronson, M. B. (1995). *The right stuff for children birth to 8: Selecting play materials to support development.* Washington, DC: National Association for the Education of Young Children.

Jalongo, M., & Isenberg, J. (1995). *Teachers' stories: From personal narrative to professional insight.* San Francisco: Jossey-Bass.

Sadker, M., & Sadker, D. (1994). *Failing at fairness: How America's schools cheat girls.* New York: Charles Scribner's Sons.

References

American Association of University Women (AAUW). (1990). *Short-changing girls, shortchanging America.* Washington, DC: Author.

Burkhardt, D. H. (1993, April). Building blocks, building skills. *Scholastic Pre-K today,* 42–49.

Chaille, C., & Silvern, S. (1996). Understanding through play. *Childhood Education, 72*(5), 274–277.

Church, E., & Miller, K. (1990). *Learning through play: Blocks. A practical guide for teaching young children.* New York: Scholastic.

Frost, J. (1992). *Play and playscapes.* Albany, NY: Delmar.

Harms, T., Clifford, R., & Cryer, D. (1998). *Early childhood environment rating scale–Revised edition.* New York: Teachers College Press.

Henniger, M. (1999). *Teaching young children: An introduction.* Columbus, OH: Merrill.

Hughes, F. (1995). *Children, play, and development.* Boston: Allyn & Bacon.

Kieff, J., & Wellhousen, K. (2000). Planning family involvement in early childhood programs. *Young Children, 55*(3), 18–25.

National Association for the Education of Young Children (NAEYC). (1998). *Accreditation criteria and procedures.* Washington, DC: Author.

Pereira, J. (1994, September 23). Oh boy! In toyland, you get more if you're male. *Wall Street Journal,* p. B1.

Prescott, E. (1994, November). The physical environment—A powerful regulator of experience. *Child Care Information Exchange,* 9–12.

Schlank, C., & Metzger, B. (1997). *Together and equal: Fostering cooperative play and promoting gender equity in early childhood programs.* Boston: Allyn & Bacon.

Serbin, L. (1980). Play activities and the development of visual-spatial skills. *Equal Play, 1*(1), 6–9.

Smilansky, S. (1968). *The effects of sociodramatic play on disadvantaged children.* New York: John Wiley & Sons.

Stritzel, K. (1995, May/June). Block play is for all children. *Child Care Information Exchange,* 42–47.

Vygotsky, L. S. (1978). *Mind in society: The development of higher psychological processes.* Cambridge, MA: Harvard University Press.

Wassermann, S. (1990). *Serious players in the primary grades.* New York: Teachers College Press.

Weiss, K. (1997). Let's build. *Scholastic Early Childhood Today, 12*(2), 31–39.

Wellhousen, K. (1996). Do's and don'ts for eliminating the hidden bias in preschool/primary classrooms. *Childhood Education, 73*(1), 36–39.

Wolfgang, C., & Wolfgang, M. E. (1992). *School for young children: Developmentally appropriate practices*. Boston: Allyn & Bacon.

Wood, D., Bruner, J., & Ross, G. (1976). The role of tutoring in problem solving. *Journal of Child Psychology and Psychiatry and Allied Disciplines, 17*, 89–100.

Including Everyone in Block Play

Guiding Questions

- *What are the general benefits of block play for children with special needs and abilities?*

- *What environmental and instructional supports could be used to foster block play among children with special needs and abilities?*

- *Describe intervention strategies that foster block play in inclusive classrooms.*

When children with special needs and abilities are included in environments serving children who are developing typically, all children benefit (Guralnick, 1990; Jenkins, Speltz, & Odom, 1985; Spodek & Saracho, 1994). Children with special needs or abilities have opportunities to improve their self-concept, gain cognitive skills, and develop friendships (Bergen, 1993; Perske, 1988), whereas children who are developing typically have the opportunity to develop respect for others and truly appreciate individual differences and contributions made by all (Biklen, 1992; Stainback & Stainback, 1990). Furthermore, when young children are able to work through their fears regarding differences among people, society benefits (Covert, 1995). In full inclusion programs, children who are developing typically and those with special needs and abilities attend the same program on a full-time basis. This is recognized as the preferred service delivery model in early childhood care and education by the National Association for the Education of Young Children (NAEYC; Bredekamp & Copple, 1997) and the Division for Early Childhood (DEC) of the Council for Exceptional Children (DEC Task Force on Recommended Practice, 1993). Developmentally appropriate early care and education programs serve as ideal environments for the development of inclusive programs because teachers are able to imbed instruction on targeted skills into naturally occurring activities throughout the day (Carta, 1995; Udell, Peters, & Templeman, 1998). These activities include small and large group instruction, self-chosen projects, routines, and play.

All children, regardless of their developmental differences, play and learn through play (Hughes, 1998), and the play of children with special needs is richer and more sophisticated when they have opportunities to play with peers who are typically developing (Esposito & Koorland, 1989; Kohl & Beckman, 1984). Block play is an important addition to inclusive settings because it provides sensory-rich opportunities for children to explore their physical environment, initiate and sustain social play, and form mental representations while working with children of differing abilities.

However, the mere presence of children with special needs or abilities in inclusive settings does not automatically result in the kind of play that will help all children, children who are developing typically as well as those with special needs and abilities, develop cognitive and social skills, empathy, and tolerance or capitalize on the benefits of friendship and social acceptance (Bergen, 1993; Esposito & Koorland, 1989; Jenkins, Odom, & Speltz, 1989; Kohl & Beckman, 1984; Lamorey & Bricker, 1993; Pickett, Griffith, & Rogers-Adkinson, 1993). Teachers must carefully design play activities and environments and choose interaction strategies that foster optimal learning for all children.

This chapter offers suggestions for planning and monitoring block play so all children are not only included, but also encouraged to develop appropriate cognitive, language, and social skills. This chapter is not meant to provide a comprehensive discussion regarding the philosophy or development of inclusive programs, the laws pertaining to inclusion, or the process of developing an Individualized Education Plan (IEP) or Individualized Family Service Plan (IFSP).

Our goal is to demonstrate how, through block play, children with special needs and abilities can satisfy certain IEP or IFSP goals, while developing self-esteem and the friendships associated with learning through play.

Play in Special Populations

Play provides all children opportunities to develop cognitive, language, physical, social, and emotional skills. However, the play behaviors children exhibit and the support they will need to foster optimal learning through play will vary according to age and individual differences (Hughes, 1998; Roopnarine, Johnson, & Hooper, 1994). As infants and young children play, they learn to effectively integrate sensory-motor experiences and gather knowledge about their world. However, children with disabilities related to the organization and integration of sensory information, such as vision, hearing, motor, or central nervous system impairments, will have more difficulty gathering and using information. Therefore, they will need additional specialized support to sustain play and learn through play.

Most children who are developing typically are easily engaged in play and consistently seek challenge through their play. When they master one skill or set of skills, they spontaneously move forward and create for themselves a new set of challenges; when they recognize a need for assistance, they generally do not hesitate to ask for it. However, a child with special needs may lack concentration skills, the drive to sustain play for an extended period of time, the ability to challenge herself through play, or the means of asking for help (Pugmire-Stoy, 1992). In a review of research regarding play and children with special needs and abilities, Hughes (1998) concluded:

> *"1)* all *children play regardless of their physical condition, level of intellectual functioning, emotional state, or environmental circumstances, and*
>
> *2) children with disabilities may play less effectively than those without them, since they are less likely to explore their physical environment, and/or to form mental representations of reality, and/or initiate and sustain social play."*
> *(pp. 183–184)*

The specific reasons for the differences in play among children with special needs will vary according to their disability. In some cases, differences in play behaviors are due to developmental delays, severity of the disability, or type of disability. For example, among children with a cognitive disability, such as Down syndrome, difference in play behaviors can be attributed mainly to developmental delays. For children with physical or sensory disabilities, such as cerebral palsy or blindness, the differences in play behaviors can be attributed to the inability of the child to access play materials (Hughes, 1998).

There are other factors that may deprive children with special needs and abilities the opportunity to learn through play. Environmental barriers such as inadequate space, lack of time for play, and absence of adapted play equipment may create situations in which children are not able to play with peers. Adults' attitudes regarding the value of play for children with special needs or abilities can also create barriers to children's opportunities to learn through play. Family members, teachers, and therapists may choose to use direct instruction instead of play as a teaching strategy. Or, teachers may lack the knowledge and skills needed to adapt activities and materials and support children's playful interactions with peers. Children with special needs and abilities can learn through play; however, they will need guidance and support that reflects their individual developmental capabilities and interests.

Promoting Block Play in Inclusive Settings   In inclusive settings, curricula, materials, and learning strategies provide experiences that are equally meaningful and enjoyable for children at different developmental levels and abilities (Recchia, 1999). Block play is an important addition to inclusive settings because it provides sensory-rich opportunities for children to explore their physical environment, initiate and sustain social play, and form mental representations while working with children of differing abilities. Therefore, it is important that all children receive the appropriate **supports** necessary for meaningful participation. Supports are those modifications that enable children to participate in activities, such as block play, at the highest level possible so they will receive maximum benefit from their experience. Some supports are environmental in nature and include ramps, widened entryways, extended time for an activity, or modified materials. Other supports are instructional in nature and are aimed at fostering the communication of concepts and skills and at developing a sense of community among people in the learning environment. Examples of instructional supports include creating buddy systems, increasing expected response time for the child, or allowing partial participation in certain activities.

When developing supports that foster inclusion, Erwin and Schreiber (1999) suggested that teachers consider these principles:

> *"1) Supports should be as ordinary, non-stigmatizing, and as unobtrusive as possible.*
>
> *2) Supports provided by peers should always be considered.*
>
> *3) Supports must reflect children's rights to exercise control over the environment and their own lives.*
>
> *4) Families should be involved in identifying supports.*
>
> *5) Monitoring and evaluating the effectiveness of supports are vital.*
>
> *6) A climate that promotes membership and community spirit must exist."*
> *(pp. 168–170)*

Most children will need a series of different supports that, when linked together in a seamless fashion, will promote opportunities for involvement in activities that foster learning. For example, widening the entryway to the block center will allow a child in a wheelchair to enter the block area, but the child may need additional support to interact successfully in the ongoing play.

Whether a child has a medical diagnosis such as spina bifida or an educational assessment such as developmental delay, it is critical that teachers and caregivers consider the uniqueness of each child when designing supports. Children with the same disability may have similar characteristics, but each child will have individual differences regarding strengths and needs for assistance and thus will require different supports. A simple list suggesting environmental or instructional supports for children with specific disabilities would not provide teachers enough information to create specific supports appropriate for a particular child. In fact, such lists might lead teachers into stereotypical thinking or biased expectations, thus preventing them from creating opportunities for the child to use all the strengths she possesses. It is important that teachers, family members, and specialists work as a multidisciplinary team to design the specific supports necessary for each child to become fully engaged in inclusive classrooms.

Environmental Supports That Foster Block Play

Procedures and techniques for creating environmental supports for a child with special needs fall into four main categories: space, time, materials, and special positioning. We consider examples in each category with the understanding that supports must be specifically chosen to fit the individual needs of the child and must be linked together with other supports to provide maximum benefit.

Space   When designing space for block play in inclusive classrooms, consideration must be given to the comfort of all children. Block play areas must be large enough to accommodate groups of children playing together and some children playing alone. Overcrowded areas will inhibit interactions and limit the development of creative designs and rich dramatic play. Some children may be overwhelmed when confronted with areas busy with activity. They may be distracted by noise, movement, or even bright lights and therefore not be able to fully concentrate on building. It may be appropriate to define specific spaces for these children to use within the block area. This could be done by using masking tape to mark the floor and would allow children to understand their boundaries. If the block center is not large enough to comfortably accommodate all children who want to participate, children could be allowed to take blocks and accessories to other designated areas within the classroom.

Accessibility, not only to the area but also to the materials in the area, is another factor to consider when designing space for block play. Certainly, entryways need to be wide enough to accommodate wheelchairs. In addition, blocks and accessories need to be stored at a height that all children can reach independently. Accessibility will encourage children to initiate play and take responsibility for materials.

Consider an alternative to floor and tabletop building, as these surfaces may not always be accessible to children in wheelchairs or prone standers. To encourage appropriate positioning and access to materials among all children, it may be necessary to devise a modification for building blocks at a height easily accessible to all children. For example, a child in a wheelchair may need an extension to a table, attached at an appropriate height, allowing the chair to slide under it. A child using a prone stander may need to work on an elevated tabletop, whereas other children can simply stand while they play with the blocks.

Predictability and consistency are also important factors to consider when designing space that fosters inclusive block play. Children need to know that certain materials are always going to be available and that these materials will be easy to find. The block area and the materials within it should be marked so all children can find, enter, and interact confidently. Using a combination of pictures and written languages, including Braille, to mark block center and storage shelves will foster a community spirit that celebrates similarities as well as differences. Hanging a wind chime in the block area would also help children and adults locate it easily.

Time   In inclusive classrooms, teachers develop flexible time schedules. Some children will need extended time frames for play because it may take longer for them to physically gather and manipulate materials or to engage in conversations that promote interaction among peers. Pressure to hurry will add stress and may create feelings of inadequacy. Children who are highly distractible may be more successful when play time is shortened. All children's activities should be monitored carefully so neither boredom nor frustration becomes associated with the idea of play.

Above all, teachers will need to protect the play time available for all children, particularly for children with special needs or abilities. Family members and therapists may believe that specific skill training should take precedence over play and therefore schedule therapy during free play or center time. However, children who are removed from the classroom during free play will miss the opportunity to learn many functional, academic, and social skills. Teachers must advocate for children by informing others of the importance of play in the lives of all children, incorporating learning goals into playful activities, and communicating with specialists and family members when children make progress through play.

Materials   Many materials typically used in early childhood settings can be adapted so children with special needs can use them independently. For example, some children may need special scissors to participate in art activities. As mentioned previously, supports, such as adapted materials, should be as ordinary and unobtrusive as possible. Blocks, because they come in so many sizes, shapes, textures, and weights, generally do not need to be adapted when chosen to fit individual needs and abilities of children in the classroom. In inclusive classrooms, there should be a variety of blocks in different textures, sizes, and weights. Children with visual impairments may initially be most comfortable playing with blocks that interlock, such as LEGO®, because they are able to feel the blocks fit together. Because these blocks come in a variety of sizes, teachers can adjust the size of the blocks as children's skills and abilities change. In such cases, the children continue to work with familiar materials while adding only one additional challenge, that of size. Children with physical impairments will find soft or light blocks easier to handle and manipulate. However, when a child shows an interest in playing with a certain set of blocks, teachers need to make innovative changes either to the block, the playing surface, or the assistance the child receives as she plays. For example, if wooden unit blocks are particularly intriguing to a child who has difficulty gripping and holding such blocks, teachers could wrap the midsection of the block with strips of rubber. This would make the block softer and provide a texture that is easier to hold on to than wood.

Accessories add important dimensions to block play and will often move simple constructive play into the realm of cooperative dramatic play. Common accessories used in block play are wooden or plastic vehicles, signs, and figures. It is important that these accessories represent the philosophy of inclusion. Following are some ideas for using accessories to create inclusive block play experiences:

1. Create models of adaptive equipment such as phones with lighting devices.
2. Include figures using wheelchairs, canes, hearing aids, or glasses.
3. Include pretend seeing-eye dogs.
4. Mark several toy vans as handicap accessible.
5. Use handicapped parking signs.

When children make accessories or signs for their constructions, help them to consider the needs of all people in the community.

Toys or accessories operated by a battery, switch, or **microswitch** motivate children who have multiple disabilities or difficulty with large or fine motor control to interact during play and sustain play for longer periods of time. Microswitches come in many shapes and sizes, with varying degrees of sensitivity. It may be possible to rig microswitches to existing block accessories that could be activated with a slight movement of the chin, by sipping or blowing into a strawlike device or tilting the head. These adaptations encourage the development of motor, language, cognitive, visual, and social skills. Adapting toys with microswitches is affordable and can often be done locally. However, finding the correct match between the type of microswitch and the needs of a particular child will require evaluation of child's movement capabilities and should be done collaboratively with family members and specialists. Figure 8–1 provides resources for adaptive toys, equipment, and microswitches.

Special Positioning   It is important that children be placed in positions that are comfortable and allow them to relax and focus, and that foster maximum independence of movement and interactions. For example, one child

Able Net, Inc.
1081 10th Avenue S.E.
Minneapolis, MN 55414
800/322-0956

Adapted Devices Group
1278 North Ferris
Fresno, CA 93728
800/723-2783

Creative Switch Industries
P.O. Box 5256
Des Moines, IA 50306
800/257-3485

Jesana, Ltd.
P.O. Box 17
Irvington, NY 10533
800/443-4728

Therapeutic Toys, Inc.
Cinta
34 North Moodus Road
Moodus, CT 06469
800/638-0676

Figure 8–1   *Resources for adapted toys and equipment.*

with motor impairment may be more comfortable and relaxed when lying on her side, whereas another child will engage better when standing in a prone stander. Children with visual impairments are easily distracted by background noise and could be encouraged to play in areas that are away from hallways and doors. An individual assessment of a child's needs regarding positioning in a variety of centers and activities should be made collaboratively with family members and specialists and reevaluated frequently.

Instructional Supports That Foster Block Play

Successful inclusion of children with disabilities or special abilities will depend, in large measure, on the individual teacher's and caregiver's ability to design and implement inclusive curricula that provide all children an age-appropriate context for social interaction, collaboration, and problem solving (Karagiannis, Stainback, & Stainback, 1996; Stainback & Stainback, 1992). Mallory (1998) stated that in high-quality early childhood programs, little modification of the curriculum is necessary to meet the needs of children with disabilities or special abilities. This is true, in part, because materials and strategies used in developmentally appropriate classrooms are applicable to children with a range of abilities; the discrepancies in ability between children with and without disabilities will be less in the preprimary and primary years; and the curriculum is integrated, thematic, activity-centered, and evolves for children's interests.

One of the elements of successful inclusion is the presence of activities that allow teachers to foster individualized skill development. The use of thematic and activity-centered curricula provides authentic opportunities for the simultaneous acquisition of academic skills, appropriate for some children in the class, as well as the acquisition of **functional skills** that may be more appropriate for other children in the same class (Barnes & Lehr, 1993). A functional skill is one that enables a child to participate, in a meaningful way, within a variety of integrated environments. For example, during block play, one child may develop academic skills related to numeric understanding by sorting and stacking blocks, whereas another child develops functional skills related to reaching and grasping.

Incorporating IEP and IFSP Goals into Ongoing Curricular Activities   It is important that teachers incorporate both the functional goals and the academic goals that are stated in a child's IEP or IFSP into motivating activities and daily routines in the classroom or child care center (see Figure 8–2). The *Individual Curriculum Sequencing Model* (see Guess, Jones, & Lyon, 1981; Helmstetter & Guess, 1987) was developed for children with severe disabilities and provides a systematic framework for organizing objectives. The major focus of this model is skill chaining or developing skill clusters. Several targeted skills are linked together and children are encouraged to practice these skills while

Figure 8–2   *Block play provides children with many opportunities to develop IEP or IFSP goals. Robert is developing fine motor skills and concentration.*

engaged in highly motivating and naturally occurring activities. The following vignette provides an example of how this model works:

> *Billy, a 4-year-old who has significant disabilities, is positioned in a corner chair (a piece of adaptive equipment that allows a child who uses a wheelchair to sit at the same level as other children) in the block area where three other 4-year-olds are playing. Billy's IFSP indicates a need to develop head control, focus attention, and operate a microswitch. His teacher, a member of a multidisciplinary team of specialists, clustered the three skills together to create a system that encourages Billy to practice these skills while engaging in block play. Several other children have built a track with blocks and are racing cars. Billy has a race car connected to a microswitch. He can activate the race car by lifting his head. As the teacher sits with Billy in the block area, she encourages him to pay attention to the race track, and when it is appropriate, she supports his efforts to raise his head and operate his car.*

Because the task is motivating and Billy receives encouragement, he is likely to accomplish the task and even attempt it several times. This model requires pre-planning and direct teacher intervention, but it can be successfully incorporated into block activities and routine. Cards can be created that outline a skill cluster, provide directions for encouraging the chain of actions, and offer suggestions for rewarding a child's accomplishment of the cluster. These cards can be kept in the block area and used by individuals who work with a particular child.

Activity-Based Instruction (see Bricker & Cripe, 1992) is another model for incorporating IEP or IFSP goals into ongoing classroom activities and routines. Teachers and specialists analyze the environment and daily routines, and identify natural opportunities for children to engage in the practice of target skills. They then encourage children to engage in activities that provide opportunities for skill development. Teachers become familiar with targeted skills and are able to take advantage of a child's spontaneous interests and self-initiated activities. Again, we offer a vignette as an example of how this model could be implemented during block play:

> *During center clean-up time, Cynthia, a 7-year-old child diagnosed with autism, is encouraged to work with her classmate Ramona to put away 10 blocks. Ramona has been taught exactly how to assist Cynthia. Later in the day, the teacher tells the children it is time to clean up the room and get ready to go home. Cynthia responds to the word clean up and turns to find Ramona. The teacher steps in and assists both Ramona and Cynthia as they pick up waste paper.*

The functional goal for Cynthia is to increase her interactions with peers. The teacher used the routine of block clean up to support the development of the skill. Throughout the day, classroom routines offer additional opportunities to practice interaction skills. It is important that teachers use naturally occurring activities to incorporate the development of both academic goals and functional goals. There are many opportunities inherent in block play that can be used to facilitate the development of specific IEP or IFSP goals. Figure 8–3 lists some of these opportunities.

Awareness:

- Increase body awareness
- Improve self-concept
- Increase awareness of individual differences

Creativity:

- Encourage creativity
- Encourage creative problem solving
- Stimulate curiosity

Feelings:

- Increase awareness of own and others' feelings
- Provide outlet for expressing feelings
- Increase feelings of group belonging

Language Skills:

- Improve expressive language
- Increase vocabulary
- Follow directions
- Increase understanding (receptive language)

Math Skills:

- Improve measurement concepts
- Improve number concepts
- Improve shape concepts
- Improve size concepts

Motor Skills:

- Improve large motor coordination
- Improve small motor coordination
- Improve eye–hand coordination
- Improve balancing skills
- Develop the ability to relax at will

Sensory Skills:

- Improve auditory association, closure, comprehension, discrimination, identification, memory
- Improve tactile association, closure, comprehension, discrimination, identification, memory
- Improve visual association, closure, comprehension, discrimination, identification, memory
- Localize sound
- Improve sensory integration

Figure 8–3   *Examples of IEP or IFSP goals that can be fostered through block play. (Continues)*

Social Skills:

- Cooperate with peers/adults
- Improve ability to take turns
- Improve ability to share
- Improve interaction skills

Thinking and Reasoning Skills:

- Improve color concepts
- Increase attention span
- Improve cause-and-effect reasoning
- Improve classification skills
- Improve decision-making skills
- Improve logical reasoning
- Improve problem-solving skills
- Make predictions

Figure 8–3   *Examples of IEP or IFSP goals that can be fostered through block play. (Continued)*

Creating a Social Climate That Fosters Interactive Block Play   Block play provides an interesting context for interaction and skill development, but research shows that children with special needs and their peers who are developing typically may need encouragement to play together effectively (Guralnick, 1981; Odom & McEvoy, 1988). Children who are developing typically interact more readily with children who are most like them, and the greater the differences between children, the less likely they are to interact (Guralnick, 1981; Stoneman, 1993).

There are, however, several ways to structure social play to foster interaction. First, play should occur frequently, for substantial amounts of time, and in small groups (Sainato & Carta, 1992). Second, children with disabilities will be more inclined to learn new skills and initiate language when in the company of competent, outgoing children (Peterson, Peterson, & Scriven, 1977). Third, more interaction will occur between same-gender classmates, although cross-gender interactions can be encouraged (Sainato & Carta, 1992). Therefore, play group composition should include children from both genders. Finally, children with disabilities appear to benefit from participation in mixed-age classes (Bailey, Burchinal, & McWilliams, 1993; Blasco, Bailey, & Burchinal, 1993; Roberts, Burchinal, & Bailey, 1994), because there are usually more sophisticated behavior models available and the activities are relevant to a greater range of abilities. Teachers can form mixed-age block play groups by inviting children from other grades to their classrooms at center time.

Another way to encourage collaborative relationships among children with differing abilities is to engage in **friendship training** (McEvoy, et al., 1988).

Training is informal and begins during teacher-led group activities such as circle time, story time, or music. The teacher leads a brief discussion about the values and importance of friendship, and involves children in songs, finger plays, or group games that have been adapted to increase the amount of physical contact or social interaction that occurs between children. Children may shake hands, pat each other on the back, smile, or say hello during the song or game. Research has shown that this type of training leads to increased social interaction during free play (Brown, Ragland, & Fox, 1988; McEvoy et al., 1988). Therefore, providing children with friendship training may increase the likelihood that all children will be included in block play.

A key element in creating an empathetic, caring classroom culture that fosters collaboration is appropriate information about differences. Some young children are naturally curious and often fearful of anything they might view as "different." They are, at the same time, naturally empathetic and kind. What all children need is specific information that will help them both understand and help others. There are many high-quality children's books that provide age-appropriate information, help children understand disabilities, and help children understand how these disabilities affect a person's actions and interactions. Often, children with special needs can talk about their disability with classmates, show adaptive devices such as hearing aids or braces, and discuss how they like to help others or be helped by others. If children themselves cannot provide classmates with this information, members of their family, medical personnel, therapists, or other specialists could be called on to answer any questions classmates might have. Adults need to remember that young children cannot always voice their questions. Observing how children interact with each other will provide adults a clearer understanding of children's fears and misconceptions, and make it possible to address unspoken questions (see Figure 8–4).

Intervention Strategies That Facilitate Block Play

Early childhood educators intuitively use many strategies during the course of the day to support learning and engage children in play. Many strategies are used simultaneously and spontaneously as they fit into the context of classroom activities and match the learning goals of individual children. However, when working with children with special needs, teachers will want to collaborate with other professionals to plan appropriate intervention strategies that can be used in a deliberate, consistent manner within the educational setting. Teachers should choose strategies that allow the child to be as independent as possible, interact in creative and useful ways, and acquire skills related to self-direction and self-control (Wolery, 1994). Here are descriptions of some common intervention strategies and examples of how they can be used to foster block play in early childhood classrooms.

Reinforcement Systems   Reinforcement systems provide a systematic way of supporting children's learning and encouraging them to explore environments,

Figure 8–4 *Children need specific information that will help them both understand and help others. Michael tells the group how he felt when he broke his leg and was confined to a wheel chair.*

experiment with materials, and engage in activities. According to behavioral theory (Skinner, 1953), a reinforcement is an event that happens after a specific behavior occurs. Positive reinforcements cause an increase in the behavior that preceded the event. Reinforcement is positive when the child being reinforced perceives it as desirable. Positive reinforcements can be intrinsic, that is, emanating from within the child (happiness, pride, or satisfaction) or extrinsic, emanating from outside the child (teacher's smile, hug, or a token). Children who are typically developing often receive intrinsic motivation or reinforcement by engaging in stimulating activities such as block play. Therefore, they continue to engage in these activities. Children with special needs may require added incentives to engage in the same activities. Therefore, extrinsic rewards may help children sustain involvement in block activities that increase their learning opportunities.

There are several guidelines for the effective use of reinforcements. The reinforcement must be given immediately after the desired behavior occurs, and consistency is important. When a child is just learning a skill or developing a desired behavior, reinforcement should occur every time the child successfully completes the skill. Later, the schedule for reinforcement can be varied, and eventually the reinforcement may not be necessary at all. It is also important to choose the correct reinforcing event. Different children will, of course, find different things rewarding. A hug or show of physical affection may reward one child, whereas another child may be fearful of this closeness. Therefore, the hug would likely cause a decrease in the desired behavior. It is necessary to consider a variety of reinforcements for any one child because the effectiveness of a particular reward may wear off with consistent use.

A behavior or skill learned in one context may not automatically transfer to other contexts. For example, a child who has learned, through a reinforcement system, to focus on building a block structure may not transfer that ability to other areas of learning. Therefore, teachers may want to employ specialized reinforcement systems to foster generalization and the transfer of skills and behaviors from one context to another. The following sections address examples of such systems.

Differential Reinforcement   Overreinforcement of one particular behavior may inhibit a child's ability to use a variety of behaviors in meaningful ways and at appropriate times. For instance, it is desirable for a child to enthusiastically explore a set of blocks and begin to construct structures on his own. However, there are times during the day, such as snack time, that this same enthusiastic exploration would not be appropriate. **Differential reinforcement** refers to rewarding specific behaviors in specific contexts but not others. Therefore, the child would be reinforced for exploration in all appropriate contexts, such as the art, music, block, and sand and water centers, but not in other contexts, such as snack or bathroom time. Children with special needs may find it particularly difficult to distinguish between appropriate settings for certain behaviors. Therefore, it is important to set priorities for skill development and target only a few skills at a time.

Correspondence Training   Often, children have particular skills but do not think to use them consistently or in the appropriate context. **Correspondence training** helps children develop the ability to decide what they need to do and then follow through and do it (Baer, 1990). For example, Evelyn has an impulsive tendency to throw blocks when playing. However, she does understand that she should not throw blocks and, through correspondence training, has demonstrated her ability to sustain appropriate block play for approximately 10 minutes. As part of this training, Evelyn's teacher intercepts her on her way to the block center and engages her in the following dialogue:

Teacher	*Evelyn, how are you going to play with the blocks today?*
Evelyn	*I will stack them. Make a building.*
Teacher	*Are you going to throw the blocks?*
Evelyn	*No. I stack the blocks. I don't throw the blocks.*
Teacher	*Great. You are going to stack the blocks today and build things.*
Evelyn	*Yes. I build and stack the blocks.*

The teacher gives Evelyn an opportunity to work in the block area and reinforces appropriate play at scheduled intervals.

Correspondence training is also an effective way to help children develop "follow-through" skills. Children are asked to match what they do with what they say they are going to do. For example, if a child has difficulty following through on choices that she makes, a teacher could employ correspondence training and ask the child, "What center are you going to play in today?" When the child responds, the teacher repeats the response, gives the child a chance to follow through on her decision, and then rewards or redirects her activity so she experiences success.

This technique can also be used to help children learn to transfer a skill from one context to another. If a child has successfully demonstrated the ability to put away personal belongings but has difficulty putting away class materials, the teacher can ask him, "Richard, what are you going to do with all those blocks on the floor?" When Richard responds, "I will put them away," the teacher repeats that response, allows Richard the opportunity to do what he says he will, and then reinforces or redirects his actions.

Behavioral Momentum **Behavioral momentum** is a reinforcement technique that helps children follow the instructions or requests of adults (Mace et al., 1988; Mace et al., 1990) or develops other skills (Davis & Brady, 1993). Children are reinforced for behaviors or skills they readily display and then are asked to engage in a skill they are less likely to initiate on their own. The teacher might approach a child at the beginning of clean-up time, but before asking her to help put away the blocks, engage her in several rapid-fire requests and rewards each compliance. This builds a momentum for compliance. In a kindergarten, momentum training might be similar to this:

At clean-up time, the teacher approaches Desire.

Teacher	*Desire, tell me your name!*
Desire	*Desire.*
Teacher	*Good! Touch your nose!*
Desire	(Touches nose)
Teacher	*Show me a block!*
Desire	(Shows the teacher a block)
Teacher	*Good! Give me a High Five!*
Desire	(Gives teacher a High Five)
Teacher	*Good! Now help us clean up this center!*

As Desire begins to clean the area, the teacher reinforces her actions and offers her as much assistance as needed to complete the task successfully.

Prompting Strategies Prompts are forms of assistance given to aid the use of a particular skill or to display a certain behavior (Wolery, Bailey, & Sugai,

1988). All early childhood educators employ a variety of prompts during the course of the day. Prompts can be pictures, words, or actions that give children an idea of what behavior is expected. Teachers may cue children to listen to a story by getting a book and sitting in a particular area, or they may give children a cue that it is time to change activities by ringing a bell or singing a song. Children who are developing typically will often learn to respond to prompts inherent in a particular classroom intuitively. However, children with special needs may require more implicit instruction, more than one prompt, and/or more time to process the meaning of the prompt.

Prompts are also useful for teaching children new skills (Demchak, 1990; Wolery, Ault, & Doyle, 1992). Verbal prompts offer children suggestions. If a child is trying to construct a bridge but has placed foundation blocks too far apart, a teacher or peer may ask a simple question that would cause the child to reevaluate her attempt. Gestural prompts are movements made by adults that cue a child to act or interact. If a child has difficulty taking turns, a nod from the teacher can cue her that it is time for her to participate or to end her turn.

Model prompts involve one person performing a skill so another person can imitate and learn to accomplish the skill independently. If the learning goal for a particular child is develop agility in grasping, placing, and releasing objects, a teacher could deliberately and systematically stack blocks on top of each other as she interacts with a play group. This would provide a model for the hand movements necessary to refine skills and accomplish the goal.

Pictorial or two-dimensional prompts are pictures or rebus signs that provide children the information they need to carry out a particular task. Many teachers label block shelves with pictures of blocks to cue children to put away materials in appropriate places.

Physical prompts involve touching and guiding a child in some way that supports her engagement in a particular activity. It may be necessary for an adult to guide a child physically through the entire sequence of an activity. A child who has difficulty grasping and holding may need physical assistance as he places one block on top of another. It is important to consider a child's personality and physical needs when choosing prompts. Some physical prompts may not be appropriate for children with emotional or physical disabilities. The multidisciplinary team that develops the child's IEP or IFSP will have valuable insight regarding the selection and use of appropriate prompts.

Wolery (1994) suggested several guidelines for using prompts in inclusive classrooms. First, choose prompts that offer the least help necessary and offer the prompt before or as the child engages in the activity. Next, use prompts only when the child is paying attention and provide the prompt in a constructive, supportive manner. For example, if you are modeling how to build a structure with blocks, make sure the child can see you, break the skill into relevant steps, and proceed at an appropriate pace. Finally, withdraw the prompt as the child begins to build the structure independently. To use prompting systems effectively, teachers must consistently evaluate and revise the prompts they use.

Assisting Children's Play   Generally, children who are developing typically will spontaneously play with toys and objects. They need few directions and will learn to use a particular toy by exploring, experimenting, or watching someone else play with it. However, children with special needs may not spontaneously engage in such exploration and experimentation. Because children learn so much about their world through exploration and play, children who do not play effectively may be at a disadvantage (Bradley, 1985). To help children develop play skills, children with special needs may require direct instruction related to the manipulation of different toys. A child may be taught to play with blocks by using physical or verbal prompts, or through modeling. An adult or peer may engage a child in structured play activities, showing her exactly how to push, pull, shake, or stack blocks.

If the learning goal for a particular child is to develop the ability to sustain play activities, the teacher provides toys in which the child shows interest. The teacher may also structure the play activity before it begins by selecting themes and roles. For example, he may select a group of blocks, discuss with the child what he might build, and reinforce the activity of building. If the goal is to develop skills related to collaborative play, the teacher may select a particular play group, help the child enter an ongoing play activity, and assist the child as he interacts during play.

Naturalistic (Milieu) Strategies   Naturalistic (milieu) strategies promote communication development and help children transfer language skills from one context to another. Naturalistic strategies take advantage of the brief interactions that occur between children and adults by giving the child the opportunity to learn new skills or practice existing ones (Halle, Alpert, & Anderson, 1984). Using these strategies, teachers make a concerted effort to create opportunities for encounters, and children gain valuable feedback and reinforcement in the naturally occurring context of the classroom. There are many variations of these strategies.

Incidental Teaching   **Incidental teaching** is a strategy that is useful for extending the language of all children. When using this strategy, teachers take advantage of a child's initiation of language by providing an expanded model or requesting more language (Kaiser, Yoder, & Keetz, 1992). For example, a child points to a particular building set sitting on the shelf in the block center. The teacher may ask the child a question, "Do you want to play with those blocks?" When the child nods in the affirmative, the teacher models by saying, "Yes." As the child begins to say yes, the teacher brings the building set to her. Teachers adjust their requests to fit the needs and abilities of each child.

Naturalistic Time Delay   **Naturalistic time delay** increases children's interactions. The teacher identifies times during the day when adults generally provide a form of assistance to a particular child. During such time, the adult stands ready to help but will delay assistance for a very short amount of time.

If the child asks for assistance, the teacher may extend the child's language through incidental teaching strategies. If the child does not ask for assistance, the teacher provides a prompt and reinforces the response (Wolery, 1994).

Transition-Based Teaching　　When using transition-based teaching, teachers use transition times as opportunities to provide children with meaningful practice of important skills (Wolery, 1994). For example, if the goal for a child is to learn the names of colors, the teacher would purposely intercept the child as he begins to make a transition from one activity to another. She would then ask the child, "Tell me the colors of these three blocks." The teacher would give the child the assistance needed to successfully answer the question. When the episode is complete, the child moves on to the next activity.

Peer-Mediated Strategies　　Peer-mediated strategies facilitate communication and promote learning among children with differing abilities (Goldstein & Gallagher, 1992; McEvoy, Odom, & McConnell, 1992). These strategies can also be used to promote social interaction skills (Odom, Hoyson, Jamieson, & Strain, 1985). Peers are taught specific strategies for engaging their less competent classmates in social and communicative exchanges and then given regular, frequent opportunities to play together and use these skills. The teacher observes and provides all children with support and reinforcement for playing and interacting together.

Research related to this strategy (McEvoy et al., 1992) suggests that teachers select peers with high social and interactive skills and teach them, in short group sessions, to use the targeted skills. The peers trained to use these skills should be given a rationale for the training and a verbal description of the skills. During training sessions, the teacher should model the desired skills, engage in role playing, and reinforce peers' efforts (Strain & Odom, 1986).

Conclusion

Block play is an important addition to inclusive settings because it provides sensory-rich opportunities for children to explore their physical environment, initiate and sustain social play, and form mental representations while working with children of differing abilities. Successful inclusion of children with disabilities into block play activities will depend on the use of appropriate environmental and instructional supports.

Theory into Practice

1.　Observe an inclusive early childhood classroom and make note of environmental and instructional supports available for children with special needs and abilities.

2. Review samples of IEPs and IFSPs, and identify functional and academic goals that can be developed through block play.
3. After extensive observations in an inclusive classroom, identify a situation where peer-mediated strategies would be appropriate interventions. Describe the situation and outline a training plan for a selected peer group.

Websites

www.cec.sped.org

Council for Exceptional Children. This website offers information and valuable links to resources and services.

www.tenet.edu/academia/earlychild.html

Hall of Early Childhood Education Resource Center. This site offers resources and support for educators and parents. There are many links that provide resources for special populations.

Related Readings

Gould, P., & Sullivan, J. (1999). *The inclusive early childhood classroom: Easy ways to adapt learning centers for all children*. Beltsville, MD: Gryphon House.

Siegel, L. M. (1999). *The complete IEP guide: How to advocate for your special ed. child*. Berkeley, CA: Nolo Press.

Wolery, M., & Wilbers, J. S. (Eds.). (1994). *Including children with special needs in early childhood programs*. Washington, DC: National Association for the Education of Young Children.

References

Baer, R. A. (1990). Correspondence training: Review and content issues. *Research in Developmental Issues, 11*, 379–393.

Bailey, D. B., Burchinal, M. R., & McWilliams, R. A. (1993). Age of peers and early child development. *Child Development, 64*, 848–862.

Barnes, E., & Lehr, R. (1993). Including everyone: A model preschool program for typical and special-needs children. In J. L. Roopnarine & J. E. Johnson (Eds.), *Approaches to early childhood education* (2nd ed., pp. 81–96). New York, NY: Macmillan Publishing.

Bergen, D. (1993). Teaching strategies: Facilitating friendship development in inclusion classrooms. *Childhood Education, 69*(4), 234–236.

Biklen, D. (1992). *Schooling without labels.* Philadelphia: Temple University Press.

Blasco, P. M., Bailey, D. B., & Burchinal, M. A. (1993). Dimensions of mastery in same-age and mixed-age integrated classrooms. *Early Childhood Research Quarterly, 8,* 193–206.

Bredekamp, S., & Copple, C. (Eds.). (1997). *Developmentally appropriate practice in early childhood programs* (Rev. ed.). Washington, DC: National Association for the Education of Young Children.

Bricker, D., & Cripe, J. (1992). *An activity-based approach to early intervention.* Baltimore: Paul H. Brookes.

Brown, W. H., Ragland, E. U., & Fox, J. J. (1988). Effects of groups' socialization procedures on the social interactions of preschool children. *Research in Developmental Disabilities, 9,* 359–376.

Carta, J. (1995). Developmentally appropriate practice: A critical analysis as applied to young children with disabilities. *Focus on Exceptional Children, 27*(8), 1–13.

Covert, S. (1995). Elementary school inclusion that works. *Counterpoint, 15*(4), 1, 4.

Davis, C. A., & Brady, M. P. (1993). Expanding the utility of behavioral momentum with young children: Where we have been and where we need to go. *Journal of Early Intervention, 17,* 211–223.

DEC Task Force on Recommended Practice. (1993). *DEC recommended practice: Indicators of quality in programs for infants and young children with special needs and their families.* Reston, VA: Council for Exceptional Children, Division of Early Childhood Education. (ERIC Document Reproduction Service No. ED 370 253).

Demchak, M. A. (1990). Response prompting and fading methods: A review. *American Journal of Mental Retardation, 94,* 603–615.

Erwin, E. J., & Schreiber, R. (1999). Creating supports for young children with disabilities in natural environments. *Early Childhood Education Journal, 26*(3), 167–172.

Esposito, B. G., & Koorland, M. A. (1989). Play behavior of hearing impaired children: Integrated or segregated settings. *Exceptional Children, 55,* 412–419.

Goldstein, H., & Gallagher, T. M. (1992). Strategies for prompting the social communication competence of young children with specific language impairment. In S. L. Odom, S. R. McConnell, & M. A. McEvoy (Eds.), *Social competence of young children with disabilities: Issues and strategies for intervention* (pp. 189–213). Baltimore: Paul H. Brookes.

Guess, D., Jones, C., & Lyon, S. (1981). *Combining a transdisciplinary team approach with an individual sequencing model for severely/multiply handicapped children.* Lawrence: University of Kansas.

Guralnick, M. J. (1981). The efficacy of integrating handicapped children in early education settings: Research and implications. *Topics in Early Childhood Special Education, 1*(1), 57–71.

Guralnick, M. J. (1990). Major accomplishments and future directions in early childhood mainstreaming. *Topics in Early Childhood Special Education, 10*(2), 1–17.

Halle, J. W., Alpert, C. I., & Anderson, S. R. (1984). Natural environment language assessment and intervention with severely impaired preschoolers. *Topics in Early Childhood Special Education, 4*(3), 36–56.

Helmstetter, E., & Guess, D. (1987). Applications of the individualized curriculum sequencing model to learners with severe sensory impairments. In L. Goetz, D. Guess, & K. Stremel-Campbel (Eds.), *Innovated program design for individuals with dual sensory impairments* (pp. 260–266). Baltimore: Paul H. Brookes.

Hughes, F. P. (1998). Play in special populations. In O. N. Saracho & B. Spodek (Eds.), *Multiple perspectives on play in early childhood education* (pp. 171–193). Albany: State of New York Press.

Jenkins J. R., Odom, S. L., & Speltz, M. L. (1989). Effects of social integration on preschool children with handicaps. *Exceptional Children, 55*, 420–428.

Jenkins, J. R., Speltz, M. L., & Odom, S. L. (1985). Integrating normal and handicapped preschoolers: Effects on child development and social interactions. *Exceptional Children, 52*, 7–18.

Kaiser, A. P., Yoder, P., & Keetz, A. (1992). Evaluating milieu teaching. In S. F. Warren & J. Reichle (Eds.), *Cause and effects in communication and intervention* (pp. 9–47). Baltimore: Paul H. Brookes.

Karagiannis, A., Stainback, W., & Stainback, S. (1996). Rationale for inclusive schooling. In S. Stainback & W. Stainback (Eds.), *Inclusion: A guide for educators* (pp. 3–16). Baltimore: Paul H. Brookes.

Kohl, F. L., & Beckman, P. J. (1984). A comparison of handicapped and non-handicapped preschoolers' interactions across classroom activities. *Journal of the Division of Early Childhood, 8*, 49–56.

Lamorey, S., & Bricker, D. D. (1993). Integrated programs: Effects on young children and their parents. In C. A. Peck, S. L. Odom, & D. D. Bricker (Eds.), *Integrating young children with disabilities into community programs* (pp. 249–270). Baltimore: Paul H. Brookes.

Mace, F. C., Hock, M. L., Lalli, J. S., West, B. J., Belfiore, P. J., Pinter, E., & Brown, D. K. (1988). Behavioral momentum in the treatment of noncompliance. *Journal of Applied Behavioral Annalysis, 21*, 123–141.

Mace, F. C., Lalli, J. S., Shea, M. C., Pinter-Lalli, E., West, B. J., Roberts, M., & Nevin, J. A. (1990). The momentum of human behavior in natural settings. *Journal of the Experimental Analysis of Behavior, 54*, 163–172.

Mallory, B. L. (1998). Educating young children with developmental differences: Principles of inclusive practice. In C. Seefeldt & A. Galper (Eds.), *Continuing issues in early childhood education* (2nd ed., pp. 213–237). Upper Saddle River, NJ: Merrill.

McEvoy, M. A., Nordquist, V. M., Twardosz, K. A., Heckman, K. A., Wehby, J. H., & Denny, R. K. (1988). Promoting autistic children's peer interaction in an integrated early childhood setting using affection activities. *Journal of Applied Behavior Analysis, 21,* 193–200.

McEvoy, M. A., Odom, S. L., & McConnell, S. R. (1992). Peer social competence interventions for young children with disabilities. In S. L. Odom, S. R. McConnell, & M. A. McEvoy (Eds.), *Social competency of young children with disabilities: Issues and strategies for intervention* (pp. 113–133). Baltimore: Paul H. Brookes.

Odom, S. L., Hoyson, M., Jamieson, B., & Strain, P. S. (1985). Increasing handicapped preschoolers' peer social interactions: Cross setting and component analysis. *Journal of Applied Behavior Analysis, 18,* 3–16.

Odom, S. L., & McEvoy, M. A. (1988). Integration of young children with handicaps and normally developing children. In S. L. Odom & M. B. Karnes (Eds.), *Early intervention for infants and children with handicaps: An empirical base* (pp. 241–267). Baltimore: Paul H. Brookes.

Perske, R. (1988). *Circles of friends.* Nashville, TN: Abingdon Press.

Peterson, C., Peterson, J., & Scriven, G. (1977). Peer imitation by nonhandicapped and handicapped preschoolers. *Exceptional Children, 43,* 223–225.

Pickett, P. L., Griffith, P. L., & Rogers-Adkinson, D. (1993). Integration of preschoolers with server disabilities into day care. *Early Education and Development, 4,* 54–58.

Pugmire-Stoy, M. C. (1992). *Spontaneous play in early childhood.* Albany, NY: Delmar.

Recchia, S. (1999). Inspiration from infants in inclusive group care. *Focus on Infants and Toddlers, 11*(4), 1–5.

Roberts, J. E., Burchinal, M. R., & Bailey, D. B. (1994). Communication among preschoolers with and without disabilities in same-age and mixed-age classrooms. *American Journal of Mental Retardation, 99,* 231–249.

Roopnarine, J. L., Johnson, J. E., & Hooper, F. H. (Eds.). (1994). *Children's play in diverse cultures.* Albany, NY: State University of New York Press.

Sainato, D. M., & Carta, J. J. (1992). Classroom influence on development of social competence in young children with disabilities. In S. L. Odom, S. R. McConnell, & M. A. McEvoy (Eds.), *Social competence of young children with disabilities: Issues and strategies for intervention* (pp. 93–109). Baltimore: Paul H. Brookes.

Skinner, B. F. (1953). *Science and human behavior.* New York: Macmillan.

Spodek, B., & Saracho, O. N. (1994). *Dealing with individual differences in early childhood classrooms.* New York: Longman.

Stainback, S., & Stainback, W. (1992). *Curriculum considerations in inclusive classrooms: Facilitating learning for all students.* Baltimore: Paul H. Brookes.

Stainback, W., & Stainback, S. (1990). *Support networks for inclusive schooling.* Baltimore: Paul H. Brookes.

Stoneman, Z. (1993). The effects of attitudes on preschool integration. In C. A. Peck, S. L. Odom, & D. Bricker (Eds.), *Integrating young children with disabilities into community programs: Ecological perspectives on research and implications* (pp. 223–248). Baltimore: Paul H. Brookes.

Strain, P. S., & Odom, S. L. (1986). Peer social initiations: Effective intervention for social skills development of exceptional children. *Exceptional Children, 52,* 543–551.

Udell, T., Peters, J., & Templeman, T. P. (1998, January-February). From philosophy to practice in inclusive early childhood programs. *Teaching Exceptional Children,* 44–49.

Wolery, M. (1994). Instructional strategies for teaching young children with special needs. In M. Wolery & J. S. Wilbers (Eds.), *Including children with special needs in early childhood programs* (pp. 119–150). Washington, DC: National Association for the Education of Young Children.

Wolery, M., Ault, M. J., & Doyle, P. M. (1992). *Teaching students with moderate and severe disabilities: Use of response prompting strategies.* White Plains, NY: Longman.

Wolery, M., Bailey, D. B., & Sugai, S. M. (1988). *Effective teaching: Principles and procedures of applied behavior analysis with exceptional students.* Boston: Allyn & Bacon.

CHAPTER 9

Assessing Children's Block Play

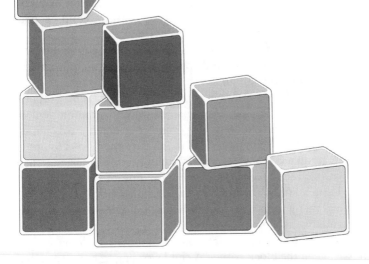

Guiding Questions

- *What are the three types of knowledge according to Piaget, and how do they differ?*

- *Describe the various methods for assessing children's learning and the different components of the Assessment of Learning Cycle.*

- *How can parents be involved in the assessment process?*

Observing and assessing children's learning is an ongoing responsibility of the teacher. Time and effort spent setting up appropriate environments, selecting quality materials, and interacting with children need to be justified with useful records that clearly document learning. This chapter provides a framework for selecting and using appropriate assessment strategies.

Assessing Children's Learning

Providing children with opportunities for play and rich learning experiences in early childhood gives them a foundation for understanding their world and the role they play in it. As children pour and sift sand, they experience the texture and fluid nature of this material. When they take on the role of doctor and patient in dramatic play, they are learning about the feelings and actions of others. Experimenting with blocks helps them understand concepts of weight and balance. Through interacting with objects and people in their world, children are building a crucial foundation of knowledge necessary for future learning.

Recognizing the Three Types of Knowledge   Piaget (1952) identified three types of knowledge that emerge from children's meaningful play, which he believed encompassed all learning. According to Piaget, the three types of knowledge are **physical, logicomathematical,** and **social-arbitrary.**

Physical knowledge is the understanding of the physical attributes of objects in the child's immediate environment. Physical knowledge can only be acquired through direct experiences with objects. Infants, for example, are naturally curious about objects within their reach and will explore them using their senses. As an infant picks up a rubber block, she visually examines it, tastes, chews, and squeezes the block. She is gaining physical knowledge of its shape, color, taste, and texture. A preschooler will explore more sophisticated properties of the same block, such as its ability to return to the original shape after being stepped on or the way in which the block holds and projects water poured into a small air hole. Through firsthand exploration, children gain physical knowledge of objects in their immediate environment.

Logicomathematical knowledge is the cognitive understanding of the relationships among and between objects. In authentic play and learning situations, children are motivated to construct an understanding of relationships to solve a real problem, which moves children to a greater level of understanding. Kamii and DeVries (1980) advocated playing games as one way to promote logicomathematical knowledge. When children play number-oriented card games, board games, and dominoes, they are motivated to improve their skills to outdo their opponents. The feedback from peers is invaluable for challenging their thinking. For children not ready for the turn-taking nature of games, teachers can devise daily living situations to promote logicomathematical knowledge. Kamii (1985) described many ways to accomplish this, including voting, settling disputes, taking attendance, keeping up with supplies, distributing materials, and planning a party. There are additional opportunities for building logicomathematical knowledge in the block corner. A child working to build an elaborate building employs problem-solving strategies as needed. Once completed, he adds a second equally challenging second floor to the building. Negotiating building strategies with a friend provides more opportunities for problem solving. With every challenge met and problem solved the child is gaining an understanding of logicomathematical relationships.

Social-arbitrary knowledge is the awareness of socially referenced knowledge that can only be learned through experiences with others. Social-arbitrary knowledge includes oral and written language as well as an understanding of rules, laws, and appropriate and inappropriate behaviors among those of a similar culture. Children demonstrate their growing awareness of the use of oral language beginning with their first words, usually signifying important people and objects in their life. As a preschooler, words are used in place of objects or actions in their play, such as "Pretend this is a horse" or "You be the waiter now" (Smilansky, 1968). Written language supports children's play as they create signs for buildings constructed with blocks or labels for shelves in a pretend grocery store. School-age children use oral language to discuss or collaborate and written language to supplement or record their endeavors, such as setting up and running a neighborhood lemonade stand.

Language is only one aspect of social-arbitrary knowledge. Knowing the difference between right and wrong at an overt and implied level is also important to competence in this area. This too is gradual and changes with age and experience. Preschool-age children may not see the importance, for example, of following arbitrary rules for a game such as taking turns or moving a playing piece the same number of spaces as designated by a cast die. However, by primary school age, children become very rigid in their interpretation of rules and anyone who does not follow them exactly is quickly labeled a "cheater" and made aware that this behavior is not acceptable. Social-arbitrary knowledge is also the ability to understand how to work cooperatively with others. Collaboration among peers in a play setting requires an understanding of give and take, and setting aside one's personal desires for the sake of the group. These social skills are learned gradually as children become less egocentric in their thinking and more capable of seeing another's point of view, around age 7.

Social-arbitrary knowledge is culture specific. Behavior that is accepted in one culture may be shunned or criticized by another. For example, a child's obsession with superheroes may be fully accepted or even encouraged by one family but cause grave concern for another. In an early childhood setting, there may be obvious or subtle cultural variations in children's and parents' attitudes toward a variety of topics, including sharing, competition, gender roles, and play.

Because the three types of knowledge are basic to all learning, encouraging and promoting physical, logicomathematical, and social-arbitrary learning is a valid and worthwhile goal for early childhood programs. It is broad enough to encompass all domains—cognitive, language, social-emotional, and physical—yet descriptive enough to facilitate planning for curriculum and assessment. Brain research shows that learning cannot be compartmentalized into subject areas (Howard, 1994). Designing curricula and assessment around the three types of knowledge gives a bigger picture of children's abilities rather than a

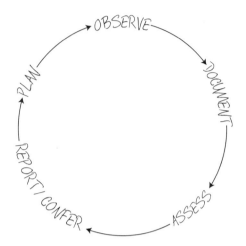

Figure 9–1 *Assessment of learning cycle.*

cross-section of their performance in isolated content areas. Setting the goal of promoting an understanding of the three types of knowledge is especially useful for assessing children's growth through their interactions with blocks. When children are introduced to new blocks and other building materials, they explore the physical properties of the blocks such as texture, weight, size, and uses. As the blocks are incorporated into play, children use logicomathematical skills to experiment and control the use of them. While playing with peers, children use oral language to express their opinions and to describe their desires in play and written language to enhance their play, as well as incorporate their skills for getting along with others.

Growth and learning in the three types of knowledge can be achieved through observing/documenting children, assessing their understanding, reporting/conferring findings, and, as a result, plan for new learning experiences. The ongoing nature of this process is depicted in Figure 9–1. There is virtually no beginning or end to evaluating children's learning, and each phase is dependent on those that come before and after. Each of these phases of evaluation are described in greater detail as follows.

Observing and Documenting Children's Learning

Observing children is crucial to understanding their learning. Through observations alone teachers can truly see what new concepts have been learned and identify concepts that children have not yet grasped. It was through observations of children and their incorrect responses on standardized tests that Piaget first began to develop his theory of cognitive development. After continued, careful observations of thousands of children over decades, he formulated the cognitive learning theory of how children of different ages think and why they think so differently from adults. Maria Montessori's observations of children living in poverty and their reactions to didactic materials resulted in her unique, prescribed method for teaching, which is still widely used. As learned in Chapter 3, Caroline Pratt's observations of children playing with unit blocks led to the realization that children move through predictable stages of building. These and other observations and findings drastically affected the field of education. Observation was as crucial to Piaget, Montessori, and Pratt in the development of their theories as it is to the classroom teacher in his discovery of what children know and understand.

Observation alone, however, is not enough. For observations to actually inform teachers and influence future learning, there must be clear documentation of the observed behaviors. According to Helm, Beneke, and Steinheimer (1997), documenting observed behaviors has the following benefits:

- Teachers who document are more often able to teach children through direct, firsthand, interactive experiences that enhance brain development.
- Teachers are more effective when they document.
- Children perceive learning to be important and worthwhile when teachers document their learning.

Documentation of observed behaviors can take many forms. Three useful methods of documenting observed behaviors as children explore and play with blocks are: 1) systematic recording, 2) project narratives, and 3) products.

Systematic Recording   Carefully observing and recording children's actions and language is crucial to recognizing when learning is taking place. There is a distinct difference between *seeing* or *watching* children and actually observing them. Observation requires specific attention to a child's progress toward an identified goal or goals. In this case, the goal is attention to children's growth and learning in the three types of knowledge—physical, logicomathematical, and social-arbitrary. Observations of children's behaviors can be systematically recorded through anecdotal records, observation guides, checklist/rating scales, and records of participation.

Anecdotal Records   Anecdotal records are brief accounts of some specific event that is currently occurring or happened only a short time prior to writing the record (Bentzen, 1992). It is important that the observer state exactly what happened in clear, concise language and avoid using descriptive words that can be interpreted inaccurately. Anecdotal records are especially useful for documenting behaviors of a single child, small group of children (McAfee & Leong, 1997), or adult–child interactions (Nicolson & Shipstead, 1998). An anecdotal record is like a snapshot of an observed encounter because it describes a single event (Wellhousen, 1994). In addition to factual descriptions of the incident observed, the record may include some direct quotes. The primary purpose of anecdotal records is to provide ongoing evidence of children's development, including behavioral patterns or changes, milestones, or unusual occurrences (Kapel, Gifford, & Kapel, 1991); therefore, the observer may record unexpected events or incidents as well as behaviors that relate to a predetermined reason for observing. In addition to describing what happened, anecdotal records also tell when and where the event took place (Wortham, 1995). It is good practice to prepare record forms ahead of time with simple labels for date, time, setting, the name of a child or children, and observer (see Figure 9–2). Nicolson and Shipstead (1998) suggested writing one or two anecdotal records for each child every week to have enough documentation for interpretation of behaviors.

Goodwin and Driscoll (1980) identified five characteristics of anecdotal records:

Child(ren): <u>Blair and Shawn</u>   Observer: <u>Miss Becky</u>

Date: 11-16-01   Time: 10:00 A.M.   Setting: 4-yr.-old class—block
                                                center

Shawn walks over to Blair and picks up three blocks from a pile next to her. Blair begins to cry, claiming Shawn has stolen her blocks. Shawn gives them back but Blair continues to cry until consoled by the teacher.

Child(ren): <u>Blair and Hannah</u>   Observer: <u>Miss Becky</u>

Date: 12-2-01   Time: 9:00 A.M.   Setting: 4-yr.-old class—block
                                              center

Blair begins to cry because she does not have enough blocks to finish her house construction. She discovers two stacks of blocks still on the shelf. After looking through them, she begins crying again because there were no pillars. Hannah takes one from her construction and gives it to Blair.

Child(ren): <u>Blair and Hannah</u>   Observer: <u>Miss Becky</u>

Date: 12-5-01   Time: 9:00 A.M.   Setting: 4-yr.-old class—block
                                              center

Blair intently removes half units from the block shelf. She carries them to an open space using a small wagon. Each block is removed and placed on its narrow edge at an angle. After making several adjustments, she creates an enclosure. Blair gives Shawn and Hannah a turn sitting in the middle of the enclosure.

Figure 9–2   *Anecdotal records.*

1. The anecdotal record is the result of direct observation.
2. The anecdotal record is a prompt, accurate, and specific account of an event.
3. The anecdotal record includes the context of the behavior.
4. The anecdotal record focuses on behavior that is either typical or unusual for the child being observed.
5. Interpretations of the incident are recorded separately from the incident.

Interpretations of anecdotal records can be made after several have been collected over a period of time. Teachers should review the collection of records, while keeping in mind all other information available on each child. Individual anecdotal records are not to be interpreted in isolation. According to McCutcheon (1981), "Interpretations are constructed through our active mental work; they are not part of the immediately given environment. They grow out of our theories, our past experiences and our present observations" (p. 5).

When writing or interpreting anecdotal records, the observer should keep in mind the following:

1. Be unobtrusive. The less obtrusive the observer, the more typical the behaviors observed. If making observational records is part of the everyday routine, children are less likely to change their behavior because they know they are being observed. When information is collected under unobtrusive situations, it is considered to be more accurate and reliable.
2. A single incident is not sufficient for interpreting behavior and does not provide enough information to draw conclusions. A substantial number of observations made over a period of time are necessary before records can be interpreted for meaning. New information should continually be collected to verify or update findings.
3. It is important for teachers to be aware of observer bias and monitor their personal feelings when observing and interpreting records so they do not dwell on behaviors that are particularly cute or distasteful. Checking for biases is crucial to producing useful, clear, and fair anecdotal records.
4. Observations of children should be kept confidential to protect the privacy of children and their families. Interpretations of anecdotal records should be shared only with authorized people, such as parents or other personnel involved in a referral process.

Observation Guide   Specific observations of each child as they play in centers need to be conducted periodically to document growth and learning (Isbell, 1995). This observation will contain questions that can either be general enough to pertain to any learning center or specific to each center in the classroom. Church and Miller (1990) suggested the following questions to guide observations of individual children in the block center:

1. What is the child doing with the blocks?
2. Does the child have the language to describe what he is making?

3. Does the child seem to make the same things over and over?
4. Does the child think of ways to solve problems, and does he try different solutions?
5. What new concepts, discoveries, or developmental abilities has the child mastered?
6. How does the child interact with others?

By answering direct, relevant questions for each child three to four times over the course of a year and comparing responses over time, children's growth and areas needing attention become obvious.

Checklists and Rating Scales   Checklists and rating scales are other methods of systematically recording children's learning. Checklists consist of a list of statements, usually arranged in a sequence, and space is provided to record the presence or absence of specific behaviors in given situations. Rating scales are similar to checklists but also record frequency and/or quality of behaviors observed. The observer is required to make a judgment about the performance when using a rating scale. The most common type of rating scale is a numerical scale in which a number correlates to the degree in which a behavior is present or performed. Teachers may choose published checklists and rating scales or create their own. Figure 9–3 illustrates a teacher-made rating scale/checklist combination for determining a child's stage of block building.

Records of Participation   Another type of systematic observation is to keep records of children's participation in the block area as well as other learning centers. This enables the teacher to design a specific plan for children who avoid or dominate a particular center at the expense of gaining new experiences from the variety of learning centers available. The teacher may take responsibility for keeping records of participation by recording daily on a grid labeled with each child's name and the names of the centers. Children can also assume responsibility for recording their participation in various centers. Teachers can color-code each center and make available a generous supply of 1-inch construction paper squares of the corresponding color in each center. Children who are 4 and 5 years of age can collect squares from the centers where they played that day and glue them to a sheet of paper that has been dated. A weekly participation chart, shown in Figure 9–4, can be used by 5- and 6-year-olds. This pictorial record has a column with the name and symbol for each learning center and a generous space for children to indicate their participation by using a date stamp. A quick glance at any of these records will show where individual children spend their time while playing in centers.

Project Narratives   Project narratives are methods of documenting learning over time, indicating growth in knowledge or skills. The project narrative provides an explanation of learning that would not have been evident to others without it. Narratives may take the form of teacher stories; journals; conversations with children, such as informal interviews or conferences; or a

Child's name _____ Observation date (s) _____

Observer's name _____ Setting _____

Section I: Circle Never, Sometimes, or Often for each behavior.

Freely selects the block center	Never	Sometimes	Often
Plays or builds with peers	Never	Sometimes	Often
Demonstrates ability to build alone	Never	Sometimes	Often
Assists in putting away blocks	Never	Sometimes	Often
Replaces blocks in designated space	Never	Sometimes	Often

Section II: Check "Observed" or "No evidence" to indicate characteristics of block building.

	Observed	No evidence
Carries blocks from one place to another	_____	_____
Stacks blocks (vertically or horizontally)	_____	_____
Stacked blocks resemble floors and walls	_____	_____
Creates a simple bridge	_____	_____
Stacks multiple bridges	_____	_____
Creates block enclosures	_____	_____
Varies the size or shape of block enclosures	_____	_____
Creates joined enclosures	_____	_____
Builds balanced structures with attention to pattern and symmetry	_____	_____
Structures are named *during or after* building is complete	_____	_____
Identifies or names structure *before* building	_____	_____
Design elements reflect authentic details of a familiar structure	_____	_____
Incorporates commercial accessories into the structure	_____	_____
Creates or uses recycled accessories as part of structure	_____	_____
Engages in dramatic play with structure and accessories	_____	_____

Comments: _____
_____
_____
_____

Figure 9–3 *Block play rating scale/checklist for preschoolers ages 3 through 5.*

NAME: WEEK OF:

Blocks 	
Computer 	
Art 	
Library 	
Home Living 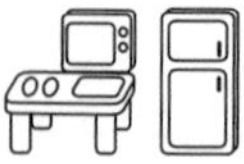	
Woodworking 	
Creative Writing 	
Music 	
Science 	

Figure 9–4   *Center participation record.*

combination of these sources (Helm et al., 1997). Whatever the form, narratives need to be ongoing and continuously updated to illustrate the learning that is taking place. Figure 9–5 is an example of a teacher story that describes a child's experiences in the block center.

I've observed and documented Lane's disinterest in the block center, so when Katy, his favorite playmate, chose to play with blocks, I suggested he join her. Lane followed Katy and began removing all the blocks from the shelf. I waited patiently for him to start using the blocks in some way, but he just kept taking them off the shelf one at a time, almost rhythmically. Knowing what an overwhelming task it is for a 4-year-old to put blocks away (even with help), I suggested he start building with some of the large assortment of blocks that almost engulfed him. He asked me to build with him, but I encouraged him to at least begin on his own.

He looked so lost, but then spotted a large switch and gothic door. He stood the switch up vertically and began stacking blocks on the narrow top. After stacking two or three blocks, the whole structure tumbled. He tried this several times unsuccessfully, and I could see he was getting discouraged. I suggested he not use the large switch and physically removed it from the block area, and I returned some of the blocks from the large pile back to the shelf.

As Lane could clearly see the 10 to 12 blocks around him, he began to look more confident and began to build a road-like structure with unit blocks. Katy suggested they make a train track and began showing Lane how to turn the blocks slightly to form an enclosure. Lane watched with interest for a few moments and then began stacking half units to form a tower.

Later when I asked Lane if he enjoyed playing with blocks he responded, "I liked stacking the blocks high so I could knock them down."

Figure 9–5 *Teacher story: Lane at block play.*

Products   A product produced by a child is an object or structure that provides evidence of a child's learning or progress (McAfee & Leong, 1997). The importance of these products as an assessment tool is often overlooked; thus, products are sent home or lost during classroom clean up. Kuschner (1989) recognized that it is extremely difficult to preserve products when they are created from nonconsumable classroom materials. Children's block structures fall into this category. When children spend a great deal of time planning and building with blocks, they often have nothing to show for their effort once clean-up time is over. To resolve this, Kuschner (1989) suggested attaching ownership and permanency to all types of children's play. This can be accomplished by the following:

1. Sending impromptu notes home to parents briefly describing when a child does or learns something new.
2. Attaching signs to products, such as block structures, that give the names of builders or reminds others "do not disturb."
3. Helping children write about the activity by dictating the story to an adult, illustrating, or using their own phonetic spellings.

Figure 9–6 *Katy Jo "saved" her Lego® house with a photograph.*

4. Photograph or videotape children's block constructions. Block play can be recorded as it is in progress or when children deem it complete. Isbell (1995) suggested posting photographs of the structure and its builders on a bulletin board near the block center, along with the children's names. Later, the photographs can be compiled into a book that is kept in the block center. Photographs of previously built structures may stimulate ideas for building new ones.

All products need to be labeled with the child's name and the date or dates in which the child worked on it (see Figure 9–6). When children give a verbal description of a product or when teachers describe why they choose to make a record of it, the product gains an additional sense of importance. When tangible evidence of a child's play exists, there is an opportunity for reflection and to think about how they might change the activity in the future. Products in conjunction with other forms of assessment will provide the whole picture of the child's progress over time.

Portfolio Assessment Systems

As observations of children's learning are documented, teachers will find they have volumes of systematic records, project narratives, and products to organize and analyze for meaning. Portfolios are useful for this purpose and have been defined as "an organized, purposeful compilation of evidence documenting a child's development and learning over time" (McAfee & Leong, 1997, p. 100); "a record of the child's process of learning: what she has learned and how she has gone about learning" (Grace & Shores, 1991, p. 3); and "a process or method whereby student performance information can be stored and interpreted" and "used for assessing and reporting the student's progress and accomplishments to parents and administrators" (Wortham, 1995, p. 186).

Portfolios have several important functions and purposes (Meisels & Steele, 1991):

- They help to integrate instruction and assessment.
- They enable children to participate in assessing their own work.
- They keep track of individual children's progress.
- They provide others with information about the child's progress.

Different categorization systems have been suggested for organization of portfolios. The Southern Early Childhood Association (Grace & Shores, 1991) recommends categorizing materials in time sequence and according to learning domains—fine motor development, gross motor development, concept development, language and literacy, and personal and social development. The Work Sampling system created by Meisels et al. (1994) uses the following categories—personal and social development, language and literacy, mathematical thinking, scientific thinking, social studies, the arts, and physical development. An organization system may be designed around the goals of the program. In our case, this would mean designing a categorization system that emphasizes and illustrates learning of the three types of knowledge—physical knowledge, logicomathematical, and social-arbitrary knowledge.

Regardless of the organization of the portfolio, it is suggested that teachers who are just beginning this type of assessment start small, focusing on only one or two domains and build from there. A portfolio reflecting children's growth and learning in block play is an ideal starting point because it focuses on only one aspect of children's activity, yet provides a broad spectrum of behaviors to observe and record. Teachers who have a portfolio assessment system in place can imbed concepts and skills learned in block play into an existing portfolio system.

In most portfolio systems, children participate in the selection, organization, evaluation, and explanation of the portfolio. Children see their own growth firsthand because they have concrete examples that learning is occurring. As a child compares a photograph of an early block structure of five blocks teetering on top of each other with a more recent airport scene, complete with runways, baggage handling area, and child-made "no parking" signs, he is captivated with his own progress. Witnessing one's own learning firsthand contributes to a healthy sense of competence and is a strong motivator for future learning.

Portfolios are designed to be shared with children's families. At designated assessment points, the teacher and child review and organize the items in the portfolio and create a list of the contents. The teacher then writes a summary of the child's growth and learning in the areas of physical knowledge, logicomathematical, and social-arbitrary knowledge. Together, they hold a conference in which family members are informed of their child's learning.

Parents should be asked to help with assessment of their child's learning by contributing information to the portfolio. Types of information that can be provided by parents include teachers' notes from informal conversations, interviews with parents about their child, conferences in which information and work samples are shared, home visits to familiarize the teacher with the child's interests, questionnaires to be completed, and specific requests for involving parents with assessment at home (McAfee & Leong, 1997). Requesting information from parents about their child upon entrance to the program or at the beginning of the school year helps teachers to establish a profile on each child and his strengths and potential weaknesses.

The Toy Preference Inventory (see Appendix A) provides teachers with information about the availability of certain play objects in the home as well as the child's interests. It also provides clues as to how the teacher might help children become familiar with classroom materials. *The Toy Preference Inventory* is completed by the parent, ideally while at home, so they can be more accurate when indicating the toys available and their child's interest in them. The inventory is then returned to the teacher, who reviews it for valuable information. It then becomes a part of the child's portfolio to be reviewed and updated at parent conferences. Teachers and parents will look for children's expanding interests in play materials over time. Also, teachers may recommend certain toys be purchased or borrowed from a toy lending library. The teacher will also see to it that children are given varied experiences with materials in the classroom. Figure 9–7 depicts one completed section of the *Toy Preference Inventory*. A quick look at this example would inform the teacher that Bristi has had few experiences with blocks at home.

Conclusion

The assessment process is a significant part of ensuring children learn through block play. Familiarity with the many types of evaluations is necessary for selecting appropriate types of assessment. Teachers can set goals for individual children and plan appropriately as they move through the Assessment of Learning Cycle.

Theory into Practice

1. Use two of the methods described to assess young children's block play. Write a summary of your findings and compare and contrast the two different methods.
2. Observe children at play and write anecdotal records documenting how they gained greater understanding in each of the three types of knowledge—physical, logicomathematical, and social-arbitrary.
3. Use photographs or sketches to document block building.

Websites

www.scholastic.com

Articles and resources on assessment.

www.ericae.net

Links to assessment-related websites and materials.

Toy Preference Inventory

Child's name: *Bristi*

Child's age (please give years and months): *3 yrs. 8 mo.*

The Toy Preference Inventory has been designed to provide important information to teachers of young children. The 65 items have been divided into six categories. Please indicate the degree to which your child typically plays with each toy by placing an "X" under one of the four options: Never, Rarely, Sometimes, or Often. *Note:* If a toy is not available to a child, select the "Never" category. Please add toys your child plays with but are not on the list at the end of each section labeled "Others."

Construction	Never	Rarely	Sometimes	Often
alphabet blocks		X		
bristle blocks	X			
connecting blocks (ex.: Lego®, Duplo®)		X		
Lincoln Logs®	X			
plastic stackable blocks			X	
set of blocks in wagon			X	
shaped sorting blocks with container		X		
Tinkertoys®	X			
waffle blocks	X			
wooden building blocks			X	
others				

Figure 9–7 *Example of the "Construction" section of the Toy Preference Inventory from Appendix A.*

Related Readings

Beaty, J. (1994). *Observing development of the young child* (3rd ed.). New York: Merrill.

Farr, R., & Tone, B. (1994). *Portfolio and performance assessment: Helping students evaluate their progress as readers and writers.* New York: Harcourt Brace.

Nilsen, B. (1997). *Week by week: Plans for observing and recording young children.* Albany, NY: Delmar.

References

Bentzen, W. R. (1992). *Seeing young children: A guide to observing and recording behavior* (2nd ed.). New York: Delmar.

Church, E., & Miller, K. (1990). *Learning through play: Blocks. A practical guide for teaching young children.* New York: Scholastic.

Goodwin, W., & Driscoll, L. (1980). *Handbook for measurement and evaluation in early childhood education.* San Francisco: Jossey-Bass.

Grace, C., & Shores, E. (1991). *The portfolio and its use: Developmentally appropriate assessment of young children.* Little Rock, AR: Southern Association on Children Under Six.

Helm, J., Beneke, S., & Steinheimer, K. (1997). Documenting children's learning. *Childhood Education, 73*(4), 200–205.

Howard, P. (1994). *The owner's manual for the brain.* Austin, TX: Leornian Press.

Isbell, R. (1995). *The complete learning center book.* Beltsville, MD: Gryphon House.

Kamii, C., & DeVries, R. (Eds.). (1980). *Group games in early education: Implications of Piaget's theory.* Washington, DC: National Association for the Education of Young Children.

Kapel, D., Gifford, C., & Kapel, M. (1991). *American educators' encyclopedia.* New York: Greenwood Press.

Kuschner, D. (1989). Put your name on your painting, but . . . the blocks go back on the shelves. *Young Children, 45*(1), 49–56.

McAfee, O., & Leong, D. (1997). *Assessing and guiding young children's development and learning.* Boston: Allyn & Bacon.

McCutcheon, G. (1981). On the interpretation of classroom observations. *Educational Researcher, 10,* 5–10.

Meisels, S., Jablon, J., Marsden, D., Dichtelmiller, M., Dorfman, A., & Steele, D. (1994). *The work sampling system: An overview* (3rd ed.). Ann Arbor, MI: Rebus Planning Associates, Inc.

Meisels, S., & Steele, D. (1991). *The early childhood portfolio collection process.* Ann Arbor: University of Michigan, Center for Human Growth and Development.

Nicolson, S., & Shipstead, S. (1998). *Through the looking glass: Observations in the early childhood classroom.* Columbus, OH: Merrill.

Piaget, J. (1952). *The child's conception of number.* London: Routledge and Kegan Paul.

Smilansky, S. (1968). *The effects of sociodramatic play on disadvantaged children.* New York: John Wiley & Sons.

Wellhousen, K. (1994). Assessment of early childhood social development. *Dimensions, 23*(1), 32–35.

Wortham, S. (1995). *Measurement and evaluation in early childhood education.* Englewood Cliffs, NJ: Merrill.

APPENDIX A

Toy Preference Inventory

Child's name: _____

Child's age (please give years and months): _____

The Toy Preference Inventory has been designed to provide important information to teachers of young children. The 65 items have been divided into six categories. Please indicate the degree to which your child typically plays with each toy by placing an "X" under one of the four options: Never, Rarely, Sometimes, or Often. *Note:* If a toy is not available to a child, select the "Never" category. Please add toys your child plays with but are not on the list at the end of each section labeled "Others."

Construction	Never	Rarely	Sometimes	Often
alphabet blocks				
bristle blocks				
connecting blocks (ex.: Lego®, Duplo®)				
Lincoln Logs®				
plastic stackable blocks				
set of blocks in wagon				
shaped sorting blocks with container				
Tinkertoys®				
waffle blocks				
wooden building blocks				
others				

Role play	Never	Rarely	Sometimes	Often
baby dolls				
cash register				
child-size kitchen appliances (ex.: stove)				
dollhouse with furniture				
dress-up clothes, hats, or jewelry				
grocery cart				
pots and pans, or plates, cups, and eating utensils				
puppets				
scenery for small figures (ex.: farm set, garage)				
small animal or people figures (ex.: Little People®)				
stuffed animals				
toy telephone, broom, or mop				
transportation vehicles (ex.: trucks, trains, cars)				
others				

Creative	Never	Rarely	Sometimes	Often
adhesives (ex.: glue, paste, glue stick)				
chalk				
crayons				
fingerpaints				
markers				
paint and brush				

	Never	Rarely	Sometimes	Often
pencils				
modeling dough				
rubber stamps and ink pad				
scissors				
stickers				
others				

Manipulative	Never	Rarely	Sometimes	Often
bathtub toys for pouring				
nesting toys				
pegboard				
plastic linking chain				
puzzles				
stringing beads, buttons, spools				
others				

Music and Literature	Never	Rarely	Sometimes	Often
audio music or story recordings				
books				
jack-in-the-box				
musical games (ex.: Ring around the Rosy)				
musical instrument (ex.: keyboard)				
See 'N Say® toy				
videotapes featuring music or stories				
winding music box				
others				

Large Motor	Never	Rarely	Sometimes	Often
ball				
basketball goal				
bean bag for tossing				
corn popper push toy				
Hippity Hop® ball				
plastic or wood workbench toy with hammer				
rocking horse				
roller skates or blades				
sandbox				
slide				
swing				
tunnel				
wading or swimming pool				
wagon				
wheeled riding toys (ex.: Big Wheel®, Little Tykes Coupe®)				
others				

Vendors of Blocks and Other Construction Materials

Childcraft® Education Corp.
P.O. Box 3239
Lancaster, PA 17604
1-800-631-5652

Community Playthings
P.O. Box 901
Route 213
Rifton, NY 12471
1-800-777-4244

Constructive Playthings®
13201 Arlington Rd.
Grandview, Missouri 64030
1-800-448-1412
e-mail: *ustoy@ustoyco.com*

Discount School Supplies
P.O. Box 7636
Spreckels, CA 93962-7636
1-800-627-2829
www.earlychildhood.com

Discovery Toys®, Inc.
Livermore, CA 94550
1-800-426-4777
www.discoverytoysinc.com

Early Childhood Direct/Chime Time
P.O. Box 369
Landisville, PA 17538
1-800-784-5717
www.chimetime.com

Lakeshore® Learning Materials
2695 E. Dominguez St.
P.O. Box 6261
Carson, CA 90749
1-800-421-5354
www.lakeshorelearning.com

Play with a Purpose: Physical Development
    Products for Young Children
220 24th Avenue NW
P.O. Box 998
Owatonna, MN 55060-0998
1-800-533-0446

Glossary

Architecture of the Brain   The intricate system of neural connections and pathways in the brain. The architecture of the brain is influenced by environmental stimuli and changes throughout one's life. The brain's architecture is also referred to as neural circuitry and the brain's wiring system. (Chapter 2)

Automaticity   The ability to produce a behavior pattern or thought sequence without focused attention or concentration. Automaticity results when certain behavior or thought patterns are repeated consistently. (Chapter 2)

Axons   Long, thin extensions of neurons that act like telephone wires carrying messages away from the nerve cell. (Chapter 2)

Behavioral Momentum   A technique designed to help children follow the instructions or requests of adults. (Chapter 8)

Big Ideas   Major concepts and issues embedded into a particular learning activity. (Chapter 6)

Circular Reaction Patterns   A chain of actions that provides children with continuous opportunities for learning and development. (Chapter 4)

Cognitive Bootstraping   The idea that activities or experiences that foster development in one area also trigger development in other areas. (Chapter 4)

Cognitive Conflict   A form of stimulation that requires children to rethink their original idea and incorporate new information. (Chapter 6)

Communication Units   The number of complete sentences spoken during a timed observation. (Chapter 5)

Consolidation of Knowledge and Skills   The ability to make connections between ideas and skills and the differing contexts in which they are used. (Chapter 6)

Constructive Play   Building or creating objects or structures from various materials. (Chapter 2)

Coordination of Secondary Circular Reactions   A substage of the sensory-motor period in which infants, 8–12 months of age, combine actions they have performed before to explore their environment. (Chapter 4)

Correspondence Training   A way to help children develop the ability to decide what they need to do and then follow through and do it. (Chapter 8)

Curriculum-Generated Play   Play designed to foster the development of concepts and skills drawn from content areas, such as literacy, math, science, and social studies. (Chapter 6)

Differential Reinforcement   Rewarding specific behaviors in some contexts but not in others. (Chapter 8)

Dimensions of the Environment   Five separate dichotomies used to show the need for balance in physical space and materials in a classroom. (Chapter 7)

Dendrites   Receptive branches of a neuron that receive input from an organism's environment or from other neurons. (Chapter 2)

Dramatic Play   Play in which children invent scenarios and pretend to be someone or something else, or pretend to be somewhere else. (Chapter 2)

Exploration   A process children use to get information. It generally precedes play and seems, to an adult's eye, much more serious than play. (Chapter 4)

Flow   A state of attentiveness that occurs when the individual's internal drive to work is balanced with appropriate challenge inherent in the task. (Chapter 6)

Friendship Training   Informal activities that support children's development of friendship and affection for each other. (Chapter 8)

Full Inclusion   Preferred service delivery model in early childhood. Children who are developing typically and those with special needs and abilities attend the same educational program on a full-time basis. (Chapter 8)

Functional Play   Repetitious behavior for mental mastery and coordination of skills. Also known as **practice play**. (Chapters 2 and 3)

Functional Skills   A skill that enables a child to participate within a wide variety of integrated environments. (Chapter 8)

Games with Rules   A form of play where children follow either implicit or explicit rules. It is the predominant form of play for children during their primary years. (Chapter 2)

Illicit Play   Play, often of a forbidden nature, that occurs when the teacher is not looking. (Chapter 6)

Incidental Teaching   A strategy for extending the language of children as they interact. (Chapter 8)

Inner Connection   A part of Froebel's theory used to describe the relationship between individual children, the spiritual world, nature, and the human race. (Chapter 1)

Interdependence   An appreciation for what can be done when working with another person. (Chapter 4)

Investigative Play   Open-ended play that encourages children to solve problems by generating multiple hypotheses and evaluating each based on logic and reasoning. (Chapter 6)

Learning Center System   The coordination of time and space to facilitate various small-group or individual activities. (Chapter 5)

Logicomathematical Knowledge   The cognitive understanding of the relationships among and between objects. (Chapters 5 and 9)

Mental Combinations   A substage of the sensory-motor period when toddlers, 18–24 months of age, can solve problems using mental images. (Chapter 4)

Metacognition   The ability to self-monitor thinking. (Chapter 6)

Metalanguage   The ability to self-monitor language. (Chapter 6)

Microswitch   A mechanism that enables toys or equipment to be activated by a slight movement of the chin, a sipping, or a blowing movement. When these mechanisms are attached to toys, children with disabilities are able to exercise more control over their play. (Chapter 8)

Microworlds   Miniature recreations of a total environment. (Chapter 6)

Model Building   The recreation of a specific form. (Chapter 6)

Naturalistic (Milieu) Strategies   Strategies used to promote the development of communication skills and help children transfer language skills from one context to another. They include incidental teaching, naturalistic time delay, and transition-based teaching. (Chapter 8)

Naturalistic Time Delay   A strategy used to increase children's interactions. (Chapter 8)

Neural Circuitry   The complex, multilayered system of synapses in the brain responsible for sending and receiving messages. Neural circuitry is also referred to as the brain's wiring system or the architecture of the brain. (Chapter 2)

Neural Pathways   A series of strong synapse connections that transport messages to and from specific areas of the brain. (Chapter 2)

Neural Plasticity   The brain's ability to adapt with experience and change the structure and chemistry of its neural circuitry. (Chapter 2)

Neural Rest   Downtime children need to process information and strengthen neural circuitry. (Chapter 2)

Neuron   Brain cell. (Chapter 2)

Neuroscience   The study of the human nervous system, the brain, and the biological basis of consciousness, perception, memory, and learning. (Chapter 2)

Neurotransmitters   Chemicals produced in the brain that carry messages from dendrites to axons across synapses. (Chapter 2)

Object Permanence   The idea that objects exist even when they cannot be seen. (Chapter 4)

Peer-Mediated Strategies   Strategies used to promote social interaction skills between children with differing abilities. (Chapter 8)

Physical Knowledge   Understanding the tangible attributes of objects in the child's immediate environment. (Chapters 5 and 9)

Play-Generated Curriculum   The incorporation of children's ideas and interests into the ongoing curriculum. (Chapter 6)

Practice Play   See **Functional Play.**

Preconceptual Stage   The time, generally between 24–36 months, when children make a transition between the sensory-motor and preoperational period. (Chapter 4)

Pretense   Play in which children represent what they are thinking through actions. They play "as if" what they are doing is real. (Chapter 4)

Primary Circular Reactions   A substage of the sensory-motor period when infants, 1–4 months of age, engage in circular reactions with their bodies. (Chapter 4)

Project Approach   A way of teaching and learning that involves children in in-depth investigations. (Chapter 6)

Project   An in-depth study of a particular topic that one or more children undertake. (Chapter 6)

Prompts   Forms of assistance that aid the use of a particular skill or display of a particular behavior. Prompts can be verbal, gesticular, physical, or pictorial. (Chapter 8)

Pruning   The process the brain uses to eliminate weak or unused synapses in the brain's neural circuitry. (Chapter 2)

Recreational Play   Play that occurs during free-choice activities or at recess. (Chapter 6)

Reflexive Period   A substage of the sensory-motor period when the actions of infants, 0–1 month of age, are a result of simple, involuntary reflexes. (Chapter 4)

Reinforcement System   A systematic way of supporting children's learning and encouraging them to explore environments, experiment with materials, and engage in activities. (Chapter 8)

Repetition Strategies   Ways children commit skills to automaticity. These skills include practice, rehearsal, and drill. (Chapter 2)

Secondary Circular Reactions   A substage of the sensory-motor period when infants engage in circular reactions that involve objects. (Chapter 4)

Sensory-Motor Schema   A response pattern children use when learning about their environment. They take in sensory information and act on it physically. (Chapter 4)

Social-Arbitrary Knowledge   Awareness of socially referenced knowledge that can only be learned through experiences with others. (Chapter 9)

Sociodramatic Play   A sophisticated form of dramatic play in which two or more children play together and coordinate pretend roles and scenarios. (Chapter 2)

Supportive Play Partner   Someone who, while playing with a child, shares the power inherent in the play episode with the child, thus extending and enriching the child's play experience. (Chapter 4)

Supports   Those things that enable children with disabilities to participate at the highest level possible in activities such as block play. (Chapter 8)

Symbolic Play   Play in which children use mental representations, thereby allowing one object to symbolize another. (Chapter 2)

Synapse   Minute gaps between axons and dendrites over which messages are carried by neurotransmitters. (Chapter 2)

Synaptic Density   The number of synapses per unit volume of brain tissue. (Chapter 2)

Tertiary Circular Reactions   A substage of the sensory-motor period where toddlers, 12–18 months of age, perform novel actions to solve problems. (Chapter 4)

Unity   A part of Froebel's theory used to emphasize the wholeness of the child's cognitive, physical, and spiritual domains. (Chapter 1)

Verbal Fluency   The total number of words spoken during a timed observation. (Chapter 5)

Vocabulary Diversity   The number of different words spoken during a timed observation. (Chapter 5)

Windows of Opportunity   Also called critical or sensitive periods, these are times in a child's life when the brain is particularly susceptible to specific stimuli. (Chapter 2)

Wiring of the Brain   The complex, multilayered system of synapses in the brain. This system is responsible for sending and receiving messages from the different areas of the brain. Wiring of the brain is also referred to as the brain's architecture or the brain's neural circuitry. (Chapter 2)

Index

*An italic page number indicates a reference to an article or book by that au-
thor.

DATE DUE